LAND EXPROPRIATION IN ISRAEL

For Ran, Matan, Noga and Yuval

Land Expropriation in Israel
Law, Culture and Society

YIFAT HOLZMAN-GAZIT
College of Management School of Law, Israel

Routledge
Taylor & Francis Group

LONDON AND NEW YORK

First published 2007 by Ashgate Publishing

2 Park Square, Milton Park, Abingdon, Oxon OX14 4RN
711 Third Avenue, New York, NY 10017, USA

Routledge is an imprint of the Taylor & Francis Group, an informa business

First issued in paperback 2017

British Library Cataloguing in Publication Data
Holzman-Gazit, Yifat
    Land expropriation in Israel : law, culture and society. -
    (Law, justice and power series)
    1. Eminent domain - Israel 2. Land tenure - Law and
    legislation - Israel 3. Palestinian Arabs - Legal status,
    laws, etc. - Israel
    I. Title
    343.5'6940252

Library of Congress Control Number: 2007931379

ISBN 978-0-7546-2543-8 (hbk)
ISBN 978-1-138-24927-1 (pbk)

Contents

List of Maps and Tables

Maps

Table

Acknowledgments

I am grateful for the opportunity to acknowledge here the assistance and support I received from a number of people. First, I would like to thank Professor Lawrence Friedman, who supervised my doctoral thesis at Stanford Law School and who introduced me to the field of law and society, which now I claim as my academic home. Throughout the years, he has been unfailingly generous with his advice and encouragement. I have greatly benefited from his wisdom and experience, as well as from his warmth and kindness. I am grateful to Professor Austin Sarat for accepting my book into the Law, Justice and Power series. I would also like to extend my appreciation to Dr. Tamar Gidron, Dean of the College of Management School of Law in Israel, for the generous grant that enabled me to complete the work. My thanks also go to Professor Yaffa Zilbershats, Dean of Bar-Ilan University Faculty of Law, for graciously placing at my disposal the facilities of the Law School.

Among the many friends and colleagues who supported me over the years it took to write this book, I would like to thank in particular Ariel Bendor, Shahar Lifshitz, Avital Margalit, Tzachi Keren-Paz, Haim Sandberg and Yofi Tirosh. Thanks are also due to Dorit Kabili. Ariane Rybski was superbly professional in preparing the maps for this book. Rotem Brikman did a wonderful job assisting me in finalizing the bibliography. Esther Snyder and Batya Razinsky of the law library at Bar-Ilan University spared no effort to locate every source I needed for my research, and I thank them both.

I owe a special debt of gratitude to my editor, Dr. Adam Vital, who provided indispensable help with my manuscript. His professional advice and endless patience have been for me a most significant source of learning and tranquility. Thanks also to Barbara Doron for her editing comments on the final manuscript. I wish to express my appreciation and thanks also to John Irwin and Alison Kirk of Ashgate Publishing for their advice throughout the process.

Most of all, I would like to extend my heartfelt gratitude to my family. My parents Meir and Hannah Holzman were tremendously supportive at all times. My husband and best friend, Ran, was an invaluable source of strength and unconditional love. And last but not least, our wonderful children, Matan, Noga and Yuval, were patient with me on this long journey. To them and to Ran I dedicate this book.

List of Abbreviations

ACRI	Association for Civil Rights in Israel
AO	Land (Acquisition for Public Purposes) Ordinance, 1943
BPI	Building Price Index
CBS	Central Bureau of Statistics
CPI	Consumer Price Index
DERs	Defence (Emergency) Regulations, 1945
D.K.	Knesset Protocols
HCJ	High Court of Justice
IDF	Israel Defense Forces
ILA	Israel Lands Administration
JNF	Jewish National Fund
L.S.I	Laws of the State of Israel
PLDC	Palestinian Land Development Company
PLO	Palestine Liberation Organization
UN	United Nations

Introduction

From its inauguration in 1948 to the present day, the Supreme Court of Israel has intervened only once to block what has otherwise been the state's unfettered hand in expropriating private property. And even that unprecedented decision, handed down in 1994, was reversed when the case was reheard.[1] How is one to explain the reluctance of Israel's Supreme Court to restrict the government's powers of expropriation? Why did it take the Court close to 50 years to make this move, and why did the Court, having finally taken this step, which in Israeli terms was quite bold, subsequently reverse itself? This book, which addresses these and related questions, is a historical study of the social, cultural and political underpinnings of Israel's land expropriation law.

Throughout much of the country's history, the Supreme Court's treatment of expropriation of private land has been characterized by extreme deference to the executive branch. This judicial record is puzzling both because of the patent inequity of some of Israel's expropriation rules and because of the traditional role of the Supreme Court as a protector of civil rights. Under Israeli law, the power to expropriate land is conferred upon the state and upon local authorities through two principal statutes: the Land (Acquisition for Public Purposes) Ordinance of 1943 (hereinafter the AO) and the Planning and Building Law of 1965 (hereinafter the Planning Law). The AO is part of the body of legislation inherited from the days of the British rule in Palestine under the mandate Britain received from the League of Nations (the precursor of the United Nations). The AO was an authoritarian and profoundly undemocratic piece of legislation. To that extent, it was typical of its era and of its colonial setting. What is more interesting is that it has never been amended by the Israeli legislature and basically it still stands today as it did in 1943. The AO does not define the public uses for which land may be expropriated, leaving the definition of this term to the absolute discretion of the Minister of Finance. Nor does it grant landowners the right to a hearing, or, for that matter, the right to know the particular public use for which their land was taken. Needless to say, the AO fails to protect landowners against abuses by the state of its expropriation powers. There is no provision for restitution when the expropriating authority abandons the public purpose or decides to transfer the land to private hands for development. Furthermore, expropriations are valid even when no agreement has been reached with the landowner on monetary compensation.

Unlike the AO, the Planning Law contains a list of statutory 'public uses.' It also places certain other (narrow) restrictions on the freedom of the expropriating authority. It requires, for instance, the existence of an approved planning scheme prior to the

---

1   H.C. 5091/91, *Nusseibeh v. Minister of Finance*, Takdin – Supreme Court Precedents 1994(3) 1765; F.H. 4466/94, *Nusseibeh v. Minister of Finance*, 49(4) P.D. 68. See discussion in Chapter 8 below.

issuance of an expropriation order. A most troubling feature of the Planning Law is the no-compensation rule. The Planning Law allows local authorities to expropriate up to 40 per cent of a plot for a public purpose without paying compensation, provided the purpose of the expropriation is one of the following: the construction or widening of roads and recreation grounds or the building of educational, cultural, religious, health and sport facilities. The AO also limits the right to compensation but to a lesser degree. Under its terms, merely up to 25 per cent of a plot may be taken without compensation and only for the purpose of construction or widening of roads or the building of recreational facilities.

Despite this grim picture, the Supreme Court of Israel has historically failed to protect the rights of property owners affected by these laws. This failure is at odds with the traditional role of the Supreme Court as a guarantor of civil rights. In the absence of a written constitution, the Israeli judiciary has developed a system of judicial protection of civil rights. Israel's Supreme Court has held that fundamental rights such as freedom of speech, occupation, religion, association, demonstration and movement have the status of legal principles in Israeli law, and the state may not curtail such rights without explicit statutory authorization. Why then has the Court been unwilling to restrict administrative excess in matters relating to land expropriation, when it has had no difficulty intervening to block executive branch actions that infringed upon fundamental freedoms such as speech and association?

The point of departure of this study is that courts in general, and supreme courts in particular, tend not to challenge the state, its centers of power and its legal ideology. The functioning of courts as institutions that support the hegemony of the state is a well documented phenomenon. Marxist scholars on the one hand, and proponents of critical legal studies on the other, are particularly rigorous in their attempts to prove and substantiate the role of law and legal institutions in legitimizing dominant economic and political interests (Hunt 1985; Stone 1985). This view is also accepted by political scientists, who note that courts depend on public support, and that therefore they are restricted in their ability (and willingness) to rule against prevailing public perceptions. A systematic judicial challenge of national narratives or public opinion might be regarded by the public as biased and political, and might therefore undermine public trust in the court system (Barzilai 1999).

Yet judicial doctrines cannot be reduced in each particular case to hegemonic interests. Once a doctrine is established, it gains autonomy and penetrates the judicial process in ways that transcend the particular ethnic/national/political context in which it was originally formulated. The theoretical structure that underpins this study may therefore be seen as one that emphasizes the autonomy of courts, in the sense that judicial doctrines have a life of their own once they have been formulated. Such was the case with respect to the effect of the legal practice of Arab land expropriation on the Israeli Supreme Court's overall approach of self-restraint in land expropriation cases. On the one hand, the Court's refusal to interfere when the state made use of its expropriation powers against the Arab minority reflects the Court's acceptance of the dominant ideology of Jewish rule in Israel. The Zionist ideology of public landownership, the pro-Jewish immigration policy and the goal of expanding Jewish settlement of the entire national territory are all manifestations of the Jewish character of the state, and as such they reflect the interests of the majority of the country's citizens. On the other hand, as this study will show, the end result of the doctrine of judicial non-intervention was that both Jews and Arabs paid the price of judicial self-restraint. Being committed to upholding its professional image as unbiased and impartial institution, the Supreme Court employed the same judicial approach to Arabs and to Jews. The logic of judicial autonomy lends thus further legitimacy to the state's interests in expropriating Arab land, but at the same time it had an unintentional result of affecting the status of Jewish landowners as well.

In 1972, Prof. Yitzhak Klinghoffer, a former Dean of the Faculty of Law at the Hebrew University of Jerusalem, published a Note on two Supreme Court cases dealing with the legality of post-expropriation changes to the designated public use for which the land was expropriated. In both cases discussed in the Note, the Court upheld the authority's right to change the intended public use after the land was taken. Prof. Klinghoffer criticized the decisions, but his abstract analysis ignored the all-too-real possibility that the political reality of Jewish-Arab relations and social and economic pressures may have affected both the political-administrative decisions to expropriate the land and the judicial decisions to let these expropriations stand. Instead, his analysis concentrated exclusively on the decisions' internal legal concepts, on statutory language and on the relevant legal categories. In his Note, Prof. Klinghoffer called for legislative reform that would protect landowners against retroactive changes to the designated public use of their land, and he formulated what he believed was the correct solution to the legal problem (namely, legislative reform) in light of his study of the comparable statutory arrangements in France, Italy and Belgium. This formulation was made without pausing to consider whether the example of these countries was relevant to the Israeli situation, or whether the political, cultural, social, historical and economic conditions of these countries, not to mention their legal traditions, might not have played a determinant role in fashioning the legal solutions that were ultimately arrived at (Klinghoffer 1972).

Prof. Klinghoffer was not alone in this narrow theoretical approach. Virtually all studies written prior to the early 1990s that addressed the case law of land expropriation had little to say about Israeli politics, history or society, and focused exclusively on a linguistic and conceptual analysis of the relevant statutes and decisions (for example, Shelach 1980). In fact, it can generally be said that until the late 1980s, the prevalent approach of Israeli legal scholarship overall was excessively formalistic. Preponderant importance was attributed to rules and concepts, and judicial outcomes were believed to be to a large extent the product of formal rules.[2]

In the 1990s, legal formalism as a dominant academic paradigm in Israeli legal scholarship began to wane, replaced by a growing perception of the law as a product of social forces rather than as an isolated and insulated system. Prominent examples of this approach in the context of land expropriation scholarship are the writings of the political geographer Prof. Oren Yiftachel and the legal scholar Dr. Alexandre Kedar. Prof Yiftachel has developed and used the theoretical concept of 'ethnocratic settler

---

2   The dominance of formalism within the Israeli legal community may be attributed in part to the fact that the majority of the legal scholars up until the mid-1960s gained their general education and legal training in Continental Europe (Salzberger and Oz-Salzberger 2000).

society' to explain the creation and maintenance of Israel's land regime. According to Yiftachel, the model of settling ethnocracy—a settler society in which the 'ethnos' (community of origins) enjoys clear legal and institutional prominence over the 'demos' (residential community of a given territory) assists in understanding the power relations within Israeli society. Ethnicity, rather than citizenship, constitutes the main criterion for distributing land and other resources of power.[3] Yiftachel pursued his empirical studies mainly on the landed power relations between Jews and Arabs in the Galilee. He showed how Israeli policies in the Galilee, including land expropriations from Arabs, Jewish settlement programs, manipulation of administrative boundaries and imposition of planning boundaries, have worked to control the spatial expansion of Arab villages and maintain the status of Arabs as an oppressed ethnic minority (for example, Yiftachel 1992, Yiftachel 1997). Dr. Kedar joined Prof. Yiftachel in adopting the model of ethnocratic society to explain the landed power relations between Jews and Arabs in Israel. His focus, however, was on the role of law in creating and enabling the Israeli ethnocratic land regime. Kedar wrote extensively on the various ways by which Israeli law interfered and legitimized the interference with Arab landholdings after the creation of Israel in 1948 (Forman and Kedar 2004; Kedar 2001; Yifatchel and Kedar 2000; see also Shamir 1996). According to both Kedar and Yiftachel, the Israeli judiciary should not be regarded as merely an objective body implementing the law as written. Rather, the Supreme Court's record in land expropriation cases that involved Palestinian-Arabs should be read as a project for legitimizing the oppressive legal order and the practice. The Court, they argued, acted in concert with the state and other Zionist quasi-governmental bodies to reduce the extent of Arab land ownership.[4] The writings of Kedar and Yiftachel join the wide-ranging academic debate that is currently taking place on various legal techniques that the state has used to discriminate against Arab citizens and on the support that these discriminatory actions has received in the courts (for example, Saban 2004; Kimmerling 2002; Kretzmer 1990).

The present study differs from such studies in that its primary focus is not on the expropriation of Arab land. This study examines the national ideologies and political, social and economic realities that constitute the real-world context in which the Supreme Court's decisions on property rights have been taken. A major point that I wish to emphasize is that, in the Israeli context, land expropriations from Arabs and from Jews are not separate issues. There can, of course, be no doubt that the scope and frequency with which Arab land rights have been violated in Israel make such violations of Jewish property rights appear paltry by comparison. However, by broadening the perspective and looking at the overall record of the Supreme Court in land expropriation cases, this study uncovers a long-ignored fact: that the Supreme Court's considerable self-restraint, which allowed the state wide discretion to abrogate the property rights of Arab landowners, had not only its intended effect on land ownership in the Arab sector,

3   According to Prof. Yiftachel, the supremacy of ethnicity over citizenship characterizes not merely Jewish-Arab relations within Israeli society but also the social division within the Jewish Israeli society between immigrants from Eastern European and from Middle Eastern countries (Yiftachel 1998a).

4   For criticism of Yiftachel and Kedar's arguments regarding the role of the courts in legitimizing Zionist interests in land control see (Sandberg 2000).

but also an unintended parallel effect on the legal treatment of private land ownership and land expropriation in the Jewish sector. It is ironic that the various mechanisms formulated by the Jewish majority to contain and suppress the land rights of the Arab minority in Israel—the tenure system of public landownership, and the preservation of the Mandatory land expropriation legislation—ultimately affected the rights of individuals who were themselves members of that same national majority.

Organization of the Study

Chapter 1 introduces the statutory scheme of land expropriation in Israel as well as the tenure system of public ownership. The law and the practice of land expropriation can only be fully understood against the background of Israel's tenure system, a unique phenomenon under which more than 90 per cent of the national territory is owned by the state. The discussion outlines the history of Israel's tenure system of public land ownership and explains why, despite the institution of public and national land ownership, expropriation powers are still of great significance in the process of urban development in Israel.

Chapter 2 focuses on the Israeli case law of land expropriation in the pre-constitutional era, from independence to the early 1990s. During this period, the concept of judicial review of legislative acts was not a recognized legal principle. Even so, and despite the fact that Israel lacked a constitution (and therefore also lacked constitutionally grounded guarantees of civil rights), the Supreme Court succeeded in establishing the protection of civil liberties. From the comparison of the Court's decisions in cases concerning infringements of non-property rights to its rulings in land expropriation cases, a clear double standard emerges. Although land expropriation is the most blatant violation of property rights, the Court failed to limit the state's powers of expropriation in any meaningful way, and its inaction amounted to a stamp of approval for expropriation orders. The Court's record in land expropriation cases cannot be attributable to an overall judicial philosophy of deference. Rather it should be viewed as influenced by the unique status of land ownership rights in Israeli legal culture and by the Israeli sociopolitical reality.

Three aspects of the cultural, social and political Israeli context will be described and analyzed as considerations that may account for the Supreme Court's hands-off approach in limiting the state's powers of expropriation. Chapter 3 examines the historical background of the disfavored status of private landownership in Israeli legal culture. Israel's existing land tenure system under which more than 90 per cent of the national territory is publicly owned is the result of a continuation of the pre-state ideology that favored public land ownership over private property as a strategy of nation-building. This ideology was implemented in the pre-state period by the Jewish National Fund, which remained a living institution after independence. Looking at the activities of the Jewish National Fund that made public land ownership a key symbol of the new Hebrew culture, the chapter examines the impact of the marginalized status of private property in Israeli legal culture on the jurisprudence of land expropriation.

Chapter 4 places the jurisprudence of land expropriation within the context of Israel's immigration policy and the various methods that were adopted at different times to resolve the country's chronic housing shortage. The discussion shows how the twin goals of maintaining a Jewish majority in the country as a whole and establishing a Jewish majority in all regions of the country have shaped the way Israeli society thinks about the desirable and efficient use of land, and how this in turn has shaped the meaning of 'public purpose' in the context of expropriation.

Chapters 5 and 6 offer an additional insight into the considerations that may have influenced the reluctance of the Supreme Court to interfere in expropriations. Chapter 5 focuses on the special statutory framework that was created in the 1950s to legalize the transfer of land from Arab ownership to collective Jewish ownership (that is, to the state) and on the patterns of Supreme Court adjudication concerning application of the special expropriation laws.

Chapter 6 shows how the special statutory framework that was enacted to facilitate expropriation from Arabs, and the Court's doctrines that were developed in this context, affected the judicial interpretation of AO. This effect has been long-lasting, and yet it is often overlooked. The legal practice pursuant to which land was expropriated from Arabs in the 1950s became the legal norm of land expropriation in Israel in general, not only from Arabs, but from Jews as well, and not only in the 1950s, but for many decades to come. In order to maintain its professional image as natural and unbiased, the Court had to decline to interfere with expropriations in the Jewish sector as it did with regard to the Arab sector. Other explanations focus on the general philosophy of legal formalism, the uncertain status of the Court and the confusion between the general and special regimes of expropriation.

With these four chapters offering explanations for the patterns of land expropriation adjudication in the 1950s, Chapter 7 moves to the post-1967 period, which witnessed an expansion of Israel's expropriation and settlement policy to the Occupied Territories and East Jerusalem. The chapter discusses the influence of the ongoing occupation of the Territories on the practices of expropriation in East Jerusalem and the Galilee. Despite the separation of the West Bank from Israel and from Jerusalem, the ongoing occupation has strengthened the domestic security discourse that advocates expansion of Jewish presence in predominantly Arab areas such the Galilee and East Jerusalem. This linkage between land, demography and domestic security led the Court to retain its traditional deferential approach in a period otherwise marked by increased judicial activism.

In 1992, the Israeli legislature enacted two Basic Laws that had the consequence of opening the door for judicial review. One of these two Basic Laws, Basic Law: Human Dignity and Liberty, states that ownership of private property is a guaranteed right. Chapter 8 assesses the impact of what is often referred to as the constitutional revolution on Israel's land expropriation jurisprudence. The chapter addresses the puzzle of why the Court did not revolutionize its approach to expropriation powers despite the formal enactment of constitutional protection to private property.

The final chapter focuses on two decisions that the Supreme Court delivered in 2001, in which it narrowed the scope of some of the troubling provisions of Israeli expropriation law. While these developments strengthen the status of landowners, it is yet to be seen whether the Supreme Court will continue in this new trend. As this study demonstrates, the history of Israel's land expropriation jurisprudence has always been closely linked to the political, social and cultural realities in which the Supreme Court acts. These realities, which the Court to a large extent is powerless to affect, are likely to continue to be of great significance in the future, as well.

Chapter 1

The Statutory Framework of Expropriation and the Land Tenure Regime

This chapter introduces the reader to the legal framework of land expropriation in Israel, as well as the context of public land ownership within which the powers of expropriation operate. The discussion clarifies the nature of expropriation powers and reviews the statutory scheme that governs their exercise in the pre-constitutional era (1948-92). Four elements of the legal doctrine are addressed in this regard: (1) the broad definition of public purpose; (2) the absence of a right to a public hearing; (3) the absence of protection from unwarranted expropriations; and (4) the no-compensation rule.

The law and the practice of land expropriation can only be fully understood against the background of Israel's tenure system, a unique phenomenon under which more than 90 percent of the country's territory is nationally owned. Situating the law of expropriation in the context of Israel's tenure system of public land, I briefly outline the history of Israel's tenure system of public land ownership. I then explain why, despite public land ownership, expropriation powers are still of great significance in the process of urban development in Israel.

The Nature of Expropriation Powers

The Hebrew term *hafka'ah* ('expropriation') does not convey the element of compulsion which is present in the English term 'compulsory purchase' (Davies 1994, 22-6). Neither the Hebrew term nor the English one indicate that historically the land taking was carried out by the Crown or the State, exercising one of its prerogative powers of sovereignty. This aspect of expropriation is reflected in the American expression 'eminent domain' (Nichols 1997, §1.12). Yet despite differences in vocabulary, each of these terms may be used to describe an acquisition of property rights pursuant to statutory powers and without the consent of the owners of those rights.[1]

In the Israeli context of land-use planning, expropriation powers should be distinguished from other means of acquiring land for public services. Expropriation

---

1   Canada, like Israel, uses the term 'expropriation' rather than 'compulsory purchase'. The term 'expropriation' is also used in South Africa (Todd 1992, 19-20; Van der Walt 1997).

powers are somewhat different from what is termed in the jargon of real estate developers 'development exactions.' Development exactions, known also as 'development agreements,' are a relatively new concept in Israel, borrowed from the context of urban and suburban planning in the United States, United Kingdom and other Western countries. In the United States, the term 'development exactions' is used to refer to a broad variety of concessions—most commonly, a range of requirements for land dedications and provision of public services—that local governments may impose on property owners as a condition for granting permits for the construction of individual buildings or subdivisions. Unlike land expropriation, a development exaction is triggered by the property owner's desire to alter the designated use of their land: the property owner wishes to make a profit from their property and, in exchange for the necessary permits, is required by the relevant authority to contribute to the community at large by providing infrastructures and community services such as roads, schools, clinics and recreational facilities that will serve others, as well. Expropriation powers, on the other hand, contain an element of compulsion; they may be exercised whether or not the owner wishes to develop their land (Alterman and Kayden 1988; Alterman 1990; Lewinsohn-Zamir 1994).

Expropriation powers also differ from another tool available to the authorities, namely land readjustment, popularly known in Israel as 'reparcellation.' Land readjustment allows local governments to re-subdivide large tracts of land and, in the process, to dedicate particular portions of such land for public purposes that are related to urban development (Doeblele 1982; Schnidman 1988). Like land expropriation, land readjustment may be undertaken without the owner's consent. However, unlike expropriation, land readjustment is a planning method that ensures that the costs and benefits of a new project are distributed equitably among all affected property owners. Under Israeli law, when land is readjusted, the authorities are required to ensure, to the extent possible, that with respect to each owner, the ratio of the value of that owner's new lot relative to the total value of all new lots, is the same as the ratio of the value of the owner's original lot relative to the total value of all original lots. If proportionality cannot be maintained, the equitability of the readjustment is attained through adjustment payments among the owners, which serve to level out relative gains and losses resulting from the otherwise unequal economic impact of the reparcellation. But such safeguards do not exist in the context of land expropriation.[2]

The Statutory Scheme

Under Israeli law, the only lawful basis for exercising the power of expropriation is an express authorization conferred by the legislature. And although authorization can be found in a number of Israeli laws (Kamar 2001, 35-85), the two laws that are central

---

2   The tool of land readjustment is used extensively in Israel. In the coastal plain, for example, where high pressures of urbanization are experienced, authorities cannot rely on the historical subdivision of the land to address modern standards of land development. Hence, to execute urban projects in such areas, authorities often consolidate land holdings and then re-subdivide the lands according to the needs of the planned project (Alterman 1990, 71-4).

to the practice of land expropriation in Israel are the Land (Acquisition for Public Purposes) Ordinance of 1943 (hereinafter the AO),[3] and the Planning and Building Law of 1965 (hereinafter the Planning Law).[4]

The AO stands as the general enabling statute for land expropriation. It contains the power to take land for public purposes and provides a standard procedure for expropriation and for assessment of compensation. The AO was introduced under the British Mandate in Palestine, which lasted from 1919 until 1948 (Goadby and Doukhan 1935, 316-31). Upon independence in 1948, it became part of Israeli law, together with numerous other items of Mandatory legislation.[5] Interestingly, the AO has survived to this day intact, despite the general tendency in Israeli law to replace Mandatory legislation with native Israeli laws. During the British rule, the acquiring authority pursuant to the AO was the High Commissioner for Palestine. After independence, the powers of the High Commissioner were transferred to the Minister of Finance.

Unlike the general enabling provision of the AO, the Planning Law establishes the power of expropriation in the specific context of land use planning. The Planning Law confers the power of expropriation on local planning commissions. These entities stand at the lowest tier of Israel's land-use planning system. The law authorizes them to take land for purposes deemed necessary for public use. Procedurally, the Planning Law adopts the rules found in the AO governing the matters of issuance of notices and power to take possession, as well as assessment of compensation. Yet there are differences in the principles of construction between the two laws that are of importance for understanding the practice of land expropriation in Israel.

One such distinction concerns the authority on whom expropriation powers are conferred. The AO confers the power of expropriation on the Minister of Finance, which suggests that the power is meant to be used for projects initiated by the central government, such as new towns and large-scale neighborhoods. The Planning Law, on the other hand, authorizes local planning commissions to issue expropriation orders. Local planning commissions are the main decision-making bodies for day-to-day local planning. In the majority of cases, they are composed solely of elected members of local councils.[6] The composition of local planning commissions and the

---

3   *Palestine Gazette*, Supp., No. 1 at 44 (1943).

4   19 L.S.I. 330 (1965).

5   The AO was absorbed into Israeli law by virtue of Section 11 of the Law and Administration Ordinance of 1948.

6   Israel's land use planning agencies are organized in a pyramid three-tier structure: At the top is the National Board for Planning and Building; below it are six District Planning and Building Commissions and at the lowest level there are more than 100 Local Planning and Building Commissions. Parallel to the hierarchy of agencies there is also a hierarchy of plans. At the top there are the national outline schemes, which may apply either to the country as a whole or to part of it. Below it are the district outline schemes, which cover entire districts, and are intended, in each case, to set out in sufficient detail the requirements for the implementation of the national scheme. At the lowest level are local outline plans and detailed plans issued by local planning commissions. Any new housing construction, whether private or public, must be anchored in a local outline or in a detailed plan. Local planning commissions maintain direct control over the use of land. They may grant development rights, provide legally binding

scope of their responsibility suggest that expropriation powers under the Planning Law, unlike the AO, are meant to be used for local community purposes such as roads, schools, libraries, recreation facilities and so on.[7]

Another distinction in the structure of the two laws relates to whether or not there is a requirement that expropriation powers be exercised by reference to an approved planning scheme. The AO does not require a connection between the act of expropriation and the planning process. It allows the taking of land for public use irrespective of whether the public use designation has been approved by planning authorities. The Planning Law, on the other hand, authorizes expropriation only if the land has been designated for public use in an approved local planning scheme (Alterman 1985). The Planning Law's requirement that a planning scheme be approved in advance is a major factor influencing the typical circumstances for applying each of the two statutory sources.

Israel has a relatively centralized land-use planning system that establishes a multi-layered approval process (Alterman 2001). Major decisions of local planning bodies, including decisions to expropriate land, require the approval of one of the six district planning commissions. The statutory structure of centralized supervision over local-level planning decisions, combined with the right of the public to challenge new planning schemes, makes for an extremely slow approval process. Seven to ten years is considered a normal timeframe for receiving approval for a proposed planning scheme. The requirement that the planning process be completed before an expropriating order may be issued has resulted in the Planning Law being used primarily for local development. Often, the local planning commission that is in charge of the planning process and responsible for the expropriation decision will relax zoning restrictions on the landowner's unexpropriated land in order to ease the economic impact of the expropriation. The AO, on the other hand, provides a time-saving route for land expropriation. It allows the Ministry of Finance to bypass the lengthy bureaucratic process of planning, and to expropriate land before completion of the multi-layered approval process. This feature of the AO makes it a preferable course of action from the viewpoint of state authorities. However, since the mid-1980s, as a result of growing public criticism of the draconian character of the AO, this statute has been saved for 'special' circumstances. The AO is typically used when the government decides to speed up the process of large-scale residential development for political reasons. Expropriations for traditional public purposes

---

directives on land use, including such matters as construction percentages, height, design guidelines and environmental mitigation. Readers familiar with the American system might view local outline plans as a cross between comprehensive plans and zoning regulations, and detailed plans as a cross between subdivision regulation and on-site plans. Readers familiar with the British system might view Israeli local outline plans as similar to the pre-1947 British Local Schemes (Alterman and Hill 1986, 131-7).

7   This distinction might be seen as a matter of formality since Section 22 of the AO authorizes the Minister of Finance to delegate their power of expropriation to a municipal corporation, local council or other local authority. The section thus permits local bodies to make use of the AO. In practice, however, authorities of the local government do not approach the Minister of Finance for delegation of powers. Development on the local level is exercised usually through the powers of expropriation established in the Planning Law.

(such as recreation facilities, school sites, and so on) are executed under the Planning Law even though this route is more cumbersome.

In addition to the aforementioned differences between the two statues, the AO and the Planning Law also diverge with respect to key elements of the legal doctrine. These refer to the public use definition; the right to a hearing; protection from unwarranted expropriations; and the right to compensation.

Legal Principles of Expropriation

Definition of Public Purpose

Exercise of expropriation powers is subject to the condition that the taking of private rights in land must be for a 'public purpose.' In some of the laws that confer specific powers of expropriation, the public purpose is defined by the legislature and appears in the text of the statute itself. However, this is not the case with the AO. The product of a Mandatory government that operated under conditions of war, the AO vested in the executive wide discretionary powers. In the original language of the AO, the High Commissioner for Palestine was empowered to decide that any project of a public nature could be considered 'public use' for purposes of land expropriation. In 1946, the 'public nature' restriction was removed from the law because of the British government's desire to prevent legal challenges to land expropriation after public investment had already been made. An Amendment to Section 2, dating from 1946 and still in force today, states that 'public purpose' means '[a]ny purpose certified by the Minister of Finance to be a public purpose.'

A narrower definition of the phrase 'public purpose' appears in the Planning Law. Section 188 of the Planning Law provides a list of public purposes that may be used to justify the use of expropriation powers. These include the construction of roads, airports, playgrounds, utility mains and other civil infrastructure projects. A comparison between the AO and the Planning Law with respect to the definition of public purpose reveals that the former grants greater leeway for exercise of expropriation powers. The AO allows the Minister of Finance to exercise the power of expropriation in cases where the common-sense meaning of 'public purpose' would not normally allow the taking of private property. Furthermore, as will be discussed in greater detail in Chapter 2, judicial review over the Minister of Finance's determinations as to what satisfied the public use requirement has been characterized by a considerable degree of deference. Beginning in the early 1950s and throughout the pre-constitutional era, Israel's Supreme Court held that 'it is not within our authority to examine the legitimacy of the Minister's definition of public use ...'[8] Hence, expropriations aimed at building residential housing and commercial

---

8   H.C. 180/52, *Dor v. Minister of Finance*, 6 P.D. 908, at 910. One may argue that the deference of Israel's Supreme Court in reviewing the public use definition is not exceptional from a comparative perspective. Both English and American courts have traditionally applied a deferential approach when considering the issue of what constitutes a lawful public use. For American law see *Berman v. Parker*, 348 U.S. 26 (1954); *Poletown Neighborhood Council v. City of Detroit*, 304 N.W. 2d 455 (Mich. 1981); *Hawaii Housing Authority v. Midkiff*, 467

facilities and enabling the operation of a textile factory were upheld by the Court as falling within the flexible definition of AO.⁹ Resorting to the AO thus bears an advantage from the state's point of view, as it effectively prevents successful legal challenges to any governmental determination of public purpose. Another feature of the AO which unjustifiably handicaps property owners who wish to challenge an expropriation decision is the lack of an established and legally grounded hearing process.

A Right to a Hearing

In a landmark case handed down in the late 1950s, the Supreme Court of Israel, relying on English common law, held that administrative bodies acting as quasi-judicial bodies must 'hear the other side.' It is a basic principle of natural justice, the Court explained, that an adversely affected party must be given the right to try 'to avert the evil decree' before it occurs. As a general rule, an administrative body shall not be allowed '[t]o attack the citizen in his person, property, occupation, status and the like, unless he is given a reasonable opportunity to be heard in his own defense against the contemplated act.'

The right to a hearing which was established as a basic principle of Israeli administrative law is missing from the AO. Although the act of land expropriation violates the basic right of the individual to own private property, the AO does not grant the property owner the right to oppose the expropriation order before it is issued.¹⁰ The absence of a hearings process in the context of land expropriation is

---

U.S. 229 (1984) and recently *Kelo v. City of New London*, 545 U.S. 469 (2005). Yet there is an important difference between the Israeli legal context and its American and English counterparts. In American law, as in English law, it is common for the authorizing statute to define the public purpose for which land may be expropriated. In English law, some of the authorizing statutes identify a specific public purpose and in others the public purpose is indicated in general terms (Davies 1994, 38-41). The same applies to American law, where state legislatures indicate the public purposes for which expropriation may be exercised. Accordingly, in such circumstances judicial review of the appropriateness of the project is open to the charge of 'legislating from the bench'. In Israeli law, on the other hand, the position of the Court cannot be attributed to deference to the legislature, because the AO fails to provide even minimal guidelines as to the purposes for which land may be taken. Hence, as a matter of policy, the highly centralized power of the Minister of Finance arguably requires even closer scrutiny than it otherwise would.

9   See for example, H.C. 342/69, *Azaryahu v. Minister of Finance*, 24(1) 225; H.C. 147/74, *Spolansky v. Minister of Finance*, 29(1) P.D. 421; H.C. 114/77, *Schwartz v. Minister of Finance*, 31(2) P.D. 800.

10   Israeli law, like English common law, distinguishes between administrative actions of legislative and of executive character. The Minister's definition of public use is considered an administrative act of legislative character whereas the decision to expropriate a particular plot constitutes an executive act. The distinction has implications, for example, with respect to the right to a hearing. While an administrative action of legislative character does not entitle the adversely affected party to a right to a hearing, executive actions (and particularly those of a judicial character) may include such an obligation. However, both types of administrative powers are subject to judicial review.

particularly disturbing in light of the practice that was common until the mid-1980s of not specifying in the notice of expropriation what kind of public use the land was intended for. According to the interpretation that the Supreme Court developed concerning the AO, a notice of expropriation may state in general terms that the land is required for 'public use,' without providing further details. Since property owners do not have a legal right to be heard before the expropriation order is confirmed, in practice they are often unaware of the purpose for which their land has been taken until they bring their case to court. At that stage, however, the likelihood of a successful challenge to the public use designation will have been considerably reduced.

A significant improvement in the procedure of expropriation occurred in 1986 when the Attorney General issued new guidelines, recommending that the Minister of Finance specify in detail in the notice of expropriation the public purpose for which the land was being taken, and grant affected owners the right to a hearing.[11] The guidelines suggested that a sub-committee of the Ministry of Finance be in charge of the hearing, and that in cases of public emergency, when a right to hearing cannot be granted in advance, the committee should allow the hearing to take place as soon as possible after the land has been taken. Today, a committee composed of representatives of the central government and local authorities hears objections from affected property owners upon the issuance of an expropriation notice under the AO.

With regard to the Planning Law, the right to a hearing is part of the procedure for approval of a local outline or detailed plan. For any expropriation decision exercised under the Planning Law, the actual expropriation may occur only after the land has been designated for a public use in an approved plan. One of the requirements for the approval of an outline plan is that interested parties must have an opportunity to object to the proposed plan or to changes in a plan. Objections to proposed changes (including designation of land for expropriation) are heard before a district planning commission in charge of the district in which the land is located.[12]

Absence of Protection Against Unwarranted Expropriations

An additional area in which the law establishes inappropriate practices concerns limitation of expropriations to cases of strict necessity. Israel's expropriation laws do not fully protect property owners against unnecessary expropriations. Sometimes the private property owner claims that they are able and willing to execute the public use themselves, thus obviating the need for the authority to expropriate the land in order to achieve the desired public purpose. This could be the case, for instance, in expropriations under the AO where the designated purpose of the expropriation is

---

11   Issuance of the guidelines followed the decision of Israel's Supreme Court in H.C. 307/82, *Lubianker v. Minister of Finance*, 37(2) P.D. 141. In that case, the Court severely criticized the practice of not specifying the public purpose for which the land was taken and of denying the owner a right to bring her claims before the expropriating authority.

12   District planning commissions are composed mainly of representatives of central government offices—in effect almost all the ministries relevant to planning.

the construction of a residential neighborhood, a commercial center or other uses that lend themselves to private development. Yet neither the AO nor the Planning Law recognizes the right of a landowner to object to the expropriation on the basis of their ability to implement the proposed public use. Lack of protection also marks the instances of changes in the public use designation and delays in the implementation of the public use.

The AO is silent on whether the former owner may reacquire the land if its public use designation has changed. In the limited number of cases of this nature that reached the Supreme Court in the pre-constitutional era, the Court alluded to the injustice that was caused to the owners as a result of the change in the proposed use from a public to a private one, but nevertheless refrained from granting the owners the right to reclaim the land. As it turns out, this is a relevant issue in the Israeli setting for the following reason. Since the AO allows the use of expropriation powers independently from the planning process, land is often designated for a public purpose in the expropriation order, but subsequently the public use designation is not always fully implemented due to inconsistency with land use regulations. These were the circumstances in *Ge'ulat Hakrach Ltd. v. Minister of Finance*.[13] The petitioners' land was expropriated with compensation for the purpose of constructing a road and building facilities for an army base. It turned out that the road was narrower than intended and the property owners appealed to get back the unused land. Their petition to the High Court of Justice was dismissed on the ground that the AO does not explicitly grant property owners a right to reclaim unused expropriated land.

If *Ge'ulat Hakrach* had involved expropriation pursuant to the Planning Law, the legal status of the property owners might have been better. According to Section 196(a) of the Planning Law, when land has been taken *without compensation* and its use changed to a designation for which it could not be expropriated, the local planning authority must compensate the property owners or, alternatively, return the land to them. Section 195(b) of the Planning Law prescribes that when a public use designation of land taken *with compensation* has been changed, the property owners have a right to repurchase the land for a sum no higher than the compensation paid, before the authority sells, rents out or otherwise transfers the land. It is worth noting that the protection of the Planning Law does not always apply in practice. Prof. Rachelle Alterman, a prominent Israeli scholar in the field of land-use and planning, mentions that many local governments have adopted the habit of indicating the land-use purpose in vague or general terms such as 'public building' or 'public use.' The result is that at the time the plan is approved, the property owner may not be able to tell whether the public use designation has been changed, or even whether the 'public use' is one that is allowed for taking without compensation. Moreover, local planning authorities often require property owners who are interested in the benefits of an outline or detailed plan to sign a release form which waives their right to claim compensation upon changes in land use designation. This habit, which prevails mostly in large cities such as Haifa and Tel-Aviv, has not yet been reviewed by the courts (Alterman 1990).

---

13   H.C. 224/72, *Ge'ulat Hakrach Ltd. v. Minister of Finance*, 26(2) P.D. 155.

The failure to protect property owners from unwarranted expropriations is evident also in the statutory regime governing the question of delays in implementing the designated public use. The Planning Law and the AO do not indicate whether an unreasonably long delay in implementing the public purpose should be considered a *de facto* abandonment of the public use designation. Delays in implementing the designated public use are the norm in the Israeli landscape of expropriation. Sometimes the delay is a consequence of the division of responsibility between local and central government as to the supply of public services. Until the 1980s, local authorities were responsible for obtaining the land for public services of a local character such as schools, hospitals or museums, whereas the central government was only in charge of financing such projects. It was not uncommon for the central government to refuse or to delay its decision to participate in a given project, thus halting its execution. In other cases, delays in implementation are due to the local authority's own behavior. Since land can be taken without compensation, local authorities may take land even if they do not have resources for implementing the intended public services.

Two situations can be distinguished in this regard. The first is when the decision to expropriate has been implemented, while the designated public use has not yet been put into effect. Although the property owner has received compensation, the delay casts doubt on the necessity of the public undertaking. The other situation is when the decision to expropriate has not yet been implemented, but the land has been designated for public use in an outline plan. Here the property owners find themselves in a quandary. On the one hand, they are not entitled to compensation, since the AO provides that compensation will be paid only upon the actual transfer of title to the land. On the other hand, they have to pay property taxes, since from a legal point of view they are still the owner of the (soon-to-be-expropriated) land. Needless to say, land that has been designated for public use rarely finds buyers on the market, and the property owners thus are saddled with a virtually worthless, unmarketable property with respect to which they nonetheless continue to pays high taxes, sometimes for a decade or more.

As stated, delays in completion of the expropriation process or realization of the public utility occur often in the Israeli context.[14] Nonetheless, in the pre-constitutional era, the Supreme Court only once ordered setting aside an expropriation order for this reason. In the 1988 case of *Amitai v. District Planning and Building Commission, Central Region*, land was designated for expropriation in its entirety, but for 26 years the authority did not take possession of the land, thus leaving the property owner without compensation and with an obligation to pay property taxes. Responding to the petition, the local planning authority was unable to enunciate, even after this long delay, what the intended public use of the land was and what the timeframe for its execution was. Given these circumstances, the Supreme Court held that the extended

14   See for example, H.C. 75/57, *Kalmas v. Local City Building and Planning Commission Tel Aviv-Jaffa*, 11 P.D. 1601; H.C. 67/79, *Shmuelson v. State of Israel*, 34(1) P.D. 281 and also the discussion in Chapter 7 below.

delay amounted to *de facto* abandonment of the expropriation, and therefore the local authority could not continue with its original plan to expropriate the land.[15]

The discussion so far has emphasized the absence of statutory barriers to the powers of expropriation. Another issue that affects the legality of the expropriation is the right of the owner to compensation. As will be detailed below, in this regard, Israel's expropriation laws establish a most troubling principle of partial compensation.

The Compensation Regime

The No-Compensation Rule

It is a well-established principle of all Western legal cultures that government action that transfers possession of private property from a citizen to the state or that has the effect of depriving the owner of possession of their property entitles the owner to compensation. Various considerations support a requirement of full compensation for land expropriation. Fairness and justice suggest that a person should not be forced to give up property rights beyond their fair share of the costs of government based on planning considerations.[16] The choice of a certain individual to bear the loss or enjoy the benefit has no connection to their identity, but is determined by planning considerations such as the suitability of the land for the use needed by the public. As a result, denial or restriction of compensation for land expropriation may fail to achieve redistributive effects, to the extent that redistribution is one of the purposes of the no-compensation rule. Land was once the major component of wealth; however, other forms of wealth are more characteristic of modern times. Given that landowners are not necessarily rich, there is no justification for requiring them to sustain a disproportional share of the costs of a social undertaking.[17] Furthermore, even if landowners are assumed to be relatively wealthy, restricting the right of compensation is not an appropriate method of wealth redistribution. Denial of compensation in land expropriation cases randomly injures only a small segment of all property owners and the wealth taken from them is transferred to a heterogeneous group, consisting of both rich and poor.[18]

---

15   H.C. 174/88, *Amitai v. District Planning and Building Commission, Central Region*, 42(4) P.D. 89.

16   The justifications of fairness and justice are often referred to in the American legal setting as the Armstrong principle. See *Armstrong v. United States*, 364 U.S. 49 (1960). For a review of the fairness rationale in takings cases in the United States, see Treanor (1997).

17   This assumption has been empirically proven in the Israeli setting. A study pursued in 1992 showed that for many landowners, the plot of land that they own is their only property of substance. Almost 80 percent of the claims submitted to the Israeli planning authorities were submitted by private individuals and approximately 60 percent of the claims concerned an injury to a small, single parcel of land (Alterman and Na'im 1992, 136-7, 143, 166).

18   For a different view which suggests that progressive distributive considerations can and should influence takings doctrine see, for example, the writings of Hanoch Dagan (Dagan 1999; Dagan 2000).

Another argument in favor of compensating owners for their expropriated land is economic efficiency. Efficiency supports compensation both by ensuring that property owners do not forgo investment due to fear of uncompensated losses (Michelman 1967) and by internalizing the costs of takings to the government (Blume and Rubinfeld 1984). The argument here is that by requiring the government to pay compensation, we force government officials to internalize the costs of engaging in a forced transaction of property rights and to compare the value of the resources in government hands to its value in private use. Presumably, acquiring authorities will go forward with the expropriation only if they anticipate that the resource will produce greater value as part the public project than the compensation the government must pay to obtain it. If we do not require full compensation, authorities may engage in excessive expropriation of property resulting in the misallocation of economic resources (Heller and Krier 1999).[19]

Finally, a requirement for full compensation may provide a safeguard against certain failures of the political process. The central problem of the political process emphasized by this set of considerations is that different interest groups have different degrees of influence in a democratic political system. It has been suggested that the practice of paying full compensation may reduce the distortions caused by the influence of interested lobby groups on the decision-making process. At the local level, the problem of differential influence is likely to be of great importance. Local government—even more so than central government—may be influenced by interest groups. A compensation requirement may be an important tool to protect those property owners who are politically weak and poorly represented from bearing the costs of a public project (Dagan 1999, 774-8; Dana and Merrill 2002, 46-52).

Notwithstanding the various rationales for a compensation requirement, Israeli law includes far-reaching powers of expropriation without compensation. Section 20 of the AO of 1943 authorized the High Commissioner for Palestine to take up to 25 percent of a plot without compensation if the land is taken for playground, recreation ground or for constructing or widening roads. According to the AO, if the expropriation order relates to more than one quarter of the land, the compensation shall be reduced by a sum which bears this proportion.

Up until the replacement of the mandatory planning laws with the 1965 Planning Law, the 25 percent figure that appears in the AO constituted an upper limit for expropriation without compensation.[20] Two other Mandatory enactments which conferred powers of expropriation, the Road Construction and Improvement

---

19 The cost-internalization argument works, however, in two directions. It has been claimed that full compensation of property owners would create incentives to over-invest in land development, disregarding the risk of planning activities that may harm its value (Blume and Rubinfeld 1984; Kaplow 1985). For criticism of this argument (Lewinsohn-Zamir 1996).

20 The AO includes authority to grant *ex gratia* compensation, if the Minister of Finance thinks that undue hardship has been caused to the property owners. In practice, however, such payments have been rarely awarded. Section 20(2)(c) of the AO reads:

it shall be lawful for the [Minister of Finance], if it is established to his satisfaction that the restrictions imposed by either of those paragraphs [i.e. the rule of no-compensation] would cause hardship, to grant in his discretion such compensation or additional compensation as, having regarded to all the circumstances of the case, he shall think fit.

(Defence) Ordinance of 1943 and the Roads (Width and Alignment) Ordinance of 1926, did not go any further in terms of the percentage of land that could be taken without compensation.[21] In 1965, however, the legal rule changed. Faced with growing demand for land for municipal services as a result of rapid urbanization, the legislature expanded the percentage of expropriated land that could be taken without compensation. This arrangement, covered by the Planning Law, is the main statutory source for expropriation without compensation today.

The Planning Law expands the no-compensation rule of the AO in two aspects. First, instead of the 25 percent ceiling that appears in the AO, the Planning Law allows local planning commissions to take up to 40 percent of a plot without compensation.[22] Second, the Planning Law broadens the list of public uses for which such expropriation is allowed. In addition to the public improvements of constructing or widening roads and the creation of recreation grounds (as provided by the AO), the Planning Law allows planning authorities to take land with no compensation for sports facilities and buildings intended for educational, cultural, religious or health services.[23]

A study conducted in 1990 by Prof. Alterman found that the Planning Law's no-compensation rule served as the primary instrument of obtaining land for public facilities (Alterman 1991, 26-32, 136-42). Reviewing the practice of local planning in Tel-Aviv and Haifa, Prof. Alterman demonstrated that the 40 percent no-compensation rule was used by local authorities for a variety of purposes, including acquisition of land for schools, community medical services, synagogues, community clubs for children and adults, neighborhood recreational areas and local roads. Furthermore, in interviews with Prof. Alterman, planning officials revealed that they treat the upper limit of 40 percent of a plot as a fixed measure, irrespective of urban density and of the statutory language which directs that *up to* 40 percent of a plot may be taken without compensation. Even in neighborhoods where urban density was relatively low and the population was not composed of families with young children

---

21 The no-compensation rule was first introduced in Palestine in the Ottoman period. The Ottoman Law of 1891 concerning the construction of streets, provided for the taking of land for road construction in municipal areas without full compensation (Goadby and Doukhan 1935, 332). The existence of a local law providing only for limited compensation on the eve of the British conquest may have contributed to the decision of the British Government to allow limitations on the right to compensation.

22 To prevent recurring uncompensated expropriation, the Acquisition for Public Purposes (Amendment of Provisions) Law of (1964) states in Section 2 that the 40 percent limit under the AO and the Planning Law is a cumulative figure with respect to any given parcel of land.

23 The only proviso is that the expropriation should not decrease the value of the remaining land held by the owner. Section 190(a)(1) of the Planning Law prescribes that land shall not be taken with or without compensation if the relative market value of the remainder of the land would decline as a result of the expropriation. However, this provision has proved to be virtually toothless, because it was interpreted by the Supreme Court as pertaining to decline in value as a result of the act of expropriation itself as opposed to any negative externalities resulting from the use made of the expropriated land. Section 190(1)(a) is currently applied only in rare cases when the remaining property, after the expropriated land has been carved out, is less marketable because of its unusual or unwieldy shape (Alterman 1990, 50-52).

(which would suggest less of a need for educational and recreational facilities), local authorities demanded dedication of 40 percent without compensation (Ministry of Construction and Housing 2000).

An important reason for the pre-constitutional practice of treating the upper limit of 40 percent of a plot as a fixed measure was the lack of meaningful judicial review of authorities' decisions to utilize the no-compensation rule. To get a sense of how Israel's Supreme Court could have narrowed the legal standard allowing for expropriation without full compensation, it is useful to look at the practice developed in this regard by American and English courts.

A Comparative Perspective

Express legislative authorizations to take land without compensation along the lines of the AO and the Planning Law do not exist in any other Western legal system (Erasmus 1990). Nevertheless, methods of shifting the funding of public services from the public to private property owners are common in American and English law.[24] These methods, known as development exactions, may take the form of a requirement for land dedication included in a contract between the authority and the developer or as a condition for issuing the building or subdivision permits. At first, development exactions were limited to on-site improvements. Local authorities required developers to dedicate land for public facilities such as access roads, sewer lines, sidewalks and parks that were located within the subdivision and were intended to serve the new development. Later, however, local authorities began exacting requirements for off-site improvements. These included land dedications or agreements to pay cash to provide public services such as schools, police stations and day-care centers located outside the subdivision (Altshuler et al. 1993; Connors and High 1987; Smith 1987).

Given the global trend toward private financing of public services, a more attuned observation would be that the Israeli no-compensation rule appears exceptional in a comparative perspective not because of the policy decision it represents but because of the way it is applied in practice. Israeli courts failed to limit the ability of local planning authorities to impose extortionate costs on property owners. This danger of using development exactions inappropriately exists in American law as well, but there, within the so-called unconstitutional conditions doctrine, courts have developed nexus and proportionality requirements which limit the power of authorities to take land.[25] The nexus and proportionality tests required evidence for proportional relationship between 'need created' and 'benefit conferred.' The 'need' test is that the new development must create the need for additional public investment—sewage facilities, parks, or schools—and the amount of the exaction must correspond to the cost of satisfying such need. The 'benefit' test is that the

---

24   English law is used throughout this volume to refer to the law of England and Wales.

25   The unconstitutional conditions doctrine, in general form, says that the state may not condition the availability of some discretionary benefit on an agreement by the recipient to waive or forgo a constitutional right.

expenditure must benefit the development and that it must relate to the particular
need that justified the exaction (Breemer 2002; Dana 1997; Fenster 2004).

A requirement that means and ends be reasonably related has also been developed
and enforced by English courts. In reviewing the practice of development exactions,
English courts have laid down a three-part test for examining the validity of a building
permit condition. The condition must be demanded by planning considerations; it
must relate fairly and reasonably to the development, and it must not be manifestly
unreasonably. A planning condition that does not comply with the three requirements
is invalid (Callies and Grant 1991; Delaney et al. 1987; Heap 1996, 214-26).

There is no equivalent in Israeli law to the American and English means-ends
tests which serve to limit disproportionate shifts of the burden of public projects to a
minority of property owners. Throughout the pre-constitutional era, Israel's Supreme
Court evinced deference to the practice of treating the upper limit of 40 percent of a plot
as a fixed measure for compensation deduction. It did not require local authorities to
prove either a nexus or a rough proportionality between the extent of land dedication
without compensation and the adverse effects on the community resulting from
the development. This position is surprising, given that a judicial requirement that
there be *some* relationship between the burden imposed on the property owner and
the adverse community impacts created by the new development could have been
created, based on the language of the Planning Law. As Prof. Alterman and other
scholars have suggested, the existence of a legal distinction between public purposes
with respect to which expropriation with or without compensation is permitted opens
the door to limiting the no-compensation rule through the process of judicial review.
The Planning Law's no-compensation rule could reasonably be interpreted as applying
only to local public services (as opposed to projects of a regional character) where
the one-time economic burden imposed on the property owner may be balanced by
the long-term benefits they receive from their community (Alterman 1990; Dagan
1999; Lewinsohn-Zamir 1994, 77-9). The judicial failure to read into the language
of the Planning Law a nexus test amounted to *de facto* approval of the practice of
overusing the no-compensation rule and imposing on landowners a disproportionate
share of the costs of supplying public services.[26]

Other Issues Affecting the Right to Compensation

In general, the goal of compensation payments under the AO and the Planning Law
alike is to place the landowner in a situation in which they would have been, if
the expropriation had not been executed. Compensation payments are typically

---

26 So prevalent and unrestricted is the practice of deducting the full 40 percent that the
market automatically adjusts land values to this possibility. In the 1987 case of *Local Planning
and Building Commission Rishon Le'zion v. Hamami* (C.A. 474/83, 41 (3) P.D. 370), the Court
indicated that urban land prices reflect this norm. The price of a square meter of land with respect
to which the full 40 percent have already been deducted is proportionally higher than a square
meter of land that has not been subjected to the no-compensation rule. See also recently, C.A.
8736/04, *Cohen v. Local Planning and Building Commission Ra'anana*, Takdin Supreme Court
Precedents 2006(1) 976.

measured on the basis of the market value of the most profitable use which could have reasonably made of the land were it not for the expropriation. According to the AO, the date for assessing compensation is the date of publication of the notice of expropriation. This has the advantage of allowing compensation to be measured without taking into account the detrimental effect of the expropriation on the free market value of the land. Yet the often protracted delays between the time of the notice of expropriation and the time of taking possession and the high rate of inflation that prevailed in Israel until the late 1980s have combined to make the rate of compensation unrealistically low.[27]

In 1977, the legislature amended the AO and allowed for inflation adjustment and interest on compensation that was due for payment.[28] The 1977 amendment improved the method for calculating compensation but still did not allow landowners to be made whole. First, the amendment provided for inflation adjustment only from 1977 onward and not for the periods prior to its enactment. Secondly, according to the 1977 amendment, compensation payments were adjusted to the Consumer Price Index (CPI) and interest was paid only on the net debt (not including inflation and interest adjustments). In Israel, the Building Price Index (BPI) has traditionally been higher than the CPI.[29] Hence, the failure of the law to adjust compensation to the BPI and to allow full interest on the adjusted value of the land leaves landowners with compensation that is less than full. Similar hardship also exists in relation to expropriation under the Planning Law.[30]

Another troubling feature of the law concerning compensation is the rule allowing the authority to transfer its rights in the expropriated land even if the property owner challenges the amount of compensation offered to them. According to Section 19 of the AO, a notice published in the Gazette declaring that the Minister of Finance acquired ownership in the expropriated land automatically vests ownership of the land in the authority with effect from the date of the publication. The only obligation imposed on the authority is to pay the amount of compensation that is not contested

---

27   The total inflation in Israel between December 1948 and December 1998 came to more than 24 million percent. In 1985, for example, a year with an inflationary surge, inflation was more than 1,100 percent (*Israel Year Book and Almanac* 1998, 175).

28   Section 2 of the Acquisition for Public Purposes (Amendment of Provisions) Law of (1964).

29   The average BPI between 1988 and 1998 was 112.7 in comparison to an average CPI of 85.7 (*Israel Year Book and Almanac* 1999, 172). There were periods in which surges in real-estate prices resulted in severe economic harm to property owners whose compensation was indexed to the CPI. For example, in 1989 and 1990, the BPI was 3,441.6 and 4004.7 respectively, while the corresponding CPI figures were 139.8 and 163.8. In the period 1995 to 1999, the general economic slowdown narrowed the gap between the two indexes. For the year 1998, for example, the BPI and the CPI both stood at 170.2 (Central Bureau of Statistics (CBS) 2003).

30   According to Section 190(a)(4) of the Planning Law, the date for measuring the compensation is 60 days after publication of a notice on expropriation. The adjustment of expropriation pursuant by the Planning Law is only in the rate of 70 percent and only in relation to increases in the CPI that occurred after March 1974.

within 90 days after it has taken possession.[31] In this regard, the obligation to compensate refers exclusively to monetary payments. Although compensation in the form of alternative land may often better alleviate the damage caused by the expropriation, Israeli law fails to grant property owners such a right and the Supreme Court has consistently refused to impose such an obligation on the authorities (Kamar 2001, 457-9).

To fully appreciate the grim treatment of property rights by the law and by judicial handling of land expropriation, it is necessary to set the legal doctrines against the background of Israel's tenure system of public land. As will be detailed below, land expropriations in Israel do not take place in 'thick' markets in which affected owners can easily buy an alternative land. Rather, the law and practice of land expropriation take place in conditions of a 'thin' market in which the vast majority of land is publicly owned and cannot be sold to individuals.

Israel's Tenure System of Public Land Ownership

Israel maintains a system of land tenure which is unusual for a country with an advanced economy. Approximately 93 percent of Israel's total land area of 21.7 million dunams[32] is owned by the state and by public bodies, and by law cannot be sold to individuals. That leaves only 7 percent of Israel's land area that is classified as private land and can be privately owned. Although the institution of public land ownership is recognized in the Western world, no other democratic country runs a land regime which freezes the vast majority of the land area under ownership of the state and national institutions (Alterman 2003).

The roots of Israel's tenure system date back to the period of Ottoman rule. The Ottomans, who governed the country from 1516 until the end of World War I (1918), established a feudal tenure system in Palestine (as well as in other conquered countries in the Middle East) based on the institution of state-owned land. The Ottoman institution of state ownership of land is rooted in Islamic religious law. The Koranic decree that 'To God belongs all that is in heaven and in the earth,' has been understood in Islamic law to mean that individuals can be neither the absolute owners nor the unfettered possessors of land and its resources (Weeramantry 1988, 61-2). In the context of the land tenure in Ottoman Palestine, the Land Code of 1858 divided the territory into five classes: *mulk, miri, waqf, matruka* and *mewat* (Tute 1927). Of these, *miri* (state) land constituted by far the greater part of the area under cultivation. This land, in contrast to *mulk* (private land), was considered under the paramount ownership of the state. Its holders were regarded as tenants and were not allowed to use the land for purposes that harmed the interest of the central government.[33]

---

31   Section 9A of the Acquisition for Public Purposes (Amendment of Provisions) Law of (1964).

32   1 dunam = 1000 sq. meters = 0.25 acre. These figures refer to the total area of Israel excluding the Occupied Territories (the West Bank and Gaza Strip), but including East Jerusalem and the Golan Heights.

33   Thus, for example, tenants of *miri* land were not allowed to mortgage or sell the land without the consent of the authorities. Nor were they permitted to use the land for a

The Ottoman category of state-owned land remained intact during the period of British rule in Palestine. The British, who governed the country under military rule from 1918 to 1922, felt constrained by the conditions of war and did not seek to make radical changes in the local legal system. After the establishment of the British Mandate over Palestine in 1922, the British continued to maintain the status quo, out of concern for the potential consequences of reform to the religious foundations of Ottoman law. Enjoined by the League of Nations from interfering in matters of religious law, the British Government issued an Order in Council in August 1922 which proclaimed that the Ottoman law which existed in Palestine on November 1914 should remain in force, unless practical difficulties arose (Bentwich 1932, 274-5).

When Israel declared independence in 1948, the Ottoman land categories were absorbed into Israeli law. The Law and Administration Ordinance of 1948, the first enactment to be passed by the Provisional Council of the State of Israel, stated in Section 11 that:

> The law which existed in Palestine on 5th Iyar, 5708 (14th May, 1948) shall remain in force, insofar as there is nothing therein repugnant to this ordinance or to the other laws which may be enacted by or in behalf of the Provisional Council of the State, and subject to such modifications as may result from the establishment of the State and its authorities (Friedman 1975).

In 1960, the Knesset (Israel's single-chamber parliament) anchored the principle of public land ownership in a new statute. The Basic Law: Israel Lands of 1960 proclaimed in Section 1 that 'the ownership of Israel lands, being the lands in Israel of the State, the Development Authority or the Jewish National Fund (JNF), shall not be transferred either by sale or in any other manner.' There are few exceptions to the rule which prohibits on the sale of public land. None, however, negates the meaning of public land holding as inalienable. The Israel Lands Law of 1960 that was passed in conjunction with the Basic Law permits the state to sell a specified area of no more than 100,000 dunams of its land (but not of JNF land).[34] The law also allows sale of public land to absentees who are in Israel in substitution for lands taken under the

---

wide range of activities, including brick-making, planting vineyards and orchards, building houses or creating enclosures. Such restrictions were intended to keep the largest amount of land available for agricultural production and to ensure the revenue interests of the central government (Stein 1984, 10-11). Gradually, however, the majority of the constraints on the use of *miri* land were abolished. In 1912, following the Young Turks Rebellion, the Ottoman government enacted a series of new land laws that removed most of the restrictions on *miri* land, placing it for most practical purposes on an equal footing with privately owned land. The only limitation that was left in force was the prohibition to turn *miri* land into *waqf* land. This restriction was due to the fact that once the land was proclaimed as *waqf*, the proclamation shielded the land from arbitrary acts on the part of the state and its officials (Eisenman 1979, 63-9; Granott 1952, 89-90).

34   This permission aimed to encourage investment in housing and in industry when the investors insist on acquiring ownership rights. Public authorities, however, do not make extensive use of this provision. Some figures suggest that by 1998, less than 60,000 dunams of public land were sold, while according to a different calculation only 30,000 dunams of public

Absentees' Property Law of 1950 or in exchange or as compensation for private land that was expropriated, provided that agricultural land may not be exchanged for urban land (Weisman 1995, 228-35).

An additional stage in the legal anchoring of the principle of nationally-owned land took place in 1969. Israel's legislature enacted a new Land Law in which it repealed the Ottoman land categories. Still, the new Land Law of 1969, currently in force, maintained the principle prohibiting the sale of 'Israel Lands.' The Land Law classifies the greater part of Israel's geographical area as 'public land' and adjusted its terms so that provisions allowing transfer of ownership over private land would not apply to public land (Weisman 1972, 6).

Israel's lands that are held under public and national ownership are owned by one of three entities.[35] The most important of these is the State of Israel itself, which owns about 74 percent of the publicly owned land area. A second owner is the Jewish National Fund (JNF), a company set up in England in 1905 to acquire land in Palestine for Jewish settlements. Its land-holdings amount to about 13 percent of Israel's total area of public land. The third entity is the Development Authority, a public company under the control of the government. The holdings of the Development Authority also comprise about 13 percent of the publicly owned land.

Since, as a general rule, land under public ownership cannot be sold, a unique pattern of leasehold contracts has developed in Israel. Land belonging to the State of Israel, the JNF or the Development Authority has been made available for private use by means of long-term leases. The authority entrusted with managing the public-land holdings in Israel is the Israel Lands Administration (ILA). The ILA is a government entity legally established in 1960 to create a unified policy for the management of public land and to cut the costs that would otherwise result from the operation of parallel land management bureaucracies by each of the three owners of Israel's public land. The Israel Lands Administration Law of 1960 stipulates that all three categories of public land will be administrated by the ILA (the managing body) and by the Israel Lands Council (the policy-making body). The Israel Lands Council is currently composed of 22 members, of which 12 are government appointees and 10 are representatives of the JNF.

Until the early 1970s, the land policy of Israel Lands Council set a definite lease period for leasehold contracts. Urban land was leased for a period of 49 years (harking back to the biblical notion of a jubilee cycle of 49 plus one year) while leases of agricultural land were signed for shorter periods which could range from

---

lands may have been sold. It should be noted that any transfer of JNF land (as opposed to state-owned land) requires the authorization of the JNF (State of Israel 1998).

35   The terms 'nationally owned' and 'publicly owned' will be used interchangeably in referring to Israel's land management policy. In the following discussion, they are both taken to mean the prohibition of land sale to private holding. In this sense, 'national land ownership' and 'public land ownership' differ from the common meaning of public property. The term public property often describes a situation where the beneficial use of the property is available to an indeterminate group, though the title is owned by a body more or less immediately accountable to the public such as a local or municipal authority. Public property, however, does not necessarily imply the prohibition of sale. For instance, a public park owned by a local authority can be sold on the market, unless the law provides otherwise (Barzel 1997, 99-101; Reeve 1986, 31-4).

three years to 49 years. At that time, the leasehold system was based on annual rent payments. Annual execution of payment by lessees to the ILA served to remind the lessees of their dependence on the real owners of the land. Under the old leasing regime, further payments to the owners were required upon any transfer of rights in public land or changes to existing buildings on the land or to the original use of the land. The leasing regime also required prior approval for each such change. In order to get approval for the transfer of leasing rights, leaseholders had to pay the ILA consent fees and, in cases in which the lessee was granted additional development rights, permission fees as well.

In the mid-1970s, the Israel Lands Council initiated a reform in the leasing system of urban land. This was because of problems of weak enforcement of the annual payments and a wish to eliminate the constant dealing with the ILA, as well as a policy decision to deepen the lessees' sense of ownership. First, the Council approved an automatic extension of urban leases for an additional 49 years. In 1999, the lease period for urban land was revised upward to 98 years, with an automatic extension for a further 98 years. Second, annual rent fees were replaced by a system of a single upfront payment. In 1973, the Israel Lands Council decided to enable lessees of urban land to capitalize the future stream of lease payments by paying 91 percent of the land value at the time the lease was issued. Capitalized leases released the lessee from the obligation of paying consent fees and permission fees. Following the reform of the leasing regime, the major restriction that has remained in force is that transactions in public land involving non-Israeli citizens are subject to ILA approval (Alterman 2003; Benchetrit and Czamanski 2004; Witkon 2004).

This reform in the leasing system of urban land achieved its goal of strengthening the lessees' sense of independence and blurring the differences between leasehold rights and private property rights under a freehold system.[36] Although well over half of Israelis who reside in cities and towns are, in fact, lessees and not owners of the land on which their homes are built, these leaseholders are normally not even aware of their true legal status.[37] Lessees treat the publicly owned land as if they were its owners and refer to the sale of their leasing rights as 'land sale,' although from a legal standpoint, the land is not sold in fee simple. Furthermore, the price of high-density apartment buildings on publicly owned land is similar to apartment buildings situated on private land. Evaluations of apartment prices in the Tel-Aviv metropolis found a gap of only 5 percent. By contrast, in the case of single-dwelling houses or industrial construction, the gap between private land and public land amounted to

---

36 The privatization of the leasing system did not apply to agricultural land. Under the new system, land for agricultural production is still leased for short periods and cannot be leased for a period of 98 years. In addition, the system of annual rent fees has remained in force and the standard agricultural lease form explicitly provides that in case of an alteration of the land use, the lease will be automatically terminated and the land will revert to the ILA. Lessees are entitled to limited compensation on the termination of their lease, intended mainly to compensate them for improvements to the land.

37 According to the ILA's records for 2003, approximately 900,000 housing units were under the arrangement of long-term leasehold contracts. *Israel Lands Administration Report* 2003-04 (Israel Lands Administration, 2003), 158. The total number of housing units in Israel in 2004 was approximately 1,700,000.

10 percent.[38] Interestingly, it is not only the reform in the leasing regime system that has blurred the distinction between the two categories of land ownership in the eyes of lessees; the property tax system does so as well. Lessees in Israel pay property taxes similar to freehold owners. The betterment levy, for example, which imposes a 50 percent tax on the value of any betterment due to plan-derived increments in land values, applies equally to lessees and real owners of land.

As will be reviewed below in Chapter 3, only in 2005 did the government approve in principle a reform in the current tenure system. According to the proposed reform, ownership rights will be transferred to private lessees of apartments and buildings. The reform will not apply to publicly owned land designated for agriculture and other non-residential uses (State of Israel 2005).

Given the fact that land in Israel is by and large publicly owned, the question immediately arises: why is there a need to resort to expropriation powers in order to obtain land for public use? The following discussion traces the factors that made land expropriation a prevalent practice in the Israeli setting.

Why Expropriate Private Land When Public Land Constitutes 93 Percent of the Land?

The main factor which makes expropriation powers an integral part of urban development in Israel is the location of private land. For historical reasons, the share of public land differs significantly between regions. Most of the land suitable for development in the large urban agglomerations—Tel-Aviv, Jerusalem and Haifa—is privately owned (Werczberger and Borukhov 1999, 134). Land held under public ownership is concentrated mainly in rural areas, the Negev desert and other peripheral regions of the country. As shown in Map 1.1, most of Israel's urban population is concentrated in the narrow coastal plain where the majority of the land is privately held. Hence, although less than 10 percent of Israel's land is privately owned, much of that private land is subject to high urban-expansion pressures.[39] As of 2003, Israel's population was 6.6 million people, 80 percent of whom are Jewish, and 90 percent of Israel's Jewish population is urban. Nearly 50 percent of the Jewish population (accounting for roughly 42 percent of the total population of the country) lives in greater Tel-Aviv; 25 percent of the population lives in the districts of Haifa and Jerusalem (CBS 2003).[40]

---

38   O. Sharvit, 'Chaos', *Ma'ariv* (Hebrew Daily)10 October 2004; Borukhov et al. 1978.

39   An exception is the city of Be'er Sheva. While considered a major urban center, private land constitutes a mere 6 percent of Be'er Sheva's municipal territory. This is due to historical reasons. Most of the Negev desert was considered state-owned land under the Ottoman Empire.

40   As an example of the high urban-expansion pressures in Israel, one can look at the population growth of four cities located in the coastal plain. Between 1972 and 1995, the population of Ra'anana grew from 15,200 to 58,400; the population of Rechovot grew from 39, 000 to 86,000; the population of Petach Tikva grew from 93,000 to 152,000 and the population of Herzliya grew from 41,000 to 83,000 (*Israel Year Book and Almanac*, 1999, 17).

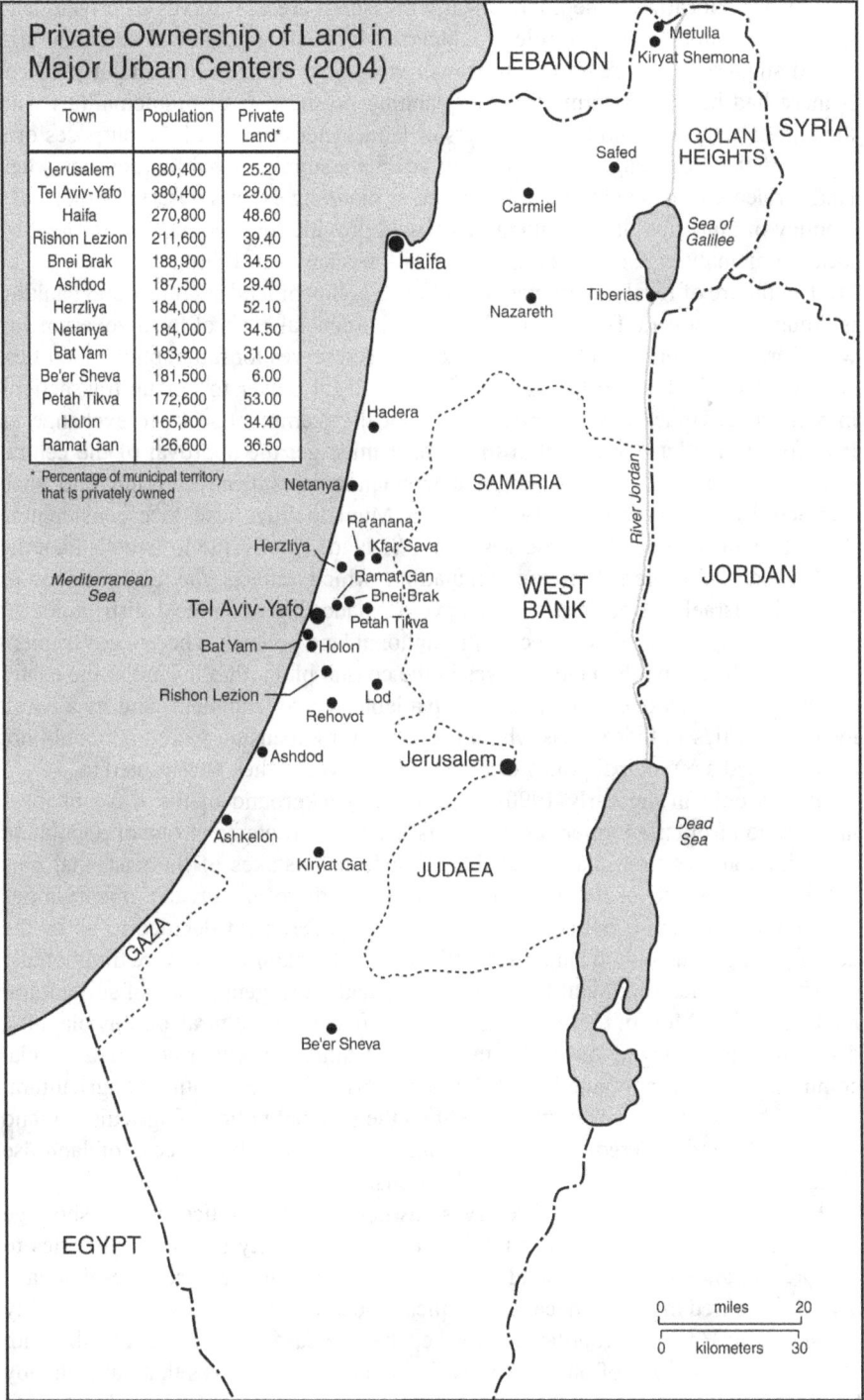

Private Ownership of Land in Major Urban Centers (2004)

Town	Population	Private Land*
Jerusalem	680,400	25.20
Tel Aviv-Yafo	380,400	29.00
Haifa	270,800	48.60
Rishon Lezion	211,600	39.40
Bnei Brak	188,900	34.50
Ashdod	187,500	29.40
Herzliya	184,000	52.10
Netanya	184,000	34.50
Bat Yam	183,900	31.00
Be'er Sheva	181,500	6.00
Petah Tikva	172,600	53.00
Holon	165,800	34.40
Ramat Gan	126,600	36.50

* Percentage of municipal territory that is privately owned

Map 1.1   Private Ownership of Land in Major Urban Centers (2004)

Given its location in demographically pressured areas, reserves of private land play a much more important role in urban development and renewal than their size would suggest. Accelerated urban growth would not have been a major problem if there had been long-term strategic planning on the part of municipalities with the aim of acquiring and banking tracts of land. After all, one of the purposes of a policy of 'land banking' is to ensure an adequate supply of public facilities when land is released for development. However, as planning experts observe, Israel lacks a policy of municipal land banking that would provide for accumulation of land by local municipalities for future public needs (Alterman et al. 1990).

The failure of local government to initiate a policy of land assembly and banking is grounded in several factors. One is the weak financial basis of local governments which prevents them from buying private land as reserves for future public facilities. Another factor relates to the lack of requisite legal power to pursue transactions in real estate. Under current laws, when a local government seeks to exchange its land for private land in a central location, it must get the approval of the central government, a condition that often deters landowners from entering into such transactions (Alterman et al. 1990, 19-23). Municipalities also face considerable difficulties in accumulating reserves of *public* land. This is due to Israel's national land policy of dispersal of the population, which reflects the commitment of successive Israeli governments to achieve a balanced geographical distribution of the Jewish population. One aspect of this national land policy has been a government decision to freeze public land reserves in the coastal plain. Public land in the center of the country has been chronically unavailable for development, and as a result local authorities in those areas where pressures for expansion were high could not have pursued a municipal policy of land banking even if they had wanted to.

It was only in the early 1990s, against the background of the wave of mass immigration from the former USSR, that Israel's deep-rooted doctrine of population redistribution was first challenged. Learning from mistakes of the past, that new immigrants wish to settle in urban areas where there are greater opportunities for employment and a better economic life, the government decided to allow the development of the public land reserves in the coastal plain which were traditionally classified as agricultural. Until then, Israel had had a stringent policy of agricultural land protection. Most of the open land was classified as agricultural and any planning decision that impinged on agricultural land required the approval of a special committee that was appointed in 1965 as a watchdog for preservation of agricultural land. In the 1990s, the government modified the national policy of agricultural land preservation and ordered the special committee to ease the process of land-use changes (Alterman 1997; Alterman and Rosenstein 1992).

Freeing up agricultural land reserves has not improved noticeably the shortage in public land for public facilities, however, nor the ability of local authorities to execute a municipal policy of land banking. The agricultural land reserves that have been declassified in the last decade are typically located on the outskirts of the highly pressured Tel-Aviv metropolis. Therefore, their release for construction has not alleviated the shortage of public land within existing urban areas that have already been built up. Furthermore, due to the weak representation of local authorities on the Israel Lands Council, which serves as a forum for national-level policy-making, a municipal policy of land banking has not been recognized as a desirable goal in Israel.

The combined effect of the lack of a municipal policy of land banking and the location of private land in areas of high urban pressure explains why, despite the tenure system of public land, local authorities look to privately owned land for the provision of public services. To complete the picture, it is necessary to examine the economic underpinnings of the system. Two economic factors drove local planning authorities to treat expropriation powers as an integral part of urban development. One is the division of responsibility between local and central government as to funding of public facilities, and the second is the statutory permission to expropriate without compensation.

As mentioned above in my analysis concerning the delays in realization of public facilities on the expropriated land, a significant factor contributing to this phenomenon has been Israel's structure of local government. Until the mid-1980s, the Israeli model of local government granted a great deal of control to the national government, and gave weak, almost non-existent powers to local government (Ben-Zadok 1993; Blank 2002). In the field of urban planning, this dependency was typically reflected in the division of responsibilities between local and central governments: local governments were in charge of providing the land for public facilities, and the central government financed the construction of the social facility and provided the services in question (education, health, welfare, etc). Even large cities that generate revenue through local taxes used to rely on state participation in the provision of public services (Kalchheim 1988). This system of funding public facilities underlined local governments' preference for land expropriation as opposed to exaction of fees. Since the only role of local authorities in the process was to provide the land for the public services, it was natural that this was the only element they focused on. Still, the acquisition of land could not have been accomplished had it not been for the no-compensation rule. Not only were local authorities freed from the cost of constructing the infrastructure, but, using their expropriation powers, they could acquire the land for free.

Reliance on expropriation powers rather than on fees in lieu of land dedication persisted into the 1990s, when the process of fiscal decentralization of local government picked up steam. From being heavily funded by the state, local governments shifted to being primarily self-funded (Ben-Elia 1999). They gained increased control over their revenues, and this in turn resulted in a variety of strategies (such as fiscalization of planning and zoning and initiating municipal boundary disputes) aimed at further increasing their revenues (Ben-Elia 2000). The 1990s were marked by growing competition among local authorities as to which would provide better public facilities and services, in order to attract and hold on to a middle-class population. This competition manifested itself in an extensive, if sometimes inefficient use of expropriation powers as a cost-free method of acquiring land for the intended public services. Because the traditional division of responsibilities between local and central government for the financing of public schools and, to a lesser extent, health, welfare and religious facilities, remained in place even after the shift to a regime of self-funding, local authorities resorted to expropriation not necessarily because of the need for additional public facilities but because land was available for free and the central government funded their facilities. A recent study found that in the field of education, for example, local governments constructed unneeded schools while existing schools were poorly maintained (Ben-Elia and Shai 1996; Blank 2004).

Given the features of the practice of land expropriation described above, the question arises as to the role of the courts, and in particular the Supreme Court, in protecting property owners and providing them relief. The statutory doctrines of the AO which ignore the basic rights of property owners, and the authority to obtain land without compensation pursuant to the Planning Law appear particularly harsh in light of the fact that they are applied mainly against a small group of citizens. Although expropriation powers could be also employed to leasing rights in public land, in practice the vast majority of the cases involving expropriation powers deal with owners of private land.[41] In the next chapter, I will explore the judicial treatment of property rights in land expropriation cases during the pre-constitutional era.

---

41   This observation should be modified with respect to the 1990s and onwards. Following the wave of immigration from the former Soviet Union, a process of middle-class suburbanization began. Since public land is typically situated on the periphery of urban centers, the process of suburbanization introduced the use of expropriation powers with respect to leasing rights of publicly owned agricultural land that was made available for urban development.

Chapter 2

Civil Rights and Land Expropriation: Double Standard in the Court in the Pre-Constitutional Era

Israel's expropriation jurisprudence in the pre-constitutional era, from the 1950s to the late 1980s, was marked by judicial deference. During that period, the concept of judicial review as applied to legislative acts was not recognized. Yet even so, and despite the fact that Israel lacked a constitution (and therefore also a constitutional guarantee of civil rights), the Supreme Court succeeded in establishing the protection of civil liberties. Declaring that the legal recognition of basic human rights was an integral aspect of Israel's democratic nature, the Court constructed what is commonly termed a 'judicial bill of rights.' This refers to a line of precedents in which the Supreme Court declared and enforced the protection of basic civil liberties such as the freedoms of speech, of association, of religion, of movement and of demonstration, as well as a number of procedural requirements which are sometimes referred to as the rules of natural justice. While these freedoms were not wholly immune from legislative interference, the Supreme Court developed tools of interpretation that protected them from administrative infringement. Government violations of civil rights were considered ultra vires and therefore void.

From comparison of the Court's decisions in cases concerning infringements of non-property rights to its rulings in land expropriation cases, a clear double standard emerges. Although land expropriation is the most blatant violation of property rights, the Court failed to ensure that private property was not infringed upon any more than necessity dictated. The Court's response to challenges to land expropriations was characterized by systematic deference to the executive branch. The Court declined to set meaningful limitations on the powers of expropriation, and its inaction amounted to a stamp of approval for expropriation orders.

This chapter examines the Israeli case law of land expropriation in the pre-constitutional period. The first section introduces the jurisdictional scope of Israel's Supreme Court. The second section outlines the pre-1992 periodization scheme of Israeli rights jurisprudence. This periodization scheme serves as a basis for the comparison between the Court's protection of civil rights on the one hand and land ownership rights on the other. The remainder of the chapter is devoted to establishing my argument regarding the lower level of legal protection afforded landowners in expropriation cases.

The Jurisdiction of Israel's Supreme Court

Israel's Supreme Court serves two functions. In one of its capacities, the Supreme Court hears cases in its role as the highest appellate tribunal for criminal and civil matters. In its other capacity, the Supreme Court sits as the High Court of Justice (hereinafter High Court or HCJ) (Edelman 1994; Maoz 1988; Shetreet 1994, 93-119). In this capacity, the Supreme Court serves as a court of first impression, with jurisdiction to review all administrative decisions over which no other court or administrative tribunal has authority. Any dispute concerning a public agency in the exercise of its legal powers may be brought directly before the HCJ. The dispute is resolved by the High Court without possibility of appeal. Ease of access to the Court is assured by minimal court fees (about $100 until 2000 and currently about $300) and by the absence of cumbersome formal requirements. A petition to the HCJ can be written by a layman, and at no stage of the proceedings is representation by a lawyer required. Hearings are based on the parties' affidavits and on their oral arguments. Oral testimony and cross examination are usually not allowed.

The High Court is able to grant petitioners immediate relief and to issue orders and injunctions, either interim or absolute, at any stage. Section 15 of Basic Law: Judicature of 1984 states:

> (C) The Supreme Court sitting as a High Court of Justice shall hear matters in which it deems necessary to grant relief in the interests of justice and which are not within the jurisdiction of any other court or tribunal.
> (d) Without prejudice to the generality of the provisions of subsection (C) the Supreme Court sitting as a High Court of Justice shall be competent ...
> (2) to order state and local authorities and the officials and bodies thereof ... to do or to refrain from doing any act in the lawful exercise of their functions, or if they have been improperly elected or appointed, to refrain from acting ...[1]

Pursuant to this authority, the High Court, like the High Court of Justice in England and Wales, has the authority to issue writs such as habeas corpus and mandamus (Goldstein 1994, 613). Moreover, judicial review by the HCJ takes place *in real time*, that is, immediately after the governmental action takes place, or even before it is completed. These institutional characteristics have contributed to the staggering increase in the number of petitions submitted to the High Court. The Supreme Court sitting as HCJ received 2000 petitions in 2001, more than nine times the number it had received 45 years earlier (CBS 1955-57).

It is through the jurisdiction of the High Court that Israel's Supreme Court has gradually extended its involvement in, and influence on, the Israeli polity. My review of the double standard in the judicial protection of property and non-property rights will therefore mainly refer to the performance of the Supreme Court in this capacity.

---

1   38 L.S.I. 101 (1984).

The Periodization of Israeli Civil Rights Jurisprudence

Scholars generally distinguish three major periods with regard to Israeli civil rights jurisprudence. The first period lasted from the inauguration of Israel's Supreme Court on September 15, 1948 until the enactment of the Judges Law in 1953.[2] This five-year period (and some extend it to the first decade) was characterized by the struggle of the Court to receive recognition as a full-fledged and equal branch of government (Lahav 1990a; Lahav 1993; Harris 1997). The status of the Supreme Court within the Israeli system of government during this period was uncertain. Judges did not have tenure, the legislature was openly involved in appointments, and termination of service was determined by the government. Furthermore, the Knesset decided in 1950 to reject its earlier commitment to enact a constitution, sending the Supreme Court a clear message regarding the supremacy of legislative acts in Israeli democracy. The ambivalent attitude of the legislative and executive branches toward the judiciary affected case law. The Supreme Court adopted a stance of judicial restraint that, in essence, accepted the political culture of the period. This is not to say that the Court did not protect basic liberties such as freedom of occupation and freedom of movement. However, application of judicial review was cautious. The early Court applied a deferential stance which focused on the procedural requirements of the laws in question. If the authority in charge violated the right of the individual in accordance with the requirements set by law, the Court refrained from substantive review. Its intervention was confined to cases where the authority did not follow the letter of the law.

The first steps toward changing the content of the Court's rights jurisprudence occurred in 1953 with the enactment of the Judges Law, which was soon followed by the landmark decision in *Kol-Ha'am v. Minister of Interior*. In this second period, which ran from the mid-1950s until the mid-1970s, the Court gradually transformed its procedural authority into a moral one, developing grounds for a substantive approach which looks at the policy considerations of the authority in charge rather than at fulfillment of procedural requirements. Yet by and large, the Supreme Court of the 1960s and the early 1970s still refrained from addressing sensitive political questions, and avoided direct confrontation with the executive branch, particularly with the security forces.

The third period began in the 1980s after the retirement of the senior Justices who had served on the Supreme Court since the early 1950s. What made the 1980s a periodization marker in the history of civil rights in Israel was the growing tendency on the part of the Supreme Court to expand the scope of judicial review. In a systematic manner, the Court developed new tools for judicial review and imposed new requirements, such as the duty of reasonableness, on administrative authorities. Moreover, it replaced the prior formalistic analysis of the legality of the governmental action (or decision) in favor of 'soft,' value-oriented analysis of interest-balancing. The constitutional decisions of the Supreme Court in the 1980s thus appear very different from the decisions of the Court in the 1950s and 1960s. For these reasons,

---

2   In my scheme of periodization, I am continuing the convention of Israeli historiography using 1948 as a central historiographical marker. For a challenge to this view, see Likhovski (1998).

it is common within Israeli legal scholarship to refer to the Supreme Court of the 1980s as the 'new Court' (Dotan 2002; Mautner 1993).

Given the sea-change in the doctrines applied by the Court to the protection of civil rights, a historical analysis of the Court's record in land expropriation cases would not be complete without situating land expropriation jurisprudence in the wider context of the developments that occurred in Israeli rights jurisprudence at the same time. Such an analysis is necessary in order to establish, with respect to any particular period, whether or not the Court's deference in land expropriation cases is attributable to an overall judicial philosophy of deference (Ackerman 1979). Where this is not the case—and I would argue that the Court's land expropriation jurisprudence was always been more deferential than its own judicial philosophy warranted—we can only conclude that its heightened judicial deference in land expropriation cases as compared to civil rights jurisprudence is attributable to the unique historical, social and political baggage that is associated in Israel with land and land ownership.

In its first five years of operation (1948-53), the Court's perception of its limited political power—and therefore its limited ability to shape Israeli law—dictated a policy of judicial restraint, which translated into a single-minded focus on procedural protection of civil rights. Yet what is noteworthy is that the Court did not accord landowners even this narrow scope of protection. Turning to the second period, from the mid-1950s to the mid-1970s, the Court's general rights jurisprudence reflected the development of a new standard of substantive judicial review. Again, however, in the area of land expropriation, the Court maintained its single-minded focus on technicalities. The third period underscores the unequal treatment accorded to the protection of civil liberties and land ownership rights. In the late 1970s and more so in the 1980s, the Court explicitly adopted a policy of judicial activism in all that concerned the protection of non-property civil rights. At the same time, however, as concerns land expropriation cases, no major jurisprudential developments took place that advanced the protection granted to landowners in a manner that was comparable to the advances in the protection of non-property civil rights.

Early Manifestations of the Double Standard, 1948-1953

Legal Formalism and Procedural Protection of Civil Rights

The early decisions of Israel's Supreme Court in defense of civil rights were characterized by cautiousness and a formalistic style of legal reasoning. In its relations with the Knesset, the Supreme Court did not seek to challenge the status of the legislature as the final authority in matters of law. In one of the very first cases that came before the High Court a few weeks after its establishment in 1948, the Court dismissed a petition to uphold the Declaration of Independence of Israel as a higher law against which the validity of laws and statues should be reviewed. Accepting the supremacy of the legislature, the Court held that '[the Declaration] gives expression to the vision of the people and its faith, but it contains no element of constitutional law which determines the validity of various ordinances and laws, and their repeal.'

Judicial self-restraint also marked the relations of the Court with the strong executive of the new state. Judicial review of administrative actions was introduced under the British Mandate. It was taken from English law current at the time and was maintained after independence. Nevertheless, although the Supreme Court's authority to review administrative actions as HCJ was not questioned, the Court opted for a narrow scope of review. This was evident primarily with regards to the 1945 Defence (Emergency) Regulations (hereinafter the 1945 DERs) that were heavily used by the executive in the early years. Upon independence, the Provisional Council of the State of Israel declared a state of emergency which resulted in the incorporation of the 1945 DERs promulgated by the British Mandatory authorities into Israeli law. The 1945 DERs, still in force today, vested the executive branch with highly intrusive powers. They authorized house demolitions, strict control over speech, deprivation of liberty without due process, deportation and even suspension of the civil judiciary in favor of military courts, as well as confiscation of private property. In reviewing challenges against the exercise of the 1945 DERs, the Court held that it was not authorized to consider the unreasonableness of the competent authority's decision to act against an individual, unless the authority in question acted in bad faith (Kretzmer 1990a).

This judicial deference to executive discretion was accompanied by a strong focus on legal formalities. The early Court was unwilling to question the validity of the decidedly anti-democratic 1945 DERs or to examine the merits of actions issued pursuant to their terms; yet it insisted that administrative agencies adhere to the letter of law, even in matters of national security and military activities. In the 1948 case of *Al-Karbuteli v. Minister of Defense*, for example, the Court set aside a detention order issued against a suspect, a Palestinian Arab, because of a technical misapplication of the law that could reasonably have been treated as a harmless error.[3]

Al-Karbuteli was detained under the 1945 DERs for more than a month without being notified of the reason for his arrest. Article 111 of the 1945 DERs allowed any military commander or a police officer to arrest without warrant any person 'whom he reasonably suspects of having committed an offence.' The officer issuing the detention order was not required to give a reason for detaining a suspect but had the power to detain persons whenever 'he is of opinion that it is necessary or expedient to make [the] order for securing the public safety, the defense of Palestine ... or the suppression of mutiny, rebellion or riot.' The 1945 DERs also provided no limits on the length of time individuals could be detained on the basis of military orders. Once the order was issued, it was not subjected to judicial review unless a writ of *habeas corpus* was submitted to the HCJ. In *Al-Karbuteli*, the military commander failed to follow the DERs' requirement of giving a suspect an opportunity to appear before an advisory committee. It turned out that at the time the detention order was issued, no such committee was yet in existence. From a practical perspective, the failure did not have immediate implications for the suspect. The 1945 DERs did not empower the advisory committee to act as an appellate court; all it could do was to issue its

---

3   H.C. 7/48, *Al-Karbuteli v. Minister of Defense*, 2 P.D. 5.

recommendation regarding the detainee. Yet despite the seemingly technical nature of the fault, the Court refused to regard it as inconsequential. In ordering the release of the suspect, the Court explained:

> since the rule of law is one of the greatest foundations of the entire State, there would be grave damage to the [public interest] if the authorities could use the powers conferred by the legislature, even temporarily, in utter disregard of [statutory restrictions] ... It is true that the security of the State, which requires the detention of a person, is no less important than the need to protect the citizen's right, but when it is possible to accomplish both purposes together, one cannot disregard one or the other.

The same insistence on the compliance of government organs with legal rules led the Court to invalidate a deportation order that was signed by a military commander rather than by the Minister of Defense,[4] and an order to seal an area that had not been published as required by the law.[5]

Perhaps the most remarkable case in which the Court invoked legal formalism as a means of protecting civil freedoms is the 1949 case of *Al-Couri v. Chief of Staff.*[6] Naif Al-Couri was a Palestinian policeman who intentionally refrained from providing assistance to Jewish members of Kibbutz Negba who were being attacked by an Arab mob. Claiming that Al-Couri was responsible for the murder of Jews *qua* Jews, the Chief of Staff issued a one-year administrative detention order against him. In the detention order, the Chief of Staff did not specify the location for detention as required by Article 111 of the DERs. Under the circumstances, the defects of the detention order could have appeared trivial. However, the Court analyzed the legality of the detention order without taking into account the specifics of the case. Adhering to strict formalism, the Court granted the petition and rejected the state's argument that the omission was merely a technicality. The Court insisted that the failure to indicate the place of detention as required by law made the order incurably defective.

The formalism that characterized the pro-civil rights decisions of the first five years may be attributed to contextual factors influencing the Supreme Court's perception of its constitutional role in Israeli society. From an institutional standpoint, the Supreme Court started at a disadvantage compared to the other branches of government. The Court was inaugurated on September 15, 1948, exactly four months after the establishment of the State, and it needed the cooperation of the two other branches in order to survive politically. The legislature did not show a favorable attitude toward the judiciary. To begin with, the Court had to fight for judicial independence (Lahav 1990a). Although Israel's first Knesset maintained a very active record of legislation, it failed to address the status of the judiciary during its four-year term (1948-52). As a result, judges continued to operate until 1953 under the Mandatory system, which did not provide for judicial tenure and allowed open and active involvement by the legislature and the executive in the appointment and dismissal of judges. Even after the enactment of the Judges Law of 1953, which established judicial

---

4   H.C. 240/51, *Al-Rachman v. Minister of Interior*, 6 P.D. 364.
5   H.C. 220/51, *Aslan v. Military Governor of the Galilee*, 5 P.D. 1480.
6   H.C. 95/49, *Al-Couri v. Chief of Staff*, 4 P.D. 34 .

tenure and changed the system of selecting judges, the legislature and executive continued to treat the Court with disrespect. The memoirs of Isaac Olshan, one of the original appointees to the Supreme Court and the second Chief Justice (1953-65), are full of complaints about the intolerance and lack of understanding of members of the government toward the judiciary (Olshan 1978, 394-452).[7]

The impression that the Court was the least important branch of government was further reinforced by the decision not to enact a constitution. Israel's Declaration of Independence of May 14, 1948 included an explicit commitment to establishing a constitutional legal regime. The Declaration called for a constituent assembly to be formed, which was to submit a proposal for a constitution 'no later than 1 October 1948.' Yet, as it turned out, the Knesset never upheld this commitment and instead it adopted what is known as 'Harari Resolution,' according to which Israel's constitution would be enacted piecemeal through a series of Basic Laws. In the debates that arose on the matter in 1951, Israel's political elite made clear that it preferred the democratic model of pure majoritarianism over a model of entrenched rights. The effect of this position was to give the Knesset the upper hand over the Court (Gavison 1985; Shapira 1993).

Aware of its political weakness and of its low status in the eyes of its political masters, the early Court retreated into procedural guarantee of the rule of law. Literal reading of statutes and a focus on the law's requirements served a dual function in the legal culture of early Israel. On the one hand, the formalistic stance which relegated all political and ethical considerations to another sphere enhanced the impression of autonomy of the judicial process and allowed the Court to establish its status in the Israeli polity and to generate respect for its decisions under the cast of 'strict objectivity' (Lahav 1990a). On the other hand, the insistence of the Court on government compliance with procedure and formal rules served an important educational purpose. Israel of 1950, as Ehud Sprinzak has observed, lacked a heritage of legalism (Sprinzak 1986; Sprinzak 1993). The Zionist movement espoused the ideology that will and practice were usually preferable to compliance with legal rules. For its leaders, who came from Eastern Europe and had never experienced a democratic culture, the conception of democracy did not include the idea of the primacy of the legal order. The Zionist leadership also shared the socialist ideology that bureaucracy, legality and formality implied false consciousness and a bourgeois mentality (Shapiro 1977, 62-3). Educating the young Israeli society to values of legalism was one of the first priority tasks of the early Court (Witkon 1962).

An additional factor shaping the purely procedural and substantively deferential approach of the early Court was the English legal tradition. In the formative period, the Supreme Court relied heavily on English legal precedents, and English legal formalism certainly had a significant impact on the scope of judicial review and on the style of legal reasoning adopted by the newly established Supreme Court (Shachar et al. 1996). Formalism also enhanced the innate desire for legal certainty.

---

7   For example, the Justices were denied diplomatic passports and they were not seated prominently at state functions. Today, Justices of the Supreme Court are invited to all major as well as minor public occasions. At all public gatherings, when the Prime Minister and the Speaker of the Knesset are present, the President of the Supreme Court is usually also present.

It may well be that the Court's refusal to advance any vision of its own as to the normative character of the Israeli 'well-ordered society' also reflected the impact of a political theory that trusted the executive to promote the common good. The turbulent domestic and international situation of the new state drove the public to trust Israel's founding political elite and its decision-making, particularly in matters of national security (Kretzmer 1990a; Lahav 1993).

Despite the rather general nature of the societal factors described above, they did not generate the same effect in all fields of constitutional adjudication. In civil rights disputes, the Court protected the individual through an insistence on the good faith of the decision-makers and on their compliance with the procedures set out in law, but when it came to a review of challenges against land expropriation it failed to do so.

Early Expropriation Cases

A prominent case which may serve as an example of the early case law of land expropriation and of the discrepancy between the judicial protection of non-property civil rights such as freedom of movement and that of land ownership is *Dor v. Minister of Finance*.[8] In that case, the petitioners' land was originally confiscated under the mistaken assumption that the petitioners, Arab Palestinians, were absentees according to the definition of the Absentees' Property Law of 1950. That law allowed the State of Israel to take possession of the property of persons who were considered absentee and to hold it in custodianship. When the authorities were apprised of their mistake, they decided to expropriate the petitioners' land again, this time pursuant to the AO. In the notice sent to the petitioners, no details were given of the purpose of the expropriation. However, an investigation conducted by the petitioners themselves disclosed that their land was designated for a project to build houses for new immigrants.

In their petition to the High Court of Justice, the petitioners raised two arguments. The first referred to the decision of the Minister of Finance to recognize the purpose of housing immigrants as a public purpose in terms of legitimizing the exercise of expropriation powers. Building housing for immigrants, the petitioners claimed, could not be regarded as a 'public purpose,' as it was not a purpose which benefited the public as a whole, but rather directed at expropriating the land of one person in order to give it to another. In addressing this argument, the Court dismissed the invitation to review the Minister's definition of public purpose. It contended that the wording of Section 2 of the AO which vests in the Minister of Finance the discretion to decide what constitutes a 'public purpose' does not leave room for review of the Minister's considerations. The Court's refusal to examine the grounds and reasonableness of the Minister's decision is not surprising. After all, this position was consistent with the general policy of the early Court of refraining from second-guessing administrative decisions. What strikes me as a deviation from the legal standard of the period is the Court's response to the second argument of the petitioners in *Dor*, which was an attack on the legality of the expropriation on the grounds that it was decided upon in

---

8   H.C. 180/52, *Dor v. Minister of Finance*, 6 P.D. 908.

bad faith. The primary purpose of the second expropriation, the petitioners argued, was retroactively to validate the illegal construction of the housing project, which had been carried out on the mistaken assumption that the land belonged to absentee landowners. The legality of the expropriation was indeed dubious, but the Court decided to reject the petition and to treat the matter forgivingly. In responding to the petitioners' argument, the Court explained:

> even if the authorities erred from the beginning, *and that everything they did at the time, they did unlawfully, there was nothing wrong in correcting the illegal action retroactively.* Instead of continuing to break the law or instead of stopping the important work, the authorities rethought the matter and, desiring to validate their action from then on, directed their actions in accordance with the law.[9] (emphasis added)

The outcome of Dor stood in contrast to the ardent concern of the early Court with prevention of illegal acts and misuse of powers. Furthermore, *Dor v. Minister of Finance* was not the only case in the formative years in which the Court failed to void an expropriation order tainted by unlawfulness and bad faith. In *Savorai v. Minister of Labor and Construction,* for example, the acquiring authority took possession of the petitioner's land without issuing an expropriation order as required.[10] Despite this omission, the authority began constructing a road on the expropriated land and ignored the petitioner's protests against the illegal action. Then, three weeks before the case was scheduled to be heard, the authority retroactively issued the required order. When the case reached the High Court of Justice, the omission at least apparently had been corrected. The Court criticized the manner in which administrative organs often ignored the formal requirements of the rule of law, but refused to intervene on behalf of the landowner. In a two-page decision, it explained that since the illegal action had already been corrected, there was no reason for the Court to undo the expropriation at that stage.

Other early examples of the discrepancy between the judicial attitudes in protecting the individual in land expropriation cases and in non-property civil rights are the cases of *Feldman* and *Dwiak.* In *Feldman,* the Court upheld an expropriation although the Minister of Finance failed to follow the requirements set by the AO as to publication of the notice of expropriation.[11] In *Dwiak,* the Court dismissed a petition to set aside an expropriation order that was issued without first obtaining funding for compensation, as required by law. Relying on the fact that authorization was received a short period after issuing the expropriation order, the Court treated the delay as a mere technical fault and upheld the expropriation.[12]

In that first formative five-year period of the Supreme Court's existence, the double standard in the treatment of land expropriation was related thus to procedural defenses. The early Court failed to grant landowners the same procedural protection it accorded to individuals in cases involving administrative infringements of non-property civil rights. In the second period, from the mid-1950s to the mid-1970s,

---

9 Id. at 911.

10 H.C. 85/49, *Savorai v. Minister of Labor and Construction,* 2 P.D. 887.

11 H.C. 136/50, *Feldman v. Minister of Finance,* 5(1) P.D. 432.

12 H.C. 124/55, *Dwiak v. Minister of Finance,* 10(1)P.D. 753.

this inconsistency continued to characterize the rights discourse of Israeli law, and it became even more pronounced following the precedent-setting *Kol-Ha'am* and the development of a new substantive standard of judicial review.

The Evolution of Israel's Judicial Bill of Rights, 1950s to 1970s

Kol-Ha'am and the Foundations of Israel's Judicial Bill of Rights

A widely acknowledged turning-point in the Court's contribution to rights and democracy in the first two decades of statehood is the opinion in *Kol-Ha'am v. Minister of Interior*,[13] which was handed down in 1953 and is the most cited Supreme Court case for the years 1948-94 (Shachar et al. 2004). It provided a theoretical model and a methodology for integrating civil rights into the Israeli legal system in spite of the lack of constitutional protection for those rights (Dorner 1999; Lahav 1990, 231-4; Kretzmer 1990a; Mautner 1993).

Kol-Ha'am arose when two newspapers affiliated with the Israeli Communist Party published an article in March 1953 that was highly critical of the relations between Israel and the United States. Relying on an erroneous report in Israel's respected daily *Ha'aretz*, according to which Abba Eban, then Israel's ambassador to the United States, had informed the American authorities that Israel was willing to commit 200,000 troops if war broke out between the United States and the Soviet Union, the Israeli Communist Party published editorials denouncing the Government in its two dailies, the Hebrew-language *Kol-Ha'am* and its Arabic counterpart, *Al-Ittihad*. The editorials called on the Ben-Gurion government to cease its profiteering from the blood of Israeli youth and suggested that 'if Abba Eban or anyone else wants to go and fight on the side of the American warmongers, let him go, but alone.'

Following the publication of these articles, the Minister of Interior suspended the publication of both Communist newspapers (but not of *Ha'aretz*) for periods of ten and fifteen days. The administrative suspension relied on the Press Ordinance, a British enactment of 1933 which stipulated in Section 19(2) that 'The [Minister of Interior] ... may, if any matter appearing in a newspaper is, in [his] opinion ... likely to endanger the public peace ... suspend the publication for such a period as he may think fit...'

The newspapers challenged the Minister's decision in the High Court. In a celebrated unanimous opinion that discussed theories relating to First Amendment jurisprudence, the Court set aside the suspension order (Lahav 1981). It is difficult to assess to what extent the boldness of this step was due to the personality of Justice Agranat (who wrote the opinion) or to the passage of the Judges Law in August 1953 which ensured the institutional autonomy of the judicial system. Yet it is beyond doubt that the decision in *Kol-Ha'am* laid the foundations for Israel's judicial bill of rights. In its doctrinal breakthrough and constitutional message, *Kol-Ha'am* was Israel's *Marbury v. Madison* (Burt 1989; Tushnet 2000). What characterizes *Kol-*

---

13   H.C. 73/53, *Kol-Ha'am Company Ltd. v. Minister of Interior*, 7 P.D. 871; translated in 1 Selected Judgments of the Supreme Court of Israel (1948-53) 90.

Ha'am and made it the cornerstone of Israeli rights jurisprudence was the readiness of the Court to state its position on substantive grounds and to make innovative use of Israel's Declaration of Independence as an indirect source of law.

Kol-Ha'am rejected the deferential judicial attitude of the early years, which limited protection of civil liberties to procedural protection. Professor Pnina Lahav provides a fine description of the judicial breakthrough in Israeli constitutionalism. *Kol-Ha'am* was the first case in which the Supreme Court moved beyond formalism and established substantive criteria for a narrow interpretation of any legislation that infringed upon basic individual rights. Section 19 of the Press Ordinance vested full discretion in the Minister of the Interior to suspend a publication for 'such period as he may think fit.' Yet Justice Agranat managed to impose limits on this broad discretion. He imported from American First Amendment jurisprudence the principle of balancing competing interests and developed a guideline principle according to which a newspaper could be suspended only if the Minister concluded, after having taken into consideration the 'high public value of the principle of freedom of the press,' that 'as a result of the publication, there is probable danger to public order.' Justice Agranat did not stop at the formulation of a substantive standard for suspending freedom of speech in light of claims about threats to national security. He reviewed the Minister's judgment according to the new substantive criteria and determined that the suspension order should be invalidated since the publication was unlikely to endanger public order (Lahav 1997, 107-12).

As Prof. Lahav has argued, Agranat's opinion in *Kol-Ha'am* vindicated 'sociological jurisprudence' (Lahav 1997, 108). For the first time, Israel's Supreme Court recognized law as a social system, and the judicial process as an enterprise of balancing interests. The function of the Supreme Court under this new understanding was to serve as a guardian of civil liberties. The Court anchored its duty to protect civil rights in the liberal statements of Israel's Declaration of Independence of May 14, 1948. The Declaration states that the State of Israel:

> [w]ill be based on freedom, justice and peace as envisaged by the Prophets of Israel; it will ensure the complete equality of social and political rights to all its inhabitants irrespective of religion, race or sex; it will guarantee freedom of religion, conscience, language, education and culture ... and it will be faithful to the principles of the Charter of the United Nations.[14]

As previously mentioned, prior to *Kol-Ha'am*, Israel's Supreme Court had refused to regard the Declaration (and this section in particular) as part of Israel's positive law. In the 1948 case of *Zeev v. Acting District Commissioner of the Urban Area of Tel-Aviv (Yehoshua Gubernik)*, the Court held that the written document did not have the legal force of a higher law.[15] Justice Agranat in *Kol-Ha'am* was aware of this holding. But in a bold leap, he reinterpreted it, opening the door for the introduction of the Declaration into Israeli law. In a widely quoted passage he explained that insofar as the Declaration of Independence 'expresses the vision of the people and

---

14 1 L.S.I. 3(1948).

15 H.C. 10/48, *Zeev v. Acting District Commissioner of the Urban Area of Tel-Aviv (Yehoshua Gubernik)*, 1 P.D. 85; translated in 1 Selected Judgments of the Supreme Court of Israel (1948-53) 68.

its faith, we [the judges] are bound to pay attention to [it] when we come to interpret and give meaning to the laws of the state.'[16]

To be sure, the Declaration does not explicitly guarantee the right to freedom of speech. But given the character of Israel as a democracy and as a freedom-loving country, Justice Agranat maintained that freedom of speech must be considered part of the Israel's legal order and hence should influence statutory interpretation. Justice Agranat thus made an innovative use of the Declaration as a source for statutory interpretation and legal recognition of extra-statutory rights (Cohen 2003; Shapira 1983, 421-3). If in the first years (1948-53) the Court based its holdings only on normative legal sources, *Kol-Ha'am* opened the door to unwritten ideas and a liberal vision of Israeli democracy as a valid source of legal rights against infringing legislation. According to the reasoning of *Kol-Ha'am*, a statute should not be construed as allowing violation of the democratic principles embodied in the Declaration of Independence, unless the legislature used unequivocal language (Barak 1987, 66-8).

In the case law that followed *Kol-Ha'am*, the Supreme Court further utilized the Declaration of Independence to develop a substantive standard of judicial review and to protect civil rights left unprotected by the Israeli legislature. Freedom of speech and its intimate relationship to freedom of association were recognized and given priority, even in the face of considerations of national security; the right of the public to know and the concomitant limitations on political censorship of movies was introduced into the legal system; and freedom of religious worship of Reform Judaism was guaranteed. Putting aside the Court's performance in expropriation cases, the constitutional jurisprudence in the two decades after *Kol-Ha'am* presented efforts on the part of the Supreme Court to transform its procedural authority into a moral one. The Court of the 1960s and early 1970s was gradually emerging as the champion of civil liberties and the number of petitions presented to it was on the rise (Goldstein 1994; Maoz 1988a; Zysblat 1996, 7).

The Failure to Set Substantive Limits to Expropriation Powers

A telling decision which may help to illuminate the double standard that permeated the case law of expropriation in this period is the judgment in *Kardosh v. Registrar of Companies* from 1960 in which the Court established the protection of freedom of association.[17] Kardosh was the leader of El-Ard (The Land), the first exclusively Arab political movement in Israel. The movement, composed of young Israeli Arab intellectuals, was highly influenced by the pan-Arab call of Egypt's President Nasser. It did not recognize the right of Israel to exist as a Jewish state and aimed at forming an Arab entity in Palestine which would form part of the awakening Arab nation, stretching from North Africa to Iraq. In April 1960, the group filed an application with the Haifa office of the registrar of companies to form a corporation. Their purpose, they

---

16   H.C. 73/53, *Kol-Ha'am Company Ltd. v. Minister of Interior*, 1 Selected Judgments of the Supreme Court of Israel (1948-53) 90, 105.

17   H.C. 241/60, *Kardosh v. Registrar of Companies*, 15(2) P.D. 1151; translated in 4 Selected Judgments of the Supreme Court of Israel (1961-62) 4.

said, was to 'engage in printing, publishing, translation, journalism, book importation and other matters related to printing.' By the time Kardosh applied for registration, the disruptive potential of *El-Ard*'s nationalist platform had sounded the alarm in the Israeli security services. Relying on the Attorney General's finding that the group was subversive, the registrar denied the group a permit to incorporate. El-Ard petitioned the High Court. Applying the reasoning of *Kol-Ha'am*, namely that statutes should be interpreted to avoid impairing civil liberties, the Court invalidated the denial, allowing the group to form a corporation to disseminate its views (Harris 2002).

The statute that vested power in the registrar of companies was inherited from the British Mandate and was a typical product of colonial legislation. It allowed the executive branch 'absolute discretion' in deciding whether to allow groups to incorporate. The registrar argued that the term 'absolute discretion' meant no or minimal judicial review of its action. The Court rejected the State's argument. Taking the jurisprudence that was developed in *Kol-Ha'am* one step further, the majority held that '[t]he general principle is that every administrative agency should act within the four corners of the purpose for which it was vested with powers by law, regardless of whether the statutory language created absolute or limited discretion.' Hence, in the absence of an unequivocal statutory authorization to censor, the powers of the registrar of companies should not be interpreted to include ideological monitoring. In a subsequent rehearing of the case, a five-Justice panel upheld the original decision.[18] It explained that Israel's democratic nature as expressed by the Declaration of Independence demanded a narrow reading of the law's wording regarding 'full and complete discretion.' These words should be construed as leaving room for judicial review that would examine the reasonableness of the limitations imposed on the right to freedom of association.

The interpretive rule which allowed substantive judicial review even in cases when the authorizing legislation granted the administrative body 'full and complete discretion' carried significant implications for the field of expropriation. As Dr. Chaman Shelach observed in a perceptive article, it was to be expected, given the *Kardosh* decision, that the Supreme Court would also examine the reasonableness of the Minister of Finance's decision to expropriate land. After all, the AO (unlike Section 14 of the Companies Ordinance at issue in *Kardosh*) did not use the language of 'absolute discretion' (Shelach 1980). Section 2 of the AO, it will be remembered, states that public purpose means '[a]ny purpose certified by the Minister of Finance to be a public purpose'; and Section 3 grants the Minister the power to order the expropriation of any land when 'he is satisfied that it is necessary or expedient for any public purpose.' Yet despite the developments in the scope of judicial review, when the issue of the AO came before it, the Court would refuse to examine the extent of the Minister's discretion in a manner consistent with its holding in *Kardosh*. Instead, the Court issued opinions in which it limited the scope of its review to matters of strict illegality or patently extraneous considerations.

---

18 F.H. 16/61, *Registrar of Companies v. Kardosh*, 16(2) P.D. 1209; translated in 4 Selected Judgments of the Supreme Court of Israel (1961-62) 32 (Cohen J. and Olshan J. dissenting).

An example of the inconsistency in the norms of judicial review employed by the Court in the period following *Kol-Ha'am* is the decision in *Committee for the Defense of Expropriated Land in Nazareth v. Minister of Finance.*[19] In this case from the mid-1950s, the petitioners, an organization of Israeli Arabs residing in the city of Nazareth, challenged the discretion of the Minister of Finance to expropriate a particular spot situated on the highest hill of the city. The expropriation order was issued so that a government center in the Galilee could be constructed on the site. Referring to the wording of Section 3 of the AO, the Court contended that discretion to choose which land to expropriate was conferred absolutely on the Minister of Finance and hence his policy considerations were immune from judicial review. Unless the petitioners could prove that the decision to expropriate a particular plot of land was tainted by bias, conflict of interest or any other similarly extraneous consideration, the Court would not intervene.

Judicial self-restraint coupled with formalistic reasoning characterized also the decisions in *Kalmas v. Local City and Planning Commission of Tel Aviv-Jaffa* and *Avivim Ltd. v. Minister of Finance.* In *Kalmas*, the petitioner challenged the necessity of the expropriation in light of a four-year delay in implementing the public purpose. [20] In *Avivim*, at issue was whether the Minister of Finance was obligated to disclose to the landowner the specific public use for which the land was designated.[21] As mentioned in Chapter 1, the AO does not indicate whether a delay in implementing the public purpose should be considered a *de facto* abandonment of the need for the expropriation, nor does it require the Minister to reveal the public purpose for which the land is taken and to conduct a hearing process. The cases thus called for an activist interpretation that would limit the state's power to expropriate land in the name of the unwritten democratic value of property rights. Although as regards freedom of speech, freedom of association and other non-property civil rights, the Supreme Court in the post-*Kol-Ha'am* period managed to integrate unwritten liberal principles into the legal system, in *Kalmas* and *Avivim* it saw an obstacle for doing do in the wording of the AO. Employing an extremely narrow reading of the text, the Court held that, since the AO does not contain explicit provisions which set a timeframe for implementation of the public purpose and obligate the Minister to reveal the specific public purpose and grant owners right to a hearing, the expropriation orders at issue should be held valid.

Formalist reasoning also characterized the Court's handling of claims against changes in the public use of the expropriated land. As recalled, the AO does limit the acts taken by the authority in the post-expropriation period and does not recognize the right of the owner to restitution upon changes in the public use designation. In *Ge'ulat Hakrach v. Minister of Finance*, the land at issue was expropriated for the purpose of constructing a road and building facilities for an army base.[22] It turned out that the road

---

19 H.C. 30/55, *Committee for the Defense of Expropriated Land in Nazareth v. Minister of Finance*, 9(2) P.D. 1261.

20 H.C. 75/57, *Kalmas v. Local City Building and Planning Commission Tel Aviv-Jaffa*, 11 P.D. 1601.

21 F.H. 29/69, *Avivim Ltd. v. Minister of Finance*, 24(2) P.D. 397.

22 H.C. 227/72, *Ge'ulat Hakrach Ltd. v. Minister of Finance*, 26 P.D. 155.

was narrower than originally planned and the property owners appealed to get back the unused land. A similar claim arose in *Banin v. Minister of Finance.*[23] In *Banin* the petitioner's land, located in the Talpiyot neighborhood of Jerusalem, was expropriated in 1960 for use as a military base. At the time, Talpiyot was on the border with Jordan. After the Six-Day War (1967) and the annexation of East Jerusalem, the Israeli army closed the base. In 1971, the owner learned from a newspaper article that the state planned to develop a residential neighborhood on the land. The owner, who had not received compensation when his land was expropriated in 1960,[24] filed a petition with the Court, claiming that the state could not change the public use designation of the expropriated land, and if it wished to do so it should re-expropriate the land and pay compensation according to the current market value of the land (which was much higher in 1971 than in 1960).

The Supreme Court dismissed both petitions. It held that since the AO did not require the acquiring authority to return land upon changes in land use designation, it was not within the authority of the Court to intervene in the expropriation, even if justice might require doing so.

The 1960s and early 1970s thus saw a continuity of the discrepancy in the judicial treatment of civil liberties and property rights. However, while in the early years, the Court's refusal to review the reasonableness of expropriation orders related to a political and philosophical disinclination to develop a substantive concept of the rule of law, this was not the case with regard to the judicial deference in the land expropriation case law of the second decade. The Court of the 1960s had gradually gained prestige and authority within Israel's system of government. Accordingly, its strengthened institutional status enabled it to shift its role from guarantor of strict legality to arbiter of the normative content of Israeli democracy. As part of this process, the Court expanded the scope of its review over the content of policies and decisions adopted by the executive. Furthermore, the gradual change in the perception of the judiciary's role as a constitutional decision-maker was reflected also in the mode of legal reasoning. In the non-property adjudication of the 1960s and early 1970s, the Court consciously resorted to external (extra-normative) principles of Israeli democracy such as those appearing in the Declaration of Independence in order to narrow the actual application of the infringing legislation. These changes did not reach the field of land expropriation. The Court based its reasoning on a literal reading of the law, the Declaration of Independence was never mentioned in the land expropriation case law of the period, and in terms of doctrines of judicial review, the Court failed to create substantive standards for limitations of expropriation powers. As will be analyzed below, the gap in the treatment of private property and non-property civil rights widened in the 1980s in consequence of the process by which the Supreme Court redefined its constitutional role in Israeli society.

---

23 H.C. 282/71, *Banin v. Minister of Finance*, 25(2) P.D. 466.

24 The owner refused to accept the below-market compensation offered him by the state, because to do so would have required him to waive any claim to further compensation.

Widening the Gap in an Age of Judicial Activism: The Late-1970s and 1980s

The Changing Role of the Supreme Court

The trend of expanding judicial review beyond the letter of the law reached a peak in the late 1970s and 1980s. As mentioned, the literature commonly treats the 1980s as a turning-point which distinguishes between the 'old Court' and the 'new Court.' This periodization scheme rests on an observation about the occurrence of two interrelated processes which are viewed as characteristic of the rights discourse of the 1980s: the decline of formalism and the rise of judicial activism (Mautner 1993).

The opinions of the High Court in the 1980s reveal a striking decline in the status of the traditional formalistic ideology and a corresponding (and important) change in the style of reasoning. Karl Llewellyn has distinguished two styles of judicial reasoning: 'grand style' and 'formal style' (Llewellyn 1960, 35-41).[25] Opinions leaning toward 'grand style' articulate both legal and non-legal arguments to explain and to justify the decision. They are a product of a legal ideology that emphasizes the normative dimension and moral consequences of law. Opinions leaning toward 'formal style,' on the other hand, present the outcome as following ineluctably or mechanically from pre-existing rules. Such reasoning is used by a judiciary that sees its function as one of finding the sole 'correct' answer to the legal problem at hand. Israel's rights jurisprudence of the 1980s was written largely in grand style. The decisions of the Supreme Court became much longer and more elaborate, and terms such as 'values of the legal system' and 'the foundational principles of Israeli law' appeared time and again in the Court's rulings. The Court also tended to invoke to a greater extent the 'interests balancing' mode of reasoning that originated in *Kol-Ha'am*.

The use of the 'grand style' in the rights jurisprudence of the 1980s signified a shift in the Court's perception of its function and duty in Israeli society. From an institution that was guided by formalistic ideology which confined the role of the judiciary to dispute adjudication, Israel's Supreme Court moved in the 1980s to a new conception. The Court of the 1980s manifestly regarded itself as an actor in the realm hitherto reserved only for the legislative bench, namely, the determination of the normative content of the law as opposed to its mere application.

Alongside the changes in the style of reasoning, there was a shift to judicial activism. The 1980s saw a revision of the rules concerning access to the High Court. In the early years, the High Court held to the concepts of standing and justiciability so as to keep itself within the safe boundaries of an institution whose main function was to decide controversies between individuals and the state, rather than issues reflecting clashes of interests between opposing sectors in society.[26] These principles

---

25   The term 'formal style' can be used interchangeably with the term 'formalistic style' used in the first part of the chapter.

26   Under the narrow concept of justiciability, the Court decided that petitions involving issues of foreign policy, military actions or other questions concerning sensitive political issues were 'unsuitable' for judicial determination and therefore non-justiciable. Under the narrow concept of standing, the petitioner had to show direct and substantial interest in the state action at stake. The Court held that a mere infringement upon religious feelings or ideological

were sharply reversed in *Ressler v. Minister of Defense*. Concerning the question of whether the deferral of military service of rabbinical students was suitable for judicial review, Justice Aharon Barak held that:

> Any [human] action is susceptible to determination by a legal norm, and there is no action regarding which there is no legal norm determining it. There is no 'legal vacuum' in which actions are taken without the law having anything to say about them. The law encompasses any action ... The fact that an issue is 'strictly political' does not change the fact that such an issue is also 'a legal issue.'[27]

The Court's activism opened the door for interest groups as well as for politicians to resort to litigation as a vehicle for initiating social and political reform. But activism was also evident in the scope of judicial review. The Court of the late 1970s and 1980s replaced the old methodology of strict formal analysis of the legality of the relevant governmental decisions in favor of supervision of the content of administrative decisions. It imposed new requirements on administrative organs such as the duty of reasonableness, rationality of the decision-making process and proportionality, all of which were now elements that the Court took into account when reviewing the legality of an alleged infringement of rights by administrative fiat (Dotan 2002; Zamir 1996). Judicial review coupled with judicial activism resulted in decisions that expanded the protection given to civil liberties in Israel. During the 1980s, the Court virtually eliminated theater censorship and reduced the impact of film censorship (Markoe 2000).[28] It prohibited gender discrimination and ordered the inclusion of women in religious councils and in the body that elected the Chief Rabbi of Tel-Aviv.[29] The Supreme Court also overturned the decision of the Central Elections Committee barring both Meir Kahane's racist party and a pro-Palestinian party from running in the 1984 parliamentary elections.[30] It recognized the freedom of demonstration (Kretzmer 1984)[31] and expanded the protection of freedom of the

---

convictions of the petitioner was unlikely to satisfy this requirement. Moreover, even when the petitioner could show that the state action caused them some material damage, they were likely to be denied standing if the same action caused similar harm to a large group of people or to the whole sector of which they formed a part. This narrow concept allowed the Court to refrain from interfering in sensitive political issues in the areas of religion and state and law-enforcement with respect to high-ranking political figures. One important implication of this policy was that it significantly reduced the ability of political parties, interest groups and other organized litigators to use the Court as an arena to promote their political agendas (Shetreet 1996).

27 H.C. 910/86, *Ressler v. Minister of Defense* 42(2) P.D. 441, 447.

28 H.C. 14/86, *Laor et al. v. Films and Plays Censorship Board*, 41(1) P.D. 421; H.C. 806/88, *Universal City Studios Inc. v. Films and Plays Censorship Board*, 43(2) P.D. 22.

29 H.C. 153/87, *Shakdiel v. Minister of Religious Affairs*, 42(2) P.D. 221; H.C. 953/87, *Poraz v. Municipality of Tel Aviv-Jaffa*, 42(2) P.D. 309.

30 E.A. 2/84, *Neiman v. Chairman of the Central Elections Committee for the Tenth Knesset*, 39(2) P.D. 225; E.A. 1/88, *Neiman v. Chairman of the Central Elections Committee to the Twelfth Knesset*, 42(4) P.D. 177.

31 H.C. 148/79, *Sa'ar v. Minister of Interior and the Police*, 34(2) P.D. 169; H.C. 153/83, *Levi v. Southern District Police Commander*, 38(2) P.D. 393; translated in 7 Selected Judgments of the Supreme Court of Israel (1983-87) 109.

press to allow the appearance of politicians who supported the Palestine Liberation Organization[32] and ultra-nationalist Jewish extremists on national television.[33]

An additional innovation of the 1980s was the willingness of the Court to employ its new substantive standards of review to decisions of the security apparatus. In the first four decades, the Court had refrained from reviewing administrative discretion in security matters. This now changed (Bracha 1991; Bracha 2003; Hofnung 1996). In the 1989 landmark decision *Schnitzer v. Chief Military Censor*, the Court set aside a decision of the military censor to suppress an article criticizing the Mossad (Israel's secret service), on the grounds that the censor had failed to show a realistic likelihood of serious injury to national security.[34] These developments led scholars to view the body of pro-civil rights rulings of the High Court as Israel's 'judicial bill of rights' (Barak-Erez 1995). Others saw in the Court's rigorous protection of civil rights a basis for comparison between American and Israeli constitutionalism (Burt 1989; Jacobsohn 1993).

The expanding involvement of the High Court in political life came as a result of major changes that took place in Israeli society and politics up to the 1980s. As Prof. Menachem Mautner observed, the rise of individualism as a social ideology, the appearance of Jewish radical groups, the change in the orientation of the legal profession—away from the English model and toward American law, and the growing institutional legitimacy of the Supreme Court[35]—all these factors combined to encourage the judiciary to redefine its role as a participant in the making of the law, in partnership with the legislature (Mautner 1993, 119-54). Yet similar to what occurred in the decade that followed *Kol-Ha'am*, the Court's changing perception of its role did not affect its holdings in land expropriation cases. As the following discussion shows, in sharp contrast to the transformations that occurred in the realm of non-property civil rights in the 1980s, in expropriation cases we encounter the 'old Court' with the characteristic features of deference to executive discretion and literal and technical interpretation of statutory language.

And while this policy of deference and restrained review was de rigueur in the formative period and to a lesser extent in 1960s, by the 1980s it seemed thoroughly outmoded.

Continuing Trends of Judicial Restraint in Expropriation Cases

Rarely does one find a remark by a Supreme Court Justice that suggests in advance that the petitioner's call for judicial review is pointless. '[T]his is yet another attempt following many previous barren attempts,' wrote Justice Berenson in the 1974 case of *Spolansky v. Minister of Finance*, 'to set aside a decision of the Minister of Finance

---

32 H.C. 243/82, *Zichrony v. Israel Broadcasting Authority*, 37(1) P.D. 757.

33 H.C. 399/85, *Kahane v. Israel Broadcasting Authority*, 41(3) P.D. 255.

34 H.C. 680/88, *Schnitzer v. The Chief Military Censor*, 42(4) P.D. 617; translated in 9 Selected Judgments of the Supreme Court of Israel (1977-90) 77.

35 By the end of the 1980s, the Court was trusted by at least 75 per cent of the public and was ranked second after the Israel Defense Forces (IDF), which had a public trust rate of 90 per cent (Barzilai et al. 1994).

to expropriate land for public use by virtue of the AO.'[36] It is noteworthy indeed that up until *Spolansky* and after more than three decades of adjudication, the Supreme Court had never invalidated an expropriation order issued pursuant to the AO. And yet it is possible to sense the influence of powerful extra-doctrinal factors between the lines. Justice Berenson's comment can be read as suggesting that no matter how solid the formal legal arguments of the petitioner, the Court must uphold the long-standing doctrine of deference and self-restraint in expropriation cases.

In *Spolansky*, the petitioner's land in southern Jerusalem was originally taken for the purpose of building a new subdivision composed of 5,000 housing units for immigrants, low-income families and young couples. After the land had been taken, the landowner discovered that although the majority of her land was indeed intended for low-income housing units, a small part of it was designated for construction of single-family units intended for wealthy immigrants and foreign investors. In her petition, the landowner asked the Supreme Court to set aside the expropriation with respect to the land on which the luxury units were to be built. Housing for wealthy immigrants and foreign investors, she contended, deviated from the original purpose for which the land was expropriated and could not be deemed a permissible public purpose justifying expropriation. A similar claim arose in 1986 case of *Aton v. Minister of Finance*.[37] In *Aton*, the intended use of the expropriated land was changed from construction the Jewish neighborhood of East Talpiyot to the planting of a forest.

While the owners in *Spolansky* and *Aton* could have expected the Court of the 1980s, which had succeeded in creating an unwritten judicial bill of rights, to reach beyond the letter of the law to its underlying premises and to find protection for property rights in the liberal vision of Israeli democracy, this apparently did not happen. The Supreme Court refused to interfere in the Minister's redefinition of public use and to grant the landowners recourse. In rejecting the petitions, the Court applied again the old formalist reasoning that viewed the language of AO as determinant in granting the Minister absolute freedom and narrowing the scope of judicial review. The Court in *Spolansky* also dismissed the landowner's request to block the expropriation of her land. In her petition, the landowner expressed her own willingness to develop the site herself and to construct the luxury accommodation (which was the stated public purpose of the expropriation). However, the Court accepted the authorities' claim that granting the landowner the right to develop her land could slow down the process of building 5,000 housing units on a large number of plots. The landowners' attempt to block the expropriation on the basis of their willingness to execute the proposed public purpose was also rejected in the 1982 case of *Lubianker v. Minister of Finance*, which will be further discussed in Chapter 7 below.[38]

The muted and deferential tone of the Supreme Court was evident in the judicial handling of challenges to the no-compensation rule, as well. Just as the judicial bill

---

36   H.C. 147/74, *Spolansky v. Minister of Finance*, 29(1) P.D. 421, 429.

37   H.C. 704/85, *Aton v. Minister of Finance*, Takdin Supreme Court Precedents 1986(3) 14.

38   H.C. 307/82, *Lubianker v. Minister of Finance*, 37(2) P.D. 141.

of rights may be traced to *Kol-Ha'am*, the landmark decision that advanced civil liberties jurisprudence in Israel, so the disfavored status of land ownership when it came to the right of full compensation for expropriated property may be traced to a single case dating from 1979, *Feitzer v. Ramat Gan Local Planning and Building Commission.*[39] In *Feitzer*, the owners' six parcels of land were expropriated in their entirety for a school. The planning commission offered to pay the landowners cash compensation of 60 percent of the value of the land, which was located in a wealthy residential area of the city of Ramat Gan. The rationale invoked by the planning commission to justify the lower amount of compensation was that the Planning Law of 1965 permitted the taking of up to 40 percent of a plot without compensation for educational buildings.

Until *Feitzer*, the Court displayed great deference to authorities' decisions to utilize the no-compensation rule while invoking a justification known as betterment rationale. According to this justification, landowners benefit from the execution of development plans associated with land expropriation. The betterment that landowners enjoy is not a result of their own effort and thus it is justifiable to require them to hand over some of the benefit by dedicating part of their land for public use without monetary compensation.[40] The betterment rationale by its nature calls for a precise calculation of the benefits received by each individual plot and the burden imposed on the landowner. Yet the Supreme Court treated it as an abstract idea and not as a matter of fact. In none of the cases of uncompensated expropriation did the Court examine the relative value of the land taken and of the benefits provided (Lewinsohn-Zamir 1994, 67). Moreover, even in cases in which the public use adversely affected the value of the remainder, the Court enforced the no-compensation rule as a matter of course.[41]

In *Feitzer*, the Court had the opportunity to reconsider its policy in deferring the authorities' decision to make maximum use of the no-compensation rule. According to the betterment rationale, the benefit derived by the landowners from the execution of the development plans may stand as compensation for the taking. But the circumstances in *Feitzer* were extreme, as the landowners' property was expropriated in its entirety. In such a case, clearly, a betterment rationale could not justify an uncompensated taking. The landowners in *Feitzer* argued that when the entire plot is taken, the authority cannot apply the no-compensation rule since the landowners had been left with no property to which betterment could attach. They

---

39 C.A. 377/79, *Feitzer v. Ramat Gan Local Planning and Building Commission*, 35(3) P.D. 645.

40 C.A. 676/75, *Estate of Fred Khayatt v. Haifa Local Planning and Building Commission*, 31(3) P.D. 785; C.A. (T.A.) 216/48, *Pardes Yanay Co. v. Municipality of Ramat Gan*, 6 P.M. (District Court's Reports) 380.

41 In H.C. 43/79, *Goldenberg v. Local Planning and Building Commission Tel-Aviv District*, 33 (3) P.D. 122, a private passage between two buildings was expropriated for a public road. The owners submitted that they did not receive any benefit from the improvement since the passage was available for their private use even before the expropriation and that its conversion into a public road caused increased levels of noise and pollution. The Court nevertheless approved the application of no-compensation rule.

called on the Court to close the gap between theory and practice and limit the no-compensation rule to actual circumstances of betterment to the remaining property.

The Court rejected the landowners' argument. While acknowledging that the landowners could not reap any benefit from the expropriation under the betterment rationale, the Court offered an alternative rationale for the no-compensation rule—the tax rationale, that is, that expropriation without compensation should be viewed as a form of general property tax. '[S]imilarly to traditional property taxes which require landowners to allocate betterment tax from the profit they gained on selling their property,' the Court held, 'the Israeli lawmaker required landowners to contribute 25 percent or 40 percent of their land for public improvement.' This reasoning, as Prof. Lewinsohn-Zamir and others have shown, leads to unjust results. Viewing expropriation without compensation as a kind of property tax aggravates the burden imposed on landowners. On the one hand, the tax rationale allows local authorities to take the maximum permitted 40 percent of any plot of land, without assessing the economic impact on the remaining 60 percent. On the other hand, the rationale justifies ignoring the connection between the burden imposed on the landowner and their share in creating the particular expenditure. By adopting a tax rationale, the Court in *Feitzer* rejected the type of nexus and proportionality tests developed by American courts, the purpose of which is to prevent the shifting of a disproportionate share of the cost of local public projects to an arbitrarily chosen subset of local residents.[42] The landowners in *Feitzer* were singled out to bear the burden of financing a school although they received no betterment from the public improvement and they did not generate the need for it (Alterman 1985, 220-25; Lewinsohn-Zamir 1994, 67-72).[43]

This harsh and morally troubling result remained the law for over two decades, until it was overturned in 2001.[44] For present purposes, the important point is that the judicial deference of the *Feitzer* Court stood at odds with the concurrent judicial activism in other areas, notably civil liberties. Even a superficial reading of the opinion reveals that the *Feitzer* Court had retreated from the grand style. The Court (per Justice Landau) pursued a highly legalistic analysis of subtle changes in the language of various statutes. Justice Landau failed to discuss the reasons for the authority's decision to deduct 40 percent of the compensation payments and failed to consider whether a dismissal of the petition might have an impact on society. Instead, he spoke of a 'correct interpretation' and of an 'inevitable conclusion.' The impression that one gets from reading the opinion is one of linguistic and technical

---

42 See Chapter 1 above.

43 As a practical remedy, the Court in *Feitzer*, per Justice Barak, suggested that the landowners could receive *ex gratia* compensation by virtue of Section 190(a)(2) of the Planning Law. This section gives the Minister of the Interior authority to instruct the Local Planning Commission to pay compensation when, in his judgment, undue hardship has been caused to the landowner. The Minister of the Interior refused, however, to grant the landowners such relief. After another appeal to the High Court of Justice in 1986, the Court ordered the Minister to consider compensation for the petitioners favorably. H.C. 839/86, *Heirs of Edith Feitzer v. Minister of Interior*, 42(2) P.D. 157.

44 See Chapter 9 below.

arguments winning out over moral values and a commitment to protect property rights.

The *Feitzer* case is the last to be discussed in this chapter concerning the double standard in the Court's treatment of civil rights and land ownership rights in the pre-constitutional era. Situating the Court's record in land expropriation cases within the wider context of the developments that occurred in Israeli rights jurisprudence during this period, one cannot but reach the conclusion that the Court's patterns of behavior cannot be attributable to an overall judicial philosophy of deference. Rather, the heightened judicial deference in land expropriation cases should be viewed as influenced by the unique status of land ownership rights in Israeli legal culture. In the following chapters, I shall explore the extra-legal factors that have shaped the disfavored status of private land ownership in Israeli law and have created a culture of legitimacy for the extensive use of expropriation powers.

Chapter 3

Nation-Building and the Ideology of Public Land Ownership

The preceding discussion demonstrated the disfavored status of private land and private land ownership in Israel's rights jurisprudence. Throughout the pre-constitutional era, Israel's Supreme Court treated land expropriation very differently from state infringements of other rights. It is now time to seek an explanation for the Court's land expropriation record. The present chapter and those that follow are an attempt to understand the Court's behavior by situating it within a broader historical, cultural and political context. I have chosen to explore three basic components of the Israeli setting. In this chapter, I discuss the historical background for the disfavored status of private land within Israeli legal culture, and the effects of this attitude on the jurisprudence of land expropriation. In the next chapter, I examine the role played by Israel's immigration policy in shaping the doctrine of 'public use.' Chapters 5, 6 and 7 focus on the implications of the Arab-Israeli land conflict for land expropriation adjudication in the Jewish sector.

The current status of private land ownership within Israeli legal culture can be traced to the pre-state process and ideology of nation-building. The leaders of the Zionist movement saw in private property an invalid nation-building strategy and favored instead the land regime of public ownership. In the pre-state period, the Zionist movement executed its preference for public land ownership through the Jewish National Fund (JNF). The JNF remains active as a quasi-governmental institution in modern Israel, and it continues to adhere to this ideology of national land ownership. Aside from the State of Israel itself, the JNF is the largest owner of cultivated land in the country, and it retains a key role in shaping policies affecting all public land in Israel. The discussion below will trace the ways by which the JNF has imbued the apparatus of the state with its pre-state ideology. This was made possible because the JNF's ideologically driven dislike for, and suspicion of, private property in favor of public land ownership coincided with the structure of political power in the pre-state Jewish community and later in the State of Israel. Furthermore, the JNF initiated an array of symbolic practices by which it succeeded in presenting national land ownership as apolitical ideology and in making it a key symbol of Jewish national revival and the new Hebrew culture.

Looking at the continuity between the pre-state and the state periods from a sociological point of view, it should not come as a surprise that ideas about land ownership maintained their long-term influence. While social covenants that bear upon matters of technology or intellectual property rights change rapidly, attitudes that frame our reference as a society to real estate are much slower to change. The argument presented in this chapter suggests that the pre-state experience of acquiring land under the policy of public ownership generated a unique Israeli land regime and tradition. The disfavored status of private land in Zionist ideology has contributed to the formation of Israel's existing land tenure, under which 93 percent of the land is publicly owned, and this in turn has reinforced a legal culture in which private landownership discourse is marginalized.

The Zionist Settlement Drive and the Establishment of the JNF

Zion, or Eretz Israel (the Land of Israel), is a central pillar of the Jewish religion and of Jewish group identity. As a people without a land for nearly 2000 years, Jews strove wherever they were to maintain the sense of vital ties to the Land of Israel. They prayed for rain in Eretz Israel during the rain-abundant seasons in the countries in which they resided; they celebrated the annual harvest festival (*Shavuot*) according to the seasonal agricultural cycle in Eretz Israel, and studied the body of law governing agriculture that applies to Eretz Israel. On a more routine basis, pious Jews express three times a day the desire to return to Zion and to rebuild Jerusalem, and the daily prayers themselves, no matter where, are always recited facing East— the direction of Jerusalem. These rituals expressed and institutionalized the belief that there exists an exceptional relationship between the people of Israel, its God and its Land: that the Land of Israel is the Promised Land and that the promise is irreversible.[1] If Jews obey God's commandments and maintain a high level of morality, they will have the right to expect a messianic Redemption (*ge'ula*), which is to say, an ending of their exile. Redemption according to the Jewish religion will take place in the spiritual realm of life and can occur only in Eretz Israel (Davies 1982).

Zionism, the movement of national liberation of the Jewish people, built upon the age-old theological concept of the Promised Land and the expectations for Redemption in the Land of Israel. Yet modern Zionism differed from the vision of religious Judaism. Zionism did not accept, but in fact reacted against, the conception of the Jewish commitment to live in the Land of Israel solely (or at least primarily) in religious, Messianic terms. Zionism meant a renaissance: a reconstruction of the Jewish people and of the Jewish person. The traditional vision of the link between the Jewish people and the Land of Israel was reconstructed to mean the building in Eretz Israel of a new society around the themes of social equality and an actual, physical connection to the soil (Laqueur 1972; Lucas 1975).

Modern Jewish settlement in Palestine began with the consolidation of the Lovers of Zion (*Hovevi Zion*), a name given to the dozens of groups in Russia and Romania, and later in Western Europe that began arriving in Palestine at the end of the nineteenth century (1882). Upon their arrival, the settlers realized that the common perception of the 'Promised Land' as empty of any people and waiting for over 2000 years for Zionist Jews to redeem it was not at all compatible with reality (Avneri 1984, 61; Gerner 1991, 13-18). In the territory that would later become known as

---

1 *Genesis*, the first book in the Bible, states that 'the Lord made a covenant with Abram, saying, Unto your seed have I given this land'(*Gen.* 15:17).

Palestine, there were close to 500,000 inhabitants of whom only 7 percent were Jewish (McCarthy 1990, 1-24). Facing this reality, Zionism developed the ideology and practice of achieving Jewish sovereignty in Palestine by acquiring and settling the land, 'dunam by dunam' (Horowitz and Lissak 1978, 49-52; Kimmerling 1983, 1-30, 106-21). The Zionist strategy of a gradual and incremental process of land acquisition was pursued under the policy of public land ownership.[2] The institution that represented and implemented this policy, converting it into an ideology and turning it into a symbol of the new emerging Hebrew culture in Palestine, was the JNF.

The JNF was the executive organ of the Zionist movement for Jewish land purchases in Palestine, and it pursued its activities under the principle of the Jewish people's common ownership of the land. The JNF was established in 1901 when the Fifth Zionist Congress accepted the proposal of Zvi Hermann Schapira of Heidelberg (1840-98), a rabbi and professor of mathematics, to institute a fund to acquire 'Jewish territory' (Hurwitz 1932; Klausner 1966). Schapira suggested that the money for acquiring the Jewish territory would come from world Jewry, and that the fund would be characterized by two qualities: it was to be perpetual, and the land acquired had to be forever the common and inalienable property of the Jewish people. It should not be sold to individuals but rather leased for renewable periods of no more than 49 years to those who were willing to work it.[3]

These two qualities of the Fund constituted and manifested links between modern Zionism and traditional Jewish values (Berlin 1932, 8). The principle of land inalienability implemented the biblical notion of the Land of Israel as divine property that 'shall not be sold for ever, for the land is Mine' (*Lev.* 25:23). The other aspect of the principle of land inalienability was the 49-year lease, which corresponded to the Biblical jubilee law, according to which all lands are redeemed every fiftieth year and restored to their original owners at no cost (*Lev.* 25: 14-17). The idea of viewing the entire Jewish people as owners of the land also gave modern meaning to the ancient belief that every Jew has a portion in Eretz Israel. Finally, even the very act of collecting donations to form the Fund's capital rested upon a well-based tradition of monetary support from Diaspora Jews to the Jewish community in Eretz Israel.[4]

Schapira presented his proposal as early as in the First Zionist Congress which took place in 1897. However, because of legal and organizational difficulties, it was

---

2   The first wave of modern Jewish immigration to Palestine (1882-1903) favored private ownership of land. But starting with following waves of immigration, attitudes favoring public ownership became most dominant (Shafir 1993).

3   The Hebrew name of the Jewish National Fund, *Keren Kayemet Le 'Israel*, emphasizes the quality of the fund as inexhaustible. The name derives from the Talmudic dictum about good deeds 'the fruits of which man enjoys in this world, while the capital abides [*keren kayemet*] for him in the world to come' (Mishnah Pe'ah 1,1).

4   Monetary support of Diaspora Jews for the Jews of Eretz Israel was a tradition originating as early as the time of the Second Temple. Beginning in the seventeenth century, the system of support was institutionalized into what came to be known as the *chalukah* (apportioning) system. This system was based on the organization of the Jewish community in Palestine into groups, with each group receiving financial support as a matter of charity from its community of origin.

not until the Fifth Zionist Congress in 1901 that the delegates voted unanimously to establish the Fund. The JNF was incorporated in England in 1907 as a limited liability company with the authority to buy—but not to sell—land in Palestine and to finance Jewish settlement of the land it acquired. Control of the JNF was permanently vested in the members of the Action Committee of the Zionist Organization.

From the outset, the JNF's principle of national land gained wide support among the rank and file of the Zionist movement. Alongside the appeal to Jewish religion on the one hand, and to Labour Zionism revolutionary aspirations on the other hand, the policy of public land ownership was essentially favored as a practical means by which to advance the objective of settling Palestine and achieving Jewish sovereignty.

The Alleged Ills of Private Land Ownership

A central concern underlying the rejection of private property as a strategy for nation-building was its connection to land speculation and the rise in land prices. The economy of Palestine had two characteristics that favored land speculation. It was a pre-industrialized country in which land could be purchased relatively cheaply and, given an increase in immigration, resold at a profit; and in the period beginning in the mid-1920s there were no alternative investment opportunities in the Palestinian economy for the Jewish capital which flowed into the country (Granott 1936; Kimmerling 1983).

Zionism struggled against land speculation since it was destructive to its goal of buying as much land as possible for Jewish settlement. The only method to acquire land in Eretz Israel was through purchases from Arab landowners on the open market. Zionism regarded national land ownership a more efficient strategy than private property for gaining ownership of large tracts of land and maintaining them under Jewish ownership. The prices of land in Palestine were high for the Jewish immigrant-settlers, both because the land was already settled and because the wide range of territorial ownership patterns under Ottoman land law made transfer of ownership difficult.[5] Furthermore, given the status of land as the central resource in the conflict between Arabs and Jews, there was also a political price that needed to be added to the land's value in order to persuade the Arabs to sell their land to Jews. The phenomenon of land speculation by Jews did not make this cheaper, nor did it help make the supply of Arab land greater. Zionist leaders feared that because of competition among Jews over land, Arabs would receive the impression that 'Jews can buy everything' and that indeed everything would be bought by Jews if the Arabs did not resist. Land speculation thus had two negative effects: it caused a rise

---

5   The two main patterns of land tenure in Palestine had very different degrees of fluidity. The most common form was collective village ownership, *mushaa*. *Mushaa* land was very difficult or often impossible to sell. The other major form of land tenure in Ottoman Palestine was private ownership of large estates. Large estates were owned either by local estate owners or by absentee (i.e. foreign) effendis. If they contained arable land, large estates were cultivated by sharecroppers, tenants, or secondary tenants (Kimmerling 1983, 31-38; Stein 1984, 65-71).

in land prices and at the same time, it increased the reluctance of Arabs to sell their land (Kimmerling 1983, 69).

The policy of public land ownership was intended to prevent or at least control speculators by keeping the responsibility for all Jewish land purchases in Palestine in the hands of the JNF. The idea was that by putting as much land as possible under national ownership, the land would cease being a marketable commodity to be bought and sold at will. In addition, the JNF as a major buyer had the advantage of being able to buy large tracts of land that were mostly uncultivated and therefore relatively inexpensive, and it would also be in a favorable position to influence land prices (Bohm 1932, 25-26; Metzer 1979).

Another important concern which fueled the dislike of private land ownership was the fear of resale of land to Arabs. Given the escalating real estate prices, Zionist leaders feared that individual Jewish landowners, lacking Zionist zeal, might be tempted to resell their land for profit. Public ownership and land inalienability, so it was argued, averted this danger and freed Jewish ownership of land from the potential impact of individual caprice.

Private land ownership was also frowned upon for reasons of social ideology. Zionist ideology drew its inspiration as much from the egalitarian doctrines heralded by the French revolution and European socialism as from the ancient call of the prophets of Israel (Avineri 1981, 88-100; Frankel 1981). Theodore Herzl, the father of political Zionism, in his book *Altneuland (Old-New Land)* (1902) depicted the new Jewish society as founded for the most part on cooperatives, with the most modern labor legislation, including a seven-hour work day. For him and for other Zionist thinkers who sought to link classical economic theory with socialist thought, public land ownership and the holding of large tracks of land by the JNF were an appealing means of preventing the formation of large private estates and the consequent introduction of the social ills of exploitation of human labor and the creation of a land-starved agricultural workforce.[6] The control of the JNF over its land would enable it to allocate to farmers only as much land as they could cultivate themselves without the need to resort to hired labor (Rudensky 1932). Furthermore, public land ownership also corresponded to the Zionist endeavor to promote social equality through land reform. Central leaders within the Zionist movement echoed the social justice ideology of the American land reformer Henry George (1839-97), who in his book *Progress and Poverty* (1879) called for the abolition of private land ownership as a cure for economic privation.[7]

---

6   'History has shown how grave are the evils arising from private ownership of land,' wrote Adolf Bohm, a General Zionist, in one of the informative pamphlets issued by the Head Office of the JNF in 1932. 'First there are those of political nature. The decline of whole empires such as Roman, has been attributed to the system of large landed estates (*latifundia*). This leads to the substitution of badly paid day laborers for independent peasants; the latter then flock to the cities and it follows that where large estates are the rule, neglect of the soil inevitably results' (Bohm 1932, 11).

7   Already in *Alteuland* (1902) Theodore Herzl supported his utopian socialism by citing Henry George's land-poverty nexus. Later on, Franz Oppenheimer (1864-1943), an economist and sociologist, published a book, *Collective Ownership and Private Ownership of Land* (1914), in which he relied on George's ideas to support the concept of cooperative

Finally, another important category of reasons for advocating collective land ownership originated in the goal of transforming as many Jews as possible into farmers. The emphasis of Zionism upon agricultural settlement derived from two sources. One was the important role of agriculture as a means by which to increase the area under Jewish ownership. Given the fact that the territory in Palestine was occupied by close to half a million Arabs, the Zionist movement sought a cheap and fast way to expand Jewish presence. Agriculture was considered the most efficient way of establishing an extended Jewish territorial basis in Palestine, since it required less investment in physical and human capital and a shorter turnaround period than manufacturing. Agricultural settlements also provided an economic framework to absorb a large influx of Jewish immigrants who were expected to arrive in Palestine (Metzer 1978).

The other group of arguments that tilted the balance toward agricultural settlement over urban life reflected the revolutionary ideology of the Labour leadership within the Zionist movement. Zionism's revolutionary state-building philosophy envisioned not only the establishment of a sovereign Jewish state, but also the creation of a 'new Jew' who would be the antithesis of the Diaspora Jew. Zionism called for transformation of the Jews from peddlers, beggars, yeshiva students and minor craftsmen into a nation of hardy laborers. In 1925, only about 4 percent of the European Jewish workforce was engaged in agricultural activity. Zionism strove to address what it regarded as an unhealthy void in the nation's occupational structure (Granott 1956, 19; Kimmerling 1983a). Agriculture therefore was assigned an important revolutionary role in Zionist ideology. In the words of a popular song of the early settlement era of the 1920s, 'we have come to the homeland to build and be rebuilt in it.' The new society would be not only the creation of the 'new Jew,' but its creator, as well.[8]

Jewish agricultural work and private land ownership were deemed incompatible in Zionist thinking (Kimmerling 1983a). First, this was because private capital had, to that point, proved unsuccessful in establishing viable agricultural settlements. The first *moshavot* (Jewish agricultural settlements) established between 1882 and 1901 by the Lovers of Zion were all a result of private initiatives. The setters bought the land with their own funds and needed to sustain themselves until the first crop yielded income. However, due to insufficient means and unforeseen difficulties in cultivating the land, the first moshavot were soon on the verge of collapse (Bein 1945, 8-9; Gvati 1985, 8-17; Penslar 1991). Given this early experience, Zionist leadership assumed that private capital as a general rule would be attracted to the

---

Jewish settlements in Palestine (Bein 1971, 71). George's book was translated into Hebrew (with the assistance of the JNF), and was read not only by the dominant socialist sector within the Zionist movement but also by middle-class Zionists.

8   The association between the Jewish return to the Land of Israel and economic transformation was well-nigh universal in Zionist ideology, resisted only by Revisionism, which glorified the individual entrepreneur and admired the Jew as a pioneer of modern capitalism. The Revisionists yearned to reshape Jews politically and militarily, but intended to leave their occupational structure intact (Penslar 2001).

city where smaller investments were required than for rural settlement, and where the demand for real estate made profitability more likely (Granott 1940, 10-16).

Private land ownership and its close connection to large estates and hired work also appeared an incorrect strategy for handling the Jewish-Arab conflict over land. It was a firm belief among the majority of Zionists that the national character of a settlement derives from those who actually till the land, rather than from those who merely own it. If we let Arabs work the land of Palestine, the leaders claimed, Palestine will become Arabized and this in turn will damage the legitimacy of the Zionist undertaking.[9]

The problem was that Jewish laborers could not compete with the local Arab labor force. For one thing, Arab laborers were cheaper. Jewish farmers did not have to provide accommodation for Arab workers (who returned at the end of the day to their villages). It was also initially believed that Arabs were better skilled and more suited to the local conditions than the new immigrants from Europe. In addition, hiring Arab workers from villages constituted a sort of insurance against attack from these villages and a form of protection against theft. Finally, Arab workers, unlike the well-educated Jewish immigrants, did not 'criticize, demand an 8-hour work day, and the right to strike' (Shafir 1989).[10]

While the above-mentioned considerations underlined the primacy of public land ownership in the Zionist worldview, in reality it was not feasible for the *Yishuv* (the pre-state Jewish community in Palestine) leadership to exclude private capital due to the absence of sovereignty. In fact, as the discussion below details, private capital made a meaningful contribution to the goal of acquiring ownership of large tracts of land in Palestine. Nevertheless, it was the JNF and its ideology of keeping the land the common and inalienable property of the Jewish people which became a key symbol of the modern Jewish life in Palestine. Private property, despite its contribution to the national cause, was frowned upon ideologically.

---

9   The Zionist Menahem Ussishkin succinctly captured the political importance of Jewish labor when he wrote in *Our Program* (1905): 'The day will come when the oppressed Arab laborer will open his eyes and see before him a flourishing Jewish settlement, with few people in it. He will know that his hands and the sweat of his brow created this abundance, and he will find the opportunity to stake all the claims on it.'

10   It was a fundamental principle of the JNF to consider capacity of the soil and intensity of cultivation and to allocate land to farmers only according to what they could cultivate on their own with the assistance of their families. So important was this principle, that the JNF sought to retain the right of reducing the size of plots even after the land had been settled. This in fact occurred in Kfar Malal, north of Tel-Aviv on the coastal plain. It was settled in 1913 by 40 families who jointly cultivated 600 acres of grain fields, or 15 acres per family. In 1934, when the profitable citrus industry was introduced to the area and the wheat fields were converted to orange groves, the average plot size was reduced to 5 acres in order to enable the number of Jewish farmers to be increased (Granott 1940, 110).

Patterns of Jewish Land Purchase and Settlement in Palestine 1882-1947: Actions and Politics

The history of Jewish land purchases in Palestine is divided into two distinct periods. The first started with the beginning of modern Jewish settlement in Palestine in 1882 and lasted until the end of World War I, and was characterized by a predominance of private entrepreneurship and low-level involvement of public capital. The most important land purchaser during this period was Baron Edmond de Rothschild, who invested approximately £1.6 million in Jewish agricultural settlements between 1883 and 1900 (Giladi and Naor 1982). During the latter part of this period, the JNF was still in its early years. Beset by financial difficulties, political concerns and organizational problems, it was relatively inactive (Katz 2001; Shilony 1990).[11] In the second period, which ran from 1920 and the establishment of the British civil administration in Palestine and lasted until the establishment of the State of Israel in 1948, Jewish land purchases were carried out both by the JNF and by private individuals.

Table 3.1   Jewish Land Purchases in Palestine 1882-1947

Year	All Jewish-owned land (in dunams*)	Of which JNF-owned land (in dunams)	JNF-owned land as a proportion of all Jewish-owned land (%)
Until 1882	22,000	-	-
1883-90	104,000	-	-
1981-1900	218,000	-	-
1901-14	418,100	16,400	4
1914-19	No data	25,000	-
1920-22	557,000	77,400	13
1923-27	864,700	196,700	23
1928-32	1,007,500	296,900	29
1932-35	1,232,000	371,000	30
1936-39	1,358,000	478,000	35
1940-41	1,431,000	566,000	39
1942-45	1,506,000	813,000	54
1946-47	1,734,000	933,000	54

* 1 dunam = 1000 sq. meters = 0.25 acre
Adapted from: A. Granott *Land Policy in Palestine* (1940) 91; B. Kimmerling *Zionism and Territory* (1983) 43.

---

11   At first it was believed that the Jews could get a charter for Palestine from the Ottoman rulers of the land in exchange for payment of all the debts of the Ottoman Empire (which totaled about £85 million). Theodore Herzl, the leader of political Zionism, thus favored not pursuing land purchases in Palestine in order not to jeopardize the existing political avenues for realizing Jewish nationalist goals. When it became clear in 1908 that Zionism could not raise the amount required, the voice of the 'practical school' gained dominance, and consequently the JNF began its organizational activities (Duckan-Landau, 1979, 98-171).

Private enterprise, as Table 3.1 demonstrates, was very productive in expediting the process of Jewish land purchases. Of the total area of land purchased throughout the period (1,734,000 dunams), private capital contributed to the acquisition of 801,000 dunams, or about 45 percent of the total. In the years 1923 to 1927, for example, there was an average annual land purchase of 61,400 dunams of land, to which private capital contributed about 60 percent. The contribution of private investors was also evident in the inflow of capital to Palestine during this era. Between 1918 and 1937, private foreign capital constituted 70 to 80 percent of all foreign capital invested in Palestine (Plessner 1994, 70-77; Ulitzur 1939, 246).

Yet despite this notable contribution, private enterprise was not looked upon favorably by the Zionist leadership. In 1923, Chaim Arlosoroff, the head of the Political Department of the Jewish Agency, stated that 'From the point of view of the Jewish settlement effort, private enterprise has been disappointing all the way, in agriculture as well as in industry' (Arlosoroff 1934, 145). Others, such as Arthur Ruppin and Menachem Ussishkin, prominent figures in their own right and influential in matters relating to land acquisition, adopted a more pragmatic attitude. They realized that the involvement of private capital in the land market was necessary, given the limited financial resources of the JNF.[12] Nonetheless, they drew a distinction between productive and unproductive capital (Ruppin 1926, 195-200). Many of the private land purchases were classified as 'unproductive' because in the Zionist leadership's eyes they did not advance the goals of enhancing Jewish labor and agricultural settlement.

While private capital (provided primarily by Baron Edmond de Rothschild) set the foundation for the first Zionist agricultural settlements, it did not adopt any policy with reference to Arab workers.[13] The first settlements that were established until the outbreak of World War I relied on the local Arab labor force. The most 'Arabized' settlements were those of Baron de Rothschild, where the most important agricultural activity was viticulture. Though the new agriculture succeeded economically, it was labor intensive. The result was that there was a need for a large and cheap seasonal workforce. Baron de Rothschild's settlements, notably Zichron Ya'acov (established in 1882), soon became, in the words of the Zionist leadership, 'Jewish settlements with an Arab majority' (Shafir 1989, 51-2; see also Giladi and Naor 1982).

---

12   In fact, the 1920 Zionist Conference in London resolved to resort to private capital as a short-term practical solution. According to the official resolution of the Conference, it was the duty of the JNF to find the means by which 'alongside the capital of the JNF itself, private capital can also be utilized for the purchase of land, under conditions which will assure subsequent transfer of land so brought into national possession' (Bohm 1932, 93). On the schemes and co-operative ventures that the JNF pursued in this regard, see Tuten (2002).

13   In addition to Baron Edmond de Rothschild, before the outbreak of World War I, private land purchases for agricultural settlement were also pursued by the Palestinian Land Development Company (PLDC). The PLDC was set up 1908 for the purpose of facilitating Jewish land purchases both for the JNF and also for individual investors (Duckan-Landau 1979; Katz 1994).

After the end of World War I, with the arrival of middle-class Jewish immigrants in the Fourth Aliya (1924-29) and the Fifth Aliya (1929-36),[14] private investment gradually came to be concentrated in towns and semi-urban settlements. The areas preferred by private investors were the coastal cities of Tel-Aviv and Haifa and their peripheries. Furthermore, over 50 percent of the private capital that flowed into Palestine during this period was invested in urban construction (Kimmerling 1983a, 28). This pattern of private land purchases, while enabling a massive build-up of new urban neighborhoods, stood in contrast to the stated core value of Zionism of making the agricultural village the soul of the Jewish national revival.

Unlike private investors, the JNF directed its land purchase and settlement activities in a manner that accorded with the ideological beliefs of many among the Zionist movement's socialist leadership. It invested about 70 percent of its resources in the purchase of agricultural land and only about 7 percent in urban land (Gracier 1983; Granott 1940, 98-101). The rest of its available resources were dedicated to enhancing agricultural activity by making the land ready for agricultural work. The JNF typically carried out the essential preliminary reclamation work—draining swamps, digging wells, planting groves and orchards—and exempted its leaseholders from rental payments for the first five years, or alternatively pegged such payments at below-market annual rates of 1 or 2 percent of the land value (Bohm 1932, 26-31). The location of the JNF land purchases also took into account the territorial aspirations of Zionism. While private investors avoided purchasing land far from areas already inhabited by Jews, the JNF from 1937 onwards made a consistent effort to acquire land in the rural areas of the Galilee in the north and the Negev Desert in the south, with an eye to influencing the nascent Jewish political entity's future territorial boundaries (Avneri 1984, 114-62, 180-224; Reichman 1979, 49-78). It is also worth noting that the JNF employed only Jews in pursuing the reclamation work on its land. According to its charter documents, the JNF was prohibited from leasing its land to non-Jews as well as granting non-Jews a right to work its land. The status of the JNF as an employer of Jews in blue-collar occupations contributed to its prestige and influence among the ranks of the Zionist leadership.

There were other reasons as well for the Zionist Labour leadership's high esteem of the JNF. From the beginning of the 1920s and until the establishment of the State of Israel, the JNF was a dominant factor in the Yishuv, both because it was the largest owner of land in Palestine and because land resources were allocated to various sectors through the JNF. Of the 272 settlements that were established in Palestine between 1882 and 1944 (not all of which survived), 193 were founded on JNF land. These settlements typically took the form of a *kibbutz* (an agricultural collective) or a *moshav* (a cooperative settlement). Both forms of settlement were common among those immigrants of the Second (1904-14) and Third (1919-23) Aliyot who wished to work the land, and it was ultimately from these groups that the left-wing leadership of the Yishuv and later of the State of Israel arose (Horowitz and Lissak 1978; Shapiro 1976). Only 30 percent of the JNF lands were allocated to settlements

14   *Aliya* (ascension or pilgrimage) is the Hebrew term for Jewish immigration to Palestine and later to the State of Israel. Beginning in 1882 and until 1948, there were five major waves of Jewish immigration to Palestine.

that did not belong to the left wing of the Labour movement, and only 16 percent of the total land of the JNF was allocated to the private or right-wing sectors (such as the General Zionists and the Revisionists) (Kimmerling 1983, 44-6).

The JNF and its policy of national land ownership thus formed an important component in the structure of political power in the Yishuv. The fact that adherents of the Labour alignment—the standard bearers of Zionist socialism in all its varieties—controlled the Zionist Organization and the National Institutions from the late 1920s onward enabled them to use national capital to strengthen their influence (Shapiro 1976, 126-57; Sternhell 1998). The right-wing and middle-class groups, despite their major economic contribution in terms of the inflow of capital, were denied political as well as cultural influence (Giladi 1966; Kimmerling 2001, 91). This connection between the JNF and the distribution of power in the Yishuv was downplayed in the Zionist rhetoric to the point where it was not at all noticeable. By imparting the principle of public land ownership through popular culture rather than through political discourse, the JNF succeeded in creating a perception of its role and of its actions as being above local politics and ephemeral concerns and represent itself as the vehicle for realizing the Jewish nation's links to its past and future.

From Policy to Culture: The JNF and the Symbolism of National Land Ownership

In a recent study Prof. Yoram Bar-Gil has shown how the JNF expanded its areas of activity and became an 'agent of Zionist propaganda in Eretz Israel' (Bar-Gil 1999). Understanding the process by which the JNF and its ideology became a key symbol of the national aims of Zionism is important for the study of contemporary property rights culture in Israeli law. The JNF is still active as a quasi-governmental institution in Israel to this day, and the symbols that it created in the pre-state period were carried over to the State of Israel after independence, and formed an integral part of the cultural backdrop against which Israel's land regime was formalized in the 1960s. The rituals and symbolic practices created by the JNF were not merely cultural fillers in the new Hebrew secular culture of the Jewish community in Palestine, but also served as powerful tools of acculturation and in the creation of a collective identity. By succeeding in establishing the policy of the inalienability of national land as a central theme of Palestinian Hebrew culture, the JNF was able to reach a receptive audience among various ideological and political streams within the Zionist movement and to instill a particular unified way of thinking about land and property rights. According to this way of thinking, the Land of Israel and its significance were dissociated from the individual's connection to the land, as well as from the land's practical economic uses.

The process by which the JNF de-emphasized the economic considerations associated with land ownership and land resource management involved two stages. The first was defining the policy of national land ownership in spiritual and idealistic terms unconnected with economic philosophy and political power. The second was raising this spiritual meaning to the symbolic level and making use of the mechanisms of socialization to implant these symbols in the community at large. The JNF applied various methods to imbue the ostensibly practical principle of national land ownership with spiritual content and to disseminate it in the Jewish community in Palestine. Chief among them was the terminology used by the JNF to describe its land purchase activities. 'Redeem yourself in the general redemption' was the slogan that the JNF coined to describe the act of Jewish land purchases. The term 'redemption' (*ge'ula*) was drawn from the ethical and spiritual spheres of Jewish tradition (Almog 1990; Near 1990). On the one hand, redemption is used in the Old Testament (*Lev.* 25:25) to refer to a moral obligation imposed on a person to avenge the death of his next-of-kin or to redeem property that had been leased to others. On the other hand, redemption refers to metaphysical aspects of the Jewish religion, as in the following passage (*Gen.* 68:16): 'the angel who hath redeemed me from all evil, bless the lands; and let my name be named with them.' The use of a term that bore religious connotations gave the JNF's activities a strong spiritual and idealistic importance by association. It also served the goal of facilitating the internalization of these connotations into the new system of symbols and values that developed within the Yishuv between 1882 and 1948. By using the old terminology in the modern context of Jewish national revival, the JNF created a new national, secular definition to what had previously been almost exclusively the religious content of the relationship between the people of Israel, its God and the Land of Israel. At the same time, the religious roots of the terminology of 'redemption' obscured the modern sources of the new meaning and made it difficult to reconstruct the circumstances of the term's appearance and the process of its public acceptance (Kark 1992).

Another important means of creating a personal spiritual identification with the principle of land nationalization was the array of devices used by the JNF for collecting contributions from Jews around the world. One of these was the 'blue box,' a collection box first designed in 1924 as a modern version of the traditional Jewish charity collection box. The box was painted blue and white, the colors of the Zionist flag, and it had a map of Eretz Israel and a Star of David on it. The JNF succeeded in placing its collection boxes in prominent public locations such as synagogues and Jewish institutions, as well as in private homes, both in Eretz Israel and in the Diaspora. By 1927, there were some 700,000 blue boxes in Palestine and around the world. The JNF's collection box took on an iconic status, and the ritual of collecting donations in various settings, including the school system in Eretz Israel and in the Diaspora, turned it into one of the focal elements of the project of national revival. In his 1929 book *The Voice of the Land* Menachem Ussishkin, President of the JNF, wrote:

> The penny that the child contributes or solicits for the redemption of the land is not significant in and of itself. The JNF will not be built up on it, nor can we redeem all Palestine with it. But this penny is significant as an educational element. It is not the child who contributes to the JNF, but rather the JNF which contributes to him. The JNF provides him with an ideal for all his life ... When he goes to bed at night, the child must not only think 'what did I learn today,' but also—'what have I done today for the redemption of the nation and for the redemption of the land on which this nation will rise.' (Ussishkin 1929, 7)

In 1932, the JNF published a list of 50 suggestions for occasions on which contributing to the blue box was appropriate. These occasions represented special events in the cycle of life, such as moving to a new apartment, thanking one's host for a good meal, a child's first tooth. Other means of soliciting funds that had a symbolic character included the JNF stamps which depicted Jewish holidays, Zionist leaders and public figures, landscapes in Eretz Israel and the agricultural settlement activity of the JNF; the *Golden Book* in which a contribution of a certain sum provided an inscription and a certificate; and the planting of olive trees, by which Jews could contribute to, and participate in, the afforestation of Palestine (Bar-Gil 1999).

Whereas for world Jewry, the symbolism of the JNF and its ideology was created primarily through the devices of fund collection and the rhetoric of redemption, for the Jews of Palestine they became integrated into the daily patterns of socialization. The JNF composed the 'Eretz-Israeli Song,' which had great success among Zionist youth movements in Palestine (Regev and Seroussi 2004; Shahar 1993), and it sponsored children's literature that was educational in its thrust. But the most effective strategy of implanting the land purchase activities of the JNF as a symbol of national revival was through its active involvement in the Jewish educational system in Palestine. In 1925, the JNF established the Teachers' Council for the JNF, a voluntary group of Hebrew educators who undertook to compose and disseminate new educational programs promoting the common theme of 'Education in the Spirit of Homeland' (Shavit and Siton 2004; Siton 1998). The Teachers' Council received the financial and organizational support of the JNF. In return, it placed the JNF's ideology, focusing on the central role of agricultural settlement in Eretz Israel, at the very core of Hebrew education. The act of placing JNF donations in the blue box figured prominently in the new festivals and ceremonies that the Teachers' Council introduced into the Hebrew schools. These included the birthday ceremony, the festival of the new month, the Sabbath ceremony, celebrations of traditional Jewish holidays, and others (Siton 1998; Shavit and Siton 2004). The principle of national land ownership and its related symbolic values of altruism, personal sacrifice and Hebrew agriculture were also advanced by the ideal image of the *halutz* (pioneer), the protagonist of new stories, plays and songs commissioned by the Teachers' Council. The halutz was typically depicted as a hardworking individual who lived in a communal agricultural settlement located on JNF land. He lived modestly and was willing to forgo material comfort, renouncing personal economic aspirations for the good of the nation (Doleve-Gandelman 1987; Firer 1985).

The success of the JNF in including its agenda into the system of values of the Jewish community in Palestine was facilitated to a great extent by the particular conditions of the period.[15] The Yishuv in Mandatory Palestine was a society composed exclusively of immigrants who had actively chosen to come to Zion for ideological reasons. Upon their arrival, the Jewish immigrants naturally felt the need to identify with collective symbols as part of the process of acculturation in their new society.

---

15 It is hard to assess the degree to which participants identified with the ceremony and the extent to which they internalized the message that the symbolic practices of the JNF embodied and strove to transmit. The important point here is that these symbolic practices were continually being performed—largely without attracting much criticism or comment— between 1925 and 1945, and they characterize the formative period of the Jewish political community in Eretz Israel (Shavit and Siton 2004, 54).

The symbolism of national land ownership responded to this important need. First, the institutionalization of communal land purchasing through a public and quasi-national entity such as the JNF created a fundamental sense of communal control over territory. In addition, the very principle of national land implied a certain distancing of the individual from their personal and practical ties to the land, and provided a framework for collective identification. The new sense of community that was instilled by the JNF's rhetoric of land redemption, the blue box and the range of inspired festive ceremonies celebrated the view of the Land of Israel as an asset that bore a collective historical and idealistic meaning for the Jewish people. It was not an ordinary economic asset subject to standard economic considerations of profit maximization. Finally, the symbolism of JNF ideology was further facilitated by the socialist accents of Labour Zionism, which had disproportionate influence on the social symbols of the Yishuv. The kibbutz ideology, with its emphasis on equality and common spiritual and economic objectives—all of which supported the principle of public ownership of land —was at the top of the Yishuv's hierarchy of ideological prestige (Almog 2000; Shapiro 1976; Sternhell 1998).

An integral part of the process of constituting national land ownership as a symbol was the social devaluation and even stigmatization of those who opposed the new system of values. Urban immigrants in general and land speculators in particular were often viewed in the Zionist mainstream discourse as the 'other' who selfishly impaired the collectivity's undertaking for the sake of personal profit. The social perception of landowners as antithetical to the ideology of Zionism coincided with increases in the rate of Jewish immigration, which generated demand for housing, as well as creating conditions for land speculation. There were three bursts of land speculation during the period of pre-state Jewish settlement in Palestine. The first occurred around 1890, upon the arrival of numerous Russian Jews as a result of a new edict prohibiting them from living in Moscow. At that time, favorable prospects for buying up to 500,000 dunams of land and for establishing numerous agricultural colonies were missed due to an accelerated rise in land prices that was blamed on speculators. Reflecting on the situation in Palestine after a visit in 1891, Ahad Ha'am reported in his book *The Truth from Eretz Israel* that 'whoever has not seen how land is bought and sold in Palestine at present, has never seen how contemptible and disgusting competition can be' (Granott 1940, 34).

The stigma on private landowners spread with the second and third spurts of land speculation that occurred upon the arrival of the Fourth Aliya (1924-29) and the economic boom of the years 1933-35. Between 1924 and 1929, about 65,000 immigrants arrived in Palestine to escape anti-Semitism in Poland. They came from all social and economic classes, but the majority were middle class. In that period, the wave of land speculation was much wider in scope than in 1890 and affected urban areas in particular. Landowners were depicted in those years as endangering the very existence of the Jewish collectivity. 'There is no saint in Palestine on whom we can depend never to sell his land,' Ussishkin wrote in 1933. 'This is an every day practice. There is only one sure way [of preventing it]: as long as the nation exists—and I believe it will exist forever—the land must continue to be the nation's property' (Kimmerling 1983, 76). And the daily *Ha'aretz* reported in 1936 that 'a special stratum of charlatans is created who live on money they illicitly obtained from Jews in connection with sales of land' (Kimmerling 1983, 66).

Harsh criticism of private land investment was directed not only against the speculators but also against those who bought land for permanent settlement in urban locations. Zionism viewed agricultural settlements as the essential basis of Jewish society, and it instinctively distrusted the town—even though the majority of the Jewish population lived in urban areas (Cohen 1970). The Fourth Aliya in particular evinced a clear preference for urban life. Unlike the typically young and single immigrants who arrived as part of the Second and Third Aliyot, the middle-class immigrants of the Fourth Aliya were generally older. Many had families, and they were concerned about the low level of security outside urban areas. And in their eyes the most desirable place to live in was Tel-Aviv (Giladi 1973).

The population of Tel-Aviv, the first entirely Jewish city, grew at an impressive rate. In 1914 there were 1,400 inhabitants, in 1921, 3,604, in 1933, 80,000, in 1937, 150,000 and in 1948, 220,000. In 1922, about 18 percent of the Jews in Palestine lived in Tel-Aviv, but this had grown to 30 percent by 1946 (Shavit and Biger 2000). As a result of the increasing demand, land prices in Tel-Aviv escalated, creating difficulties for immigrants who wanted to buy property. Upon the arrival of the Fourth Aliya in 1927, prices of unimproved land rose from £50 per dunam to £400 per dunam, and they soared to £2,400 per dunam in the years 1933-35 (Bein 1945, 37-8). Spokesmen for the Labour movement perceived this trend of urbanization in accord with the anti-urban orientation of Zionist ideology. The rapid growth was viewed as artificial, even dangerous, inducing most Jewish immigrants to choose city life and attracting Jewish private capital to land speculation. Hence, when the need arose to build urban working-class housing in Tel-Aviv, the General Federation of Labour in Palestine and later in Israel insisted that the workers should not be owners of the land on which their houses were situated (Gracier 1989, 293). The vast majority of the Fourth Aliya immigrants who did not ascribe to the Zionist values of collectivism and blue collar work occupied a low rank in the prestige hierarchy of the Yishuv life. Thus, for example, Avraham Harzfeld, a pioneer and Zionist leader, pointed out in a speech before the 19th Zionist Congress (1935) that there were 'two Palestines, that of the cities, such as Tel-Aviv, which is a degenerate state, and that of the agricultural colonies' (Cohen 1970, 13). Other critics pointed out that the lifestyle in Tel-Aviv imitated the 'Warsaw fashions' or 'Odessa fashions,' i.e. the lifestyle of Jews in the Diaspora (Arlosoroff 1934a, 56).

In 1940, after the three spurts of land speculation, Avraham Granott summarized his thoughts as follows:

> Economically, land values became inflated and purchase of land was made difficult by the senseless competition of Jews with one another; morally the consequences could be seen in the corrupt methods of speculators who shamelessly cut each other's throat competing with one another while they carried on their shady dealings under the name of 'Ge'ulat Ha'aretz' [the redemption of the Land of Israel] without a slightest care for our primary national interests (Granott 1940, 47).

These observations, written a mere eight years before the establishment of the State of Israel, expressed the views of a liberal Zionist who, unlike many Labour Zionists, believed that private property was a desirable economic institution. Nevertheless, the use of the rhetoric of morality and shame demonstrates that even the liberal strand of Zionist economic thought was incapable of viewing land exclusively in economic terms.[16]

This pre-state ideology, which regarded land as fundamentally a non-economic resource and the use of land for personal profit as inherently suspect, remained dominant after independence. Labour Zionism gained power in 1948 as the ruling Mapai party; the JNF preserved its role as a central actor in the land regime of independent Israel and land nationalization became the official land policy of the new state.

The Status of the JNF after Independence

The attainment of political sovereignty in 1948 pulled the rug from under the land-purchasing activity of the JNF. Israel gained territorial sovereignty over a land area of 20.6 million dunams, and the transition from non-sovereign community to full-fledged state took place against the departure—in part forced, in part voluntary—of some 80 percent of the Arab population of the territory. It is estimated that following the War of Independence, Palestinian Arabs abandoned between 4.2 and 6.5 million dunams of land in what became Israel (Golan 2001). The existence of a very large inventory of previously Arab-owned but now state-controlled land put into question the need for the JNF. David Ben-Gurion, the first Prime Minister of Israel, stressed the point in May 1949 at the end of the War of Independence:

> During the 70 years of our activities, from the establishment of Petah Tiqvah until the establishment of the State, we redeemed around 1.8 million dunams of land, an average of around 25 thousands dunams per year. Now we control above 20 million dunams. Had we kept the pre-State pace, we would have needed 800 years to reach this size ... (Sandler 1993, 54-5)

Although the leaders of the JNF shared the socialist ideology of the ruling Mapai party,[17] Ben-Gurion, whose personal ideology was statist, opposed the idea that portions of the land of the independent state should remain under the control of a non-state institution. He believed that as a result of the War of Independence, the JNF had lost its *raison d'être* (namely, acquiring land from non-Jews), and all the land of the new sovereign state should be managed by state institutions. In fact, in his opinion there was no justification for the continued existence of the JNF. The State of Israel did not need more land, Ben-Gurion explained, 'What we need now is Jews to settle the large land areas that the State of Israel has obtained' (Holzman-Gazit 2002).

---

16 On the eve of independence, privately owned urban land amounted to about 300,000 dunams out of the total 800,000 million dunams of land under Jewish private ownership (Kark 1995).

17 *Mapai* (The Palestinian Workers Party) was the socialist-Zionist party founded in 1930 in Palestine as a unified labor party. It became the governing party upon independence and maintained its power until 1977 when it lost to the right wing coalition (Medding 1972).

But Ben-Gurion's proposal to liquidate the JNF was never implemented. Seeking to justify its existence, the JNF instilled a new meaning into the activity of 'land redemption.' Post-independence rhetoric of redemption no longer meant buying land from non-Jews but redeeming the land from its desolation. After independence, the JNF shifted its focus to enterprises that were central to the infrastructure of the state. It took on the expenditure involved in the reclamation and development of Israel's lands, as well as the establishment of water projects such as dams and reservoirs, and it became the prime non-state institution engaged in preparing land for Jewish agricultural activity. For land that was not suitable for agriculture (such as mountainous terrain), the JNF shouldered the expenditure involved in afforestation, which, to Zionist eyes, was as important as agriculture to the almost sacred mission of liberating the land from its existing desolation (Zerubavel 1996).

An important milestone in strengthening the status of the JNF in the post-1948 era was reached when the Government consented to sell the JNF 2 million dunams of abandoned Arab land.[18] The JNF's offer to buy such land from the state was attractive for several reasons. First, the economy of the new country was on the brink of collapse as a result of the war, and funding, which the JNF was able to supply, was needed for acquiring arms and basic food provisions, as well as for absorbing the wave of immigrants. Second, on 11 December 1948, the UN General Assembly concluded its debate on the question of Palestine with Resolution 194, which called on the Israeli government to permit those refugees who wished to return to their homes to do so at the earliest possible date. This resolution raised concerns that a wave of refugees would indeed return. Not wishing to be seen as provoking the international community by outright expropriation of refugee property, an act which would have been interpreted correctly as an attempt to prevent the refugees' return, Ben-Gurion opted for the practical and speedy solution of transferring some of the abandoned property to non-governmental Jewish hands, i.e. the JNF (Golan 1995). Finally, the JNF's offer to buy the abandoned land was attractive to the Government because of the ability of the JNF to contribute to the effort of 'Judaizing' the land. The JNF's 1901 charter included restrictive covenants prohibiting the leasing of JNF land to non-Jews, as well as the employment of non-Jews on JNF land. As a private company, the JNF could thus accomplish goals that contradicted the State's commitment to treating all of its citizens equally, Jews and Arabs alike (Kretzmer 1990, 49-76; Lehn 1988). In January 1949, the state sold the JNF 1 million dunams of abandoned Arab land. In October 1950, a contract for the sale of a further 1 million dunams of Arab land was signed. Taken together, these land acquisitions by the JNF represented more than double the acreage that the JNF had been able to acquire in its close to 50 years of existence (Golan 1995). Furthermore, the land that the JNF purchased from the state was some of the most desirable real estate in Israel, located in areas such as the Jerusalem corridor, the southern Carmel and the central

---

18   Upon independence, the JNF had landholdings of about 935,000 dunams. This figure composed approximately 55 percent of the total Jewish landholdings in the area that became the State of Israel, but only 4 percent of the area of Mandatory Jewish Palestine (Katz, 2001, 271; Tsur 1983 61).

coastal plain. Naturally, all the newly acquired land was subjected to the existing JNF policy of the inalienability of its landholdings.

In other words, just two years after the JNF was deprived of its corporate mission, it not only avoided liquidation but succeeded in preserving (and arguably extending) its political and economic power in the new state. This power was a function not only of the expansion of its landholdings (from less than a million dunams to some 2.5 million dunams)[19] and its new role as a key partner of the State in matters such as the promotion of agricultural settlements and afforestation. Another important element was its close ties to the political elite. The key figures active in the JNF were all members of the Labour-led coalition in the World Zionist Organization, from which the leadership of the ruling Mapai coalition was drawn. As such, they had access at the highest levels to the bureaucratic hegemony that Mapai established and which governed the country until 1977. In fact, the line separating the higher echelons of the JNF administration from the political elite of the country was blurred, to the extent that it existed at all.[20] An indication of the JNF's unique status and influence is the fact that when the State began the process of settling land titles in the Galilee in the mid-1950s, representatives of the JNF were included as members of the national committees that were formed for this purpose. As members of these committees, the representatives of the JNF had considerable influence on the formation of Israel's land regime (Forman 2002*)*. Nor did anyone think to object or question the propriety (let alone legality) of the inclusion of JNF representatives on such government committees.

The fact that the JNF shared the socialist ethos of Labour Zionism while at the same time it was identified as the apolitical symbol of national revival also enabled it to maintain its extensive involvement in the educational system of the new state. Although a subsidized, general (largely secular) system of elementary education was established upon independence as part of Ben-Gurion's attempts to distance the new state from sectoral interests and affiliations, the JNF-inspired Teachers' Council was permitted to continue its curricular activities. The pre-state symbolism of the blue box, as well as the celebration of the values of self-sacrifice, Hebrew labor and the ideological importance of modest personal economic expectations, continued to be an integral part of the cultural context of Israeli schoolchildren.[21]

---

19   The JNF was ultimately unable to pay for all it had contracted to buy from the Government. As a result, the October 1950 transaction was terminated after only 500,000 dunams had been transferred to the JNF.

20   One such person was Yosef Weitz (1890-1972) who, starting in 1932, had risen to serve as the director of the JNF's Land Development Division. At the same time he was also involved in the establishment of the Histadrut, the all-encompassing Zionist Labour federation. By 1948, Weitz was one of the most knowledgeable Zionist land officials in Israel. In 1960, he was appointed as the first Israel Lands Administration's director (Weitz 1965).

21   Thus, long after independence, girls in elementary schools in all branches of the Israeli education system—secular and religious—would place a donation in the JNF's blue box on the Sabbath eve before blessing the candles. Blue boxes containing pupils' donations were opened ceremoniously in the presence of the class during the festival celebrating the new month, and the pupil who served as class treasurer would proclaim: *'The land shall not be*

The blurring of the lines between the state and the JNF as a quasi-state institution in all matters pertaining to land management was reinforced by the passage in 1953 of the Jewish National Fund Law.[22] This law, heavily lobbied for by the JNF, provided for the change of status of the JNF from an English company to an Israeli company. From a legal perspective it was an unnecessary piece of legislation. The JNF could have become an Israeli company in the same way that other companies did, namely, under the provisions of the Companies Ordinance of 1948, which governed the process of converting a foreign company into an Israeli one. The importance of the Jewish National Fund Law was symbolic. The Law was a reflection of the special status of the JNF. The passage of a special law bearing its name accorded the JNF considerable prestige. After the law's enactment, the JNF was secure; the State was clearly going to continue to engage and consult it on all matters of land planning and administration (Holzman-Gazit 2002). And this in fact is what occurred. When the time came to adopt a policy for the management of Israel's public lands, the State adopted the JNF's principle of inalienable national land ownership —the culmination of an incremental process by which the JNF consolidated its status and inscribed its land policy into the cultural, political and legal spheres of the country. The ideology that delegitimized private land ownership had become the official land policy of the State of Israel.

Enactment of Basic Law: Israel Lands (1960)

The legal regime establishing public ownership of the millions of dunams of Arab land that were abandoned in the wake of the 1948 War of Independence was accomplished in several stages (Katz 2002; Oren-Nordheim 2002). The first step was the enactment of the Development Authority (Transfer of Property) Law of 1950, which provided for the transfer of Arab property to a government entity to be known as the 'Development Authority.'[23] The Knesset then enacted the State Property Law of 1951, which established a regime of state ownership for lands that the State of Israel inherited from the British Mandatory government, as well as for all land whose owners were unknown.[24] The process was completed by the enactment of the Basic Law: Israel Lands of 1960.[25]

In the absence of a written constitution, the format of the Basic Laws is reserved for issues that carry considerable social significance. Collectively, the Basic Laws are viewed as chapters of Israel's emerging constitution. The Basic Law: Israel Lands was enacted as part of the process that the State of Israel embarked upon in the late 1950s to unify the administration of public land. Throughout the 1950s, the land regime was split between the State of Israel and the JNF, and each entity had its own administration and principles of land policy planning. In 1960, the government endeavored to create a unified body known as the ILA that would be in charge

---

sold, for the land is mine. And in all the land you possess, you shall grant redemption of the land'(Siton 1998).

  22 8 L.S.I. 35 (1953).
  23 4 L.S.I. 151 (1950).
  24 5 L.S.I. 45 (1951).
  25 14 L.S.I. 48 (1960).

of administering all public lands. But the creation of a joint administrative body required the cooperation of the JNF. The central condition of the JNF for agreeing to transfer the management of its landholdings to the ILA was the formal declaration of its policy of national land ownership as the legal regime for *all* public lands in Israel.[26]

The Basic Law: Israel Lands is the shortest of all eleven Basic Laws enacted to date, and is possibly the briefest law ever enacted by the Knesset. It contains three sections. The first provides that the ownership of 'Israel lands,' defined as lands held by the State itself, the Development Authority and the JNF, 'shall not be transferred either by sale or in any other manner.' The second section clarifies that this prohibition may be overridden and landownership transferred when explicitly provided for by legislation.[27] Finally, the third section defines 'land' for purposes of the law as 'land, houses, buildings and anything permanently fixed to land.' The Law served a declarative rather than a legal purpose. Upon its enactment in 1960, the prohibition on the sale of land owned by the government and the Development Authority had already been accepted and implemented by virtue of the laws of the early 1950s, and the Basic Law anchored it as a semi-constitutional principle. For all the Basic Law's semi-constitutional status and, consequently, its symbolic importance, the Knesset did not take the opportunity to conduct a thorough review of the country's policy of public land ownership when it enacted this law. All parties, including the bourgeois General Zionists, supported the prohibition on the sale of public land. The sole exception was the small right-wing Revisionist Party, which argued in favor of privatizing Israel's lands (Katz 2002).[28]

The Knesset debate preceding the enactment of the Basic Law revealed the majority's fixation on an ideology of nation-building that harked back to the pre-state period. National sovereignty provides a wide array of legal mechanisms to

---

26 The JNF made the transfer of the management of its lands to a unified body conditional on three other demands as well: that its lands would be administrated according to its 1901 Memorandum and Articles of Association, which prohibited the lease of the JNF's lands to non-Jews; that the reclamation and afforestation of national land would be run by the JNF alone; and that the JNF would control the appointment of 49 percent of the membership of the Israel Lands Council (the body in charge of determining the land policy of the ILA). The Government acquiesced to all the JNF's demands. In conjunction with the enactment of Basic Law: Israel Lands, the government signed a Covenant between the State of Israel and the JNF, granting the JNF sole rights to conduct development works and afforestation of Israel's lands (thereby depriving the Ministry of Agriculture of some of its central functions), and accorded the JNF the right to appoint seven of the 15 members of the Israel Lands Council even though the JNF owns only 13 per cent of the land under public ownership. Currently, the Council is comprised of 22 members; 12 represent government ministries and 10 represent the JNF.

27 As indicated in Chapter 1, along with the Basic Law, the Israel Lands Law was passed in 1960 with clauses granting the right to sell up to 100,000 dunams (25,000 acres) of state-owned land in special circumstances, such as in exchange or as compensation for private land (Weisman 1995, 228-35).

28 Whereas the Revisionist called for a capitalist economy, the Communist Party came out in favor of full nationalization of Israel's lands, and objected to the division of ownership between the JNF and the State.

counter dangers such as those that the leadership of the day perceived as posing an existential threat to Israel, namely, land speculation and the sale of land to non-Jews. Such mechanisms typically include property and capital gains taxes and restrictions on the conveyance of land to foreigners (Weisman 1980). However, the Knesset never adopted any of these methods. Instead, the pre-state mindset continued to dominate. Land speculation and sales to non-Jews were raised time and again by participants in the debate as arguments in support of the enactment of the Basic Law (Katz 2002; Plessner 1994, 66-9). Other arguments mentioned included the urgent requirements of the immigrant absorption program and the need to 'conquer the land' by creating a more evenly dispersed pattern of Jewish population settlement throughout the country. Knesset members, particularly from the ruling Mapai party, argued that private land ownership would pose an obstacle to immigrant absorption and to population dispersal. Property rights would make the necessary processes of planning and construction for the new immigrants longer and more expensive due to the need to aggregate land by purchasing relatively small tracts from many owners. For the same reason, private land ownership was also seen as undermining the process of population dispersal, which would require the cooperation of many landowners whose rights in the land were stronger than those of mere leaseholders. Finally, members of the religious parties in the Knesset emphasized the appeal of the Basic Law to Jewish tradition regarding the sacredness of the Land of Israel.

As is evident from the parliamentary records, social and political attitudes toward private land ownership were a continuation of the pre-state heritage. In the public discourse of the 1960s, private land ownership remained suspect, and land was widely considered to be a resource that should not be managed on the basis of personal financial (or emotional) interests or even national economic benefit (Aharoni 1991, 198-213; Plessner 1994, 100-02). This atmosphere of distrust towards private property and the treatment of land as a non-economic resource created the cultural context within which land expropriation cases were adjudicated.

The Ideology of Public Land Ownership and the Case Law of Land Expropriation

Judicial attitudes in general, and property law in particular, reflect the culture and societal beliefs within whose context they are formed. American property law, for example, was shaped in light of the ethos of capitalism and the role of land ownership in American history, where it is intrinsically tied to the value of personal liberty. American Takings jurisprudence also reflects this special emphasis on land as property. Judges long ago understood that the Takings Clause protects particular things or assets, rather than fungible wealth, and within this definition of property they applied the Taking Clause almost exclusively to land ownership rights (Dana and Merrill 2002, 68-85; Treanor 1995). In Israel, the pre-state experience and history of territorial expansion generated a different land regime and tradition. The expropriation case law of the 1950s and in fact up until the late 1970s was decided in accordance with a pervasive societal opposition to the ethos of capitalism and private land ownership. As the discussion above indicated, the exclusion of private land ownership from the system of values of

Zionism was not a marginal issue or a minority view. Rather, it gained the status of a key symbol of the new Hebrew culture and as such it was reflected and reproduced after independence, in the laws enacted by the Knesset. Given the clear attitude in favor of public land ownership and against private property, it is more than likely that such views also shaped and influenced the Supreme Court's perception of the underlying issues at stake in the land expropriation cases that it was called upon to adjudicate. Private land ownership was not deemed as being a particularly worthy object of protection from the power of the state. After all (it was widely held), private landowners were by and large city dwellers, bourgeois urbanites who placed their personal comfort and financial gain ahead of the common goals and aspirations of the community.

It is worth noting in this regard that the entire first generation of Justices were themselves long-time members of the Yishuv and activists in the Zionist movement (Lahav 1990a, 52). And at least two of them, Justice Olshan, the Second Chief Justice, and Justice Agranat, had actively represented the JNF in land purchase cases in their private legal practice before ascending to the bench (Olshan 1978, 179-90). The cumulative effect of the cultural atmosphere and personal ideology made it difficult to persuade the Court to set aside expropriation orders merely because of initial technical legal errors which in any case could be (and were) subsequently easily corrected.

The same could be said of the Court's position regarding full compensation for expropriated land. Zionist ideology, it will be remembered, tended to attach an economic value to land only when the land was in non-Jewish hands. Once transferred to Jewish control, the land's economic value was outweighed by wide (non-economic) interests. This approach characterized the history of Jewish settlement in Palestine and later in Israel. In the pre-state period, the JNF used to allocate its land not on the basis of demand but according to considerations of enhancement of Jewish self-labor. After independence, the State of Israel adopted a national land policy of preservation of agricultural land even though there was increasing demand for urban development in the central areas of the country and the agricultural usage of the land and communities dependent on such land use consistently and demonstrably failed to be profitable. Given this anti-economic approach at the political and administrative levels and its general acceptance in the culture of the 1950s and 1960s, it is not surprising that the judiciary deferred from construing the no-compensation rule narrowly. In fact, the expansion of the no-compensation rule in the Planning Law of 1965 could be seen as legal reflection of the social covenants of the day.

Gradually, however, the social values of collectivism that had been at the heart of the ideological rejection of private land ownership faded. In the late 1970s, personal success and economic self-fulfillment took the place of the egalitarian values which had enjoyed wide support in Israeli society during the first decades of statehood. The new profile that Israeli society began to acquire in the late 1970s related in part to the experience of the 1973 Yom Kippur War. The traumatic consequences of the failure of the political and military elites to foresee the joint Egyptian and Syrian attack, particularly in terms of the unacceptably high number of causalities, forced many Israelis to re-examine their previously unquestioned value system represented by key institutions in Israeli society such as the military, the Labour Party, the kibbutz network and the Histadrut. When political power shifted to the right in 1977, economic policy also started to reflect and promote the new value system of neoliberalism, individualism and free enterprise (Eisenstadt 1985; Horowitz and Lissak 1989; Sharkansky 1987).

The change in Israeli social ideology and economic structure brought about a dramatic change in the relative status of the major sectors of the economy. Agriculture, which in the 1950s had been the ideologically preferred sector, the one that received priority in human and economic resources, was replaced in the 1980s by the manufacturing and service sectors (Ben-Porat 1999). In 1961 there were 127,600 Jewish farmers in Israel. By 1994, this number had dropped to 61,746—a mere 3.3 percent of the Jewish workforce (Amiran 1996). Similarly, in 1957 the relative weight of agriculture in exports was 44.2 percent. Thirty years later, agriculture represented only 9 percent of exports (Aharoni 1991, 209; Plessner 1994, 121).

By the late 1980s, reduced income from agriculture resulted in economic crisis for the kibbutzim and moshavim, which were unable to repay their massive bank loans. To solve their financial problems, the influential farming lobby proposed that the government allow kibbutzim and moshavim to sell off their most valuable asset, agricultural land. Two separate questions arose in this respect. First, it was clear that the kibbutzim and moshavim could not sell their land unless it was re-zoned for urban use, since no one would buy it for agricultural use. Second, almost all the land held by kibbutzim and moshavim was public land. Legally, changes in land use designation required leaseholders to return the land to the ILA.

As will be detailed in Chapter 9, the 1992 political decision to permit changing the designation of land held by agricultural settlements to urban use was taken against the background of the urgent need for land in order to settle the wave of Jewish immigrants who arrived in Israel from the former Soviet Union. This practical need should not obscure the fact that the decision signified a dramatic change in the ideology underlying Israel's land policy: for the first time, urbanization as a form of Zionist pioneering was granted ideological legitimacy and recognition. The decision also reflected the waning of the traditional anti-economic approach to land. The new policy, which allowed leaseholders in cooperative settlements to sell their land for urban use or to return it to the ILA in exchange for compensation that would be determined in accordance with the market value of the land after its re-zoning, signified the emergence of economic criteria for land valuation.[29]

These practical and ideological changes in the attitude to land management — from agricultural to urban and from idealistic to material asset—were not sufficient, however, to bring about a wholesale reform in the public land ownership regime. In 1996, Ariel Sharon, then Minister of National Infrastructure, established a commission headed by Prof. Boaz Ronen whose task was to 'reexamine the land policy in Israel' (State of Israel 1998; Witkon 1998).[30] The Ronen Commission's recommendations

---

29 The leasing agreements between the State and the cooperative settlements stipulated that agricultural land whose use was changed would revert to the State, and the leaseholder would be entitled only to compensation to the extent of his improvements to the land.

30 The commission was established in the wake of growing criticism of the inefficiency of the state bureaucracy that managed Israel lands, and doubts about the continuing need for such extensive public land ownership. One claim was that the tenure system of public land ownership created upward pressure on land prices due to the ILA's policy of releasing small

called for a gradual privatization of national lands, beginning with residential dwellings. Yet these recommendations were rejected by Israel Lands Council, mainly due to the objection of the JNF's representatives (Israel Lands Administration 1995; Saskin and Gilai 1986). It was not until 2005 that similar recommendations of another public commission, the Gadish Commission, received the backing of both the Israel Lands Council and the government. The Gadish Commission recommended the full transfer of urban residential land ownership rights to the private lessees of apartments and buildings, and the retention of the regime of public ownership with regards to state-owned land designated for agriculture. It still remains to be seen whether the recommendations will in fact be implemented (State of Israel 2005).

Indeed, since the 1980s, traditionally accepted ideas regarding land ownership––and consequently private land ownership as well––have been the subject of re-examination in Israeli society. On the one hand, the force of the old collectivist ideals receded and land began to be viewed primarily in economic terms. On the other hand, the current Israeli land regime, which is still heavily skewed in favor of public land ownership, reflects the sustained Zionist ideology of nation-building and a pervasive suspicion of private property. The tension between these two modes of thought has formed the background against which the Supreme Court has been adjudicating land expropriation cases in the last two decades. As discussed in Chapter 8 below, the current ambiguity as to the status of private ownership of land in Israeli culture may account at least in part for the ambiguity in the land expropriation case law of the Supreme Court in the period after the constitutional revolution of 1992.

---

quantities of land for development in areas of high demand. Another argument for reform was that the existing system of public ownership was subject to considerable pressure by interest groups, in particular the agricultural lobby. Critics also pointed out that the system of public land ownership did not prevent the sale of land to foreign entities through Israeli representatives.

Chapter 4

The Public Use Requirement: The Impact of Immigration and Housing Policies

Israel is a country of immigrants. In 2002, out of the Jewish population over the age of 25, only 45 percent were native-born, and of those only 20 percent had native-born fathers (CBS 2003). Immigration on this scale has immediate implications for the practice of land expropriation. The rapid (and essentially unpredictable) population growth creates pressure on the housing supply, on national infrastructure and on community services and, not least, on Israel's limited supply of land. This chapter analyzes the ideological traditions, social ideas and political interests that have shaped the immigration and housing policies of Israel and have influenced the Supreme Court's land expropriation decisions. The long-standing ideological commitments to immigration and to the settling of all parts of the national territory contain a national security dimension whose profound effect on land expropriation is rarely discussed. The discussion below will show that the twin goals of maintaining a Jewish majority in the country as a whole and establishing a Jewish majority in all regions of the country have shaped the way Israeli society thinks about the desirable and efficient use of land, and this in turn has shaped the meaning of 'public purpose' in the context of expropriation.

Israel's Immigration Policy: Practice and Driving Forces

The ideological origins of Israel's immigration policy lie in the Zionist worldview which called on Jews to rebel against the Diaspora existence. The Zionist movement grew out of the conviction that the social discrimination and economic and political restrictions that Jews experienced as a minority population constituted a dead-end for the Jewish people and Jewish culture. The implication of this worldview was and remains that any Jew regardless of their health, age, race or economic status who wished to settle in the national homeland should be allowed to do so.

Prior to independence, immigration policies affecting Jews in Palestine were determined by the non-Jewish rulers of the land. The Turks set limitations on Jewish immigration to Palestine, and restrictions were also imposed by the British authorities. With the establishment of the State of Israel in 1948, the issue of Jewish immigration came under the control of Jews for the first time, and it was given top priority. The first act of legislation of Israel's Provisional State Council (the predecessor of the Knesset) on the very day that independence was declared was to abolish the British restrictions on Jewish immigration and on the purchase of land by Jews. In the Declaration of Independence, the founders stated that Israel would always embrace Jewish immigration (*aliya*) and that the country's foremost mission was *kibbutz galuyoth* (the ingathering of exiles); in other words, the absorption and integration of Jews from all over the world.

The principle of free immigration was legally grounded in two laws enacted shortly after independence: the Law of Return of 1950[1] and the Law of Citizenship of 1952.[2] The Law of Return permanently grants all Jews the right to immigrate to Israel.[3] The Law of Citizenship grants citizenship to anyone who has immigrated to Israel or has entered as a tourist but is eligible for immigrant status. Furthermore, Israel has not only permitted any eligible Jew to enter Israel and obtain citizenship, but from its early days it has actively stimulated and encouraged immigration. After independence, the state hired American and British companies to provide transport from Yemen's 50,000-strong Jewish community, in what was termed 'Operation Magic Carpet,' and paid the governments of Hungary, Rumania and Bulgaria what was in effect a per-head ransom to permit their Jewish citizens to emigrate for Israel (Hacohen 1994, 54-76; Segev 1986, 95-116; Stock 1988). In the 1960s and 1970s, Israel led the struggle for the rights of Soviet Jews to immigrate, and in 1991 it operated a 48-hour continuous airlift known as 'Operation Solomon,' in the course of which 14,500 Ethiopian Jews were flown to Israel.[4]

The efforts that Israel invests in promoting immigration at public expense are grounded to a large extent in the sense of responsibility for Jewish communities living under non-democratic regimes. In part as a result of the Holocaust, Israel sees itself as having a positive moral obligation not merely to leave its gates open but to actively assist Jews in distress (Brecher 1972, 229-33). No less influential, however, is the view that sees immigration as a major strategic component of state-building. All Israeli governments, past and present, have regarded the rapid growth of the Jewish population as a significant contribution to the strength and development of the state. In the early years, promotion of immigration was presented as a matter on which the fate and security of the Jewish state depended. Immigration was expected to improve the ability of Israel to face the external threat to its existence posed by its

---

1   4 L.S.I. 114 (1950).

2   6 L.S.I. 50 (1952).

3   In the 1950 version of the law, a Jew was defined as any son or daughter of a Jewish mother who has not converted to another faith, or any person who has converted to Judaism. In 1970, the Law of Return was amended to grant the right to immigrate to Israel to non-Jewish family members of Jews (Rubinstein and Medina 2005, 396-409). Interestingly, the issue of who is a Jew was not mentioned in the discussion preceding the enactment of the Law of Return in 1950. The issue captured public attention only upon the amendment of 1970 when applicants for Israeli citizenship challenged the religious definition of Judaism. In the Law of Return, there are three categories of Jewish applicants who are deprived of the right to immigrate to Israel: those who act against the Jewish people; those who endanger public heath or public security; and those who are convicted of criminal offences.

4   As might be expected, Israel's Arab citizens, who constitute 19 percent of the population, oppose the immigration policy, which is extremely open toward Jews and very restrictive toward non-Jews. The Law of Return and the active immigration policy are quintessential examples of the tension between the definition of Israel as a Jewish state and as a democratic state (Smooha 1997; Rouhana and Ghanem, 1998).

Arab neighbors, and, internally, to overcome the low Jewish birthrate compared to that of the Arab population. In 1948, the population ratio between Israel and the five Arab countries—Egypt, Syria, Lebanon, Jordan and Iraq—that fought against it in the War of Independence was 1 to 50 (Brecher 1972, 69). Clearly, no rise in Jewish immigration, however dramatic, could seriously alter this demographic disparity. Nonetheless, rapid growth of the Jewish population has had important implications for wartime as well. From 1948 and until the mid-1990s, Israel based its military force on the doctrine of a 'nation in arms.' Under this framework, in military emergencies, a reserve force of men serving until the age of 55 was available for immediate call. The Jewish male population between the ages of 18 and 55 thus constituted the maximum size of Israel's military manpower (Lissak 1995, Tal 1977).

Mass immigration was also seen as the solution for the problem posed by the existence of a large Arab population in Israel. The Arab citizens of Israel have traditionally been viewed as hostile to the interests of the Jewish state. On the eve of Israel's independence, Jews constituted only about 30 percent of Palestine's total population. Jewish immigration formed an effective mechanism for rapid population growth and a counterbalance to the high rate of natural growth of the Arab population of the country. As a result of the waves of Jewish immigration and the exodus of hundreds of thousands of Arabs during the War of Independence, the ratio between the two populations changed dramatically. Jews currently account for roughly 81 percent of the total population of Israel. Immigration has accounted for 48 percent of the total growth of the Jewish population (CBS 2003).

Another consideration underlying the importance of immigration is economic growth and the achievement of economic independence. Upon the establishment of the State of Israel, Ben-Gurion identified basic food production, arms manufacture and international air and sea transport capabilities as factors necessary for the security of Israel:

> We dare not be blind to our unique geographical location. In a quarrel with our neighbors we have no overland communication with the outside world. This grave circumstance impels us to the following conclusions: our agriculture and fishery must supply the population with food stuff ... defensive weapons must be made locally, so that we shall not be wholly dependent on outside sources; we must foster Israeli shipping and the expansion of our national marine services to all quarters of the globe; and we require improvements in domestic and international air routes. (State of Israel 1951, 12)

In the mid-1950s, the development of a strong industrial sector was added to this list of key economic goals (Aharoni 1991; Halevi and Klinov-Malul 1968). Given Israel's lack of natural resources, human resources have been regarded as the main reservoir from which economic expansion would be achieved. Economic growth would thus be based on demographic growth, human resources and the inflow of capital (Horowitz 1972; Ben-Porath 1986).

Evidence for the social treatment of immigration as a process central to the existence and strength of the state is provided by the terminology that has traditionally been used by both policy-makers and the general public regarding emigration and immigration. While the Hebrew term *aliya* (immigration) connotes 'ascension' from the Diaspora to Israel, *yerida* (emigration) describes the formerly highly stigmatized path of abandonment of the Promised Land and 'descent' to the Diaspora. In a 1976 television interview, then Prime Minister Yitzhak Rabin notoriously referred to Israeli emigrants as *nefolet nemoshot* (fallout of weaklings), and as 'moral lepers' (Eisenstadt 1985, 486). Rabin subsequently recanted these harsh statements, but the pejorative term *yordim* for emigrants remained in popular use for many years.

Between 1948 and 2002, 2.7 million Jewish immigrants entered Israel in four major waves of immigration (CBS 2003). The first and most dramatic of these waves occurred immediately after independence. Between May 1948 and the end of 1951, the Jewish population of the country doubled from 700,000 to 1,400,000. This first wave of immigration is referred to below as the 'mass immigration.' The second wave of immigration took place between 1955 and 1957, when about 165,000 immigrants from North Africa arrived in Israel. The third major immigration wave came on the heels of the 1967 War and saw 250,000 immigrants arriving from the Soviet Union, Western Europe and North America between 1969 and 1972. The final major wave of immigration began in 1990. Between 1990 and 1999 nearly 1 million immigrants arrived in Israel and were added to Israel's 1989 population of 4.5 million; 84 percent of them came from former Soviet Union and about 4 percent from Ethiopia.

Israel's Housing Policy

The national interest in promoting immigration, coupled with the sense of responsibility toward Jewish communities in distress, has been a major consideration in shaping Israel's housing policy. Throughout the country's history, Israeli governments assumed responsibility for assisting immigrants with housing. Housing composed a central facet of Israel's domestic public policy since it was perceived as a key component of the strategy of state-building and development.

Following the large wave of immigration in its first two decades, Israel's housing policy aimed primarily at achieving two national goals: absorbing immigration and encouraging a more uniform geographic dispersal of the population. The strategic goal of demographic dispersal was the result of the perception, which to a lesser extent persists to this day, that the security of the state depends on a more even geographic distribution of the Jewish population, particularly in areas where Jewish control and sovereignty are disputed (Drori 2006; Evans 2006). Jewish pioneering settlement was expected to help delineate the external borders of the Jewish state and to secure its territorial base against military invasion and against the infiltration of Arab refugees.[5] Settling Jews in outlying areas of the country was also intended to help delineate internal frontier regions which act as a powerful strategy to expand state control over the minority Arab population (Yiftachel 1998).

On the eve of independence, the call for population dispersal was particularly acute in light of the extremely polarized geographic distribution of the population.

---

5   Infiltration of Arab refugees was one of Israel's central security problems in the early years. In the first 15 months after the War of Independence, 134 people were killed and 104 injured by infiltrators. The establishment of frontier agricultural communities was intended to create a security barrier against such infiltrations, and, in case of war, to buy time for the military to organize effectively (Drory, 2006; Gvati 1985, 117-21).

Approximately 80 percent of Israel's Jewish population lived in greater Tel-Aviv and greater Haifa, while the northern and southern frontier regions were practically devoid of Jewish presence (Torgovnick 1990, 34). Seeking to take effective control of the northern and southern districts (the Galilee and the Negev respectively), in 1949 the Government adopted the first of a series of national population distribution plans. The plan envisioned the establishment of new towns and villages spread out along Israel's borders and across the country (Brutzkus 1964; Evans 2006; Torgovnick 1990, 30-32).[6] Key areas of this plan were the Galilee, where there was an Arab majority, and the sparsely populated Negev Desert, where it was important to create a 'Jewish presence' in order to prove—not least for ideological reasons—that this large and inhospitable region was an integral part of the country. Over the years, the various plans for population dispersal were implemented through mechanisms that required profound and direct involvement of the state in the housing market. In the 1950s and the 1960s, the overwhelming majority of housing units—80 percent in the 1950s, 65 percent in the 1960s—were constructed by the government. Between 1948 and 1964, the Ministry of Housing was involved in the construction of 35 new urban localities, known as 'new towns' or development towns, and about 400 small cooperative agricultural settlements located in rural areas.[7] Public housing also provided the basis for many new neighborhoods on the peripheries of existing urban centers (Gonen 1995, 32). Due to low construction standards and the fact that public housing was built on public land (and therefore free), their price was often 40 to 50 percent cheaper than housing constructed on privately owned land. The price factor and the dominance of the state in the housing supply caused the Jewish population in the peripheral areas to increase. The Jewish population in the Southern District as a percentage of all Jews in Israel rose from 1 percent in 1948 to 15 percent in 1995, and that of the Northern District grew from 7.5 percent to 10 percent over the same period (Carmon 2002, 191). Research shows, however, that the major population groups who lived in the publicly constructed housing in outlying regions were newcomers who had immigrated to Israel in the mid- and late 1950s from North African and Asian countries such as Iraq, Yemen and India. They could not afford publicly constructed homes in central urban areas and thus were directed by the state to public housing in outlying regions and on the outskirts of urban conurbations (Lipshitz, 1998; Gonen 1985; Roter and Shamai 1990).[8]

---

6   Since 1949, seven national plans of population dispersal have been prepared by the Minister of Interior. The population distribution mindset permeated into the late 1980s. It changed upon the arrival of the most recent wave of immigration from the former Soviet Union in the early 1990s.

7   Most of the development towns were established in the Galilee and the Negev. The concept was to create local centers that could provide employment opportunities, commercial services and cultural activities for the inhabitants of smaller rural settlements. In reality, however, the scheme did not work. The development towns often failed to generate employment opportunities; they offered (and still offer) relatively low standards of living, and their residents are characterized by a low socioeconomic status (Lipshitz 1998).

8   Immigrants from European countries who were sent to development towns succeeded in leaving them on average within ten years of their arrival in Israel, moving to better apartments in established cities in the central region, thanks to their sociopolitical mobility. By contrast,

The use of housing as a means for achieving Jewish demographic predominance in particular areas of the country continued in the 1970s. In that period, however, Israel's housing policy gradually became focused on the need to provide low-income populations with higher standards of living. Together with this change of focus, the governments of the day shifted from supply-side support (housing construction) to providing financing subsidies to home-buyers. By the 1980s, only 20 percent of newly built units were in state-sponsored housing developments. The vast majority of new housing starts were now carried out by the private sector, with the government offering home-buyers subsidized loans for the purchase of an apartment (Carmon and Czamanski 1990).

At the end of 1989, in light of the large wave of immigration from the former Soviet Union, public resources were mobilized once again to absorb the immigrants. Within a few months, the government stepped back into direct involvement in the construction and marketing of housing. Whereas in 1989 the number of new housing units was 20,000, 16 percent of which were publicly initiated, the comparable figures for 1991 were 42,000 and 51 percent. The share of publicly initiated housing dropped back to 20 percent or less by 1995, as the government once again pulled out of the housing construction business, all the while preserving the financial support to immigrants, to young couples, and to the needy (Carmon 2002, 187).

Housing assistance programs are not unique to Israel. But the total scope of state involvement in the housing market distinguishes Israel from other Western countries. Israel's housing policy departs from the capitalist model of market forces in favor of a socialist model; housing assistance is provided not only on a need basis, but also on the basis of the government's assessment of the potential contribution of citizens to national goals (Borukhov 1980; Carmon 2002, 186). Particularly notable in this regard is the fact that assistance programs in Israel are designed to encourage homeownership rather than rental accommodation. In 1999 homeowners (or, to be more precise, long-term leaseholders) accounted for 71 percent of all households (CBS 1999). This rate is extremely high compared to most European countries, and is of particular interest considering the fact that Israel is an immigrant society.[9] Although typically in immigration countries the most common form of dwelling is rental accommodation, the governments of Israel have historically taken a different emphasis, and have encouraged the citizens of the country—and new arrivals among them in particular—to purchase (or lease long-term) the housing units they occupy.

The encouragement of homeownership, like the policy of population dispersal, is not based solely on considerations of economic efficiency, but on the ability of housing policies to play a key role in the fulfillment of the state's strategic interests.[10]

---

immigrants from Asian and North African countries stayed in the urban periphery. According to the population census of 1961, 62 percent of the immigrants from Morocco and 72 percent of those from Algeria were housed in the new peripheral towns, compared with 1.3 percent of those from Germany and Austria and 13 percent of those from Poland.

9   In 1999, 54 percent of French households owned their homes. The comparable figure for West Germany was 43 percent. Only Spain, Ireland and Belgium had higher ownership rates than Israel (National Agency for Enterprise and Housing 2003, Table 3.4).

10   Data shows that the cost of housing in Israel is very high relative to average income. In 1999 the median price of a housing unit in the United States was $108,000 while in Israel

Homeownership is viewed as a more effective means of establishing Jewish presence and dominance than is rental housing. Since buying a home requires a considerable personal financial investment, it has the effect of reducing the homeowner's mobility. It becomes harder for the homeowner to relocate from the periphery to the center, and of course it becomes harder to emigrate. Homeownership also ties people to the land emotionally, a commitment particularly important in an immigrant society (Lewin-Epstein et al. 2004, 343). Finally, in the early years of statehood, land and housing were used as political resources to reward favored groups, as was the case with Labour party leaders and army veterans (Rabinowitz 2000).

Given the national-strategic emphasis that, in large part, dictates government housing policies in Israel, it is reasonable to ask whether this has influenced the socially acceptable definition of 'public purpose' for which land may be expropriated. As the discussion below shows, the national-strategic role that housing plays in Israel results in a social culture in which expropriation of land for housing, for infrastructure and for community services is regarded as essential for national security. It thus defines what constitutes a valid 'public purpose,' and at the same time provides a justification for imposing limits on property rights.

The implications of the social and political significance that has been devoted to housing for the practice of expropriation and the case law will be examined below with regard to three periods in the country's history. The first was the brief span of years immediately following independence, when authorities resorted to confiscating privately owned apartments in order to provide temporary accommodation for those in need. The second was the 1950s and early 1960s, a period of increasing political pressure to provide permanent housing solutions for the immigrants who had arrived immediately after independence and to develop the infrastructure of the new state. The third period is the decade of the 1970s, when expropriations were employed as a means to provide better housing and living conditions to both immigrants and underprivileged communities of long-time citizens.

Apartment Confiscation as a Means of Providing Temporary Accommodation, 1949-52

The period between 1948 and 1951 was the most intensive in terms of allocating resources for immigrant absorption. Overall, 690,000 immigrants entered Israel during

---

in 1997 it was $150,000. This price difference is astonishing considering the fact that US per capita gross domestic product (GDP) is double that of Israel (Benchetrit and Czamanski 2005, 52). Housing prices in outlying areas of the country are considerably lower than in the central region. In 1982 the average housing prices in the peripheral towns of northern and southern Israel were about half of those of metropolitan Tel-Aviv and Jerusalem. Yet given the correlation between economic status and housing values, housing is very expensive relative to average income, both for the affluent and for the poor. As a result, most households (and first-time buyers in particular) need to obtain, in addition to the subsidized mortgage offered by the Government, a private-sector mortgage, which is naturally more expensive to service. From an economic point of view it would be desirable to offer households a choice between subsidies for homeownership and rented accommodation (Gabriel 1986).

these years, compared to the 483,000 immigrants who entered Jewish Palestine in the 30-year period prior to independence. The result was a doubling of the Jewish population base to 1.4 million in less than four years (Bachi 1974, 89-111; Sicron 1957, 38-9).

Absorbing immigrants at a rate as dramatic as this would be an ambitious challenge for any country. For the Israel of 1949, a fledgling state, poor in resources and attempting to recover economically from a year-long war of independence, attempting to absorb these masses led the economic system and the existing social structure to the verge of collapse. The hardships involved in immigrant absorption were the result not only of the large volume of immigration but also of its social composition. The immigrants of these years arrived overwhelmingly from two regions of the world: Eastern and Central Europe (48.6 percent) and Arab countries (50.7 percent). All immigrants were accepted: the young and the old, the healthy and the infirm. Among the post-war remnants of European Jewry who arrived, a large number were chronically ill concentration camp survivors. Inability to support themselves economically also typified certain segments of the community of Oriental Jews (Jews originating from Moslem countries), many of whom arrived in Israel destitute, having been compelled to leave all their possessions behind. In addition, their family structure made social mobility and economic independence difficult to achieve.[11] The encounter between the veterans, who had created a relatively modern institutional and social infrastructure, and the immigrants from the Arab countries, nearly all of whom were attached to traditional cultural systems, posed a severe challenge. The interaction between the groups was not symmetric, and the establishment preferred a policy of rapid (and essentially enforced) integration over one of recognition of, and reconciliation with, cultural pluralism (Lissak 2003).

The chief proponent of a policy of unrestricted immigration was Prime Minister and Defense Minister David Ben-Gurion. Although public opinion polls taken in 1949 showed that the vast majority of the population (82 percent) was in favor of planning and regulating the stream of immigrants and adjusting it to the economic ability of the country to absorb immigration (Blander 2004; Halperen 1969), Ben-Gurion ardently opposed selective and controlled immigration (Hacohen 1998; Gelber 1998). For Ben-Gurion, immigration not only enhanced the political, social, economic, ideological and psychological image of the new state; immigration strengthened national security, and this was the prime consideration. 'A primary and deciding factor in our security is mass immigration in short order,' Ben-Gurion stated in 1949. 'No effort is as potent as the intensification of immigration in this regard ... and no economic or similar consideration can be allowed to slow down the rate of immigration, any more than it did our resistance to the Arab armies' (State of Israel 1951, 12). Ben-Gurion went on to explain why, in his view, immigration would achieve more in terms of strengthening the country's security than any other single

---

11   Nearly 40 percent of the Oriental Jews who arrived in Israel were children under the age of 14, compared to only 15 percent among European immigrants. In terms of economic independence, there were 75 dependents (including 66 children) per 100 Asian and North African immigrants of working age, compared to 49 dependents (including 28 children) per 100 Europeans (Bachi 1974, 110; Sicron 1957, 62).

measure: 'We might have captured the West Bank, the Golan, the entire Galilee, but those conquests would not have reinforced our security as much as immigration. Doubling and tripling the number of immigrants gives us more and more strength... That is the most important thing, above all else.' Of the importance of dispersing Jewish settlements over the entire national territory he spoke in similar vein: 'We have conquered territories, but without settlements they have no decisive value, neither in the Negev, nor in the Galilee, nor in Jerusalem. Settlement is the real conquest.' And as settlement of the land required a stronger demographic base, the future of the state depended on immigration (Segev 1986, 97).

Mass immigration gave rise to shortages of essential supplies such as food, clothing, fuel and building materials. The influx of immigrants coupled with the demobilization of thousands of soldiers at the end of the 1948 war also led to high levels of unemployment and to inflationary pressures as a result of the expansion of loan programs. As far as housing was concerned, immigration created critical shortages of residential units.

Upon arrival, the first immigrants of late 1948 and early 1949 were given temporary shelter in former British Army barracks. After a few weeks, most of them were able to find permanent housing in abandoned Arab villages and urban neighborhoods. About 124,000 new immigrants and thousands of discharged soldiers were settled in conditions of high density in abandoned Arab homes in Acre, Beit She'an, Be'er Sheva, Lydda, Ramla, Haifa, Jaffa and Tiberias (Lucas 1975, 273-5; Stock 1988, 84-90). As the influx of immigrants increased in the spring and summer of 1949, all vacant Arab housing in the center of the country was soon occupied. The Government realized that construction of permanent housing could not keep up with the rate of immigration, and it therefore decided to house the immigrants in what were, in effect, temporary shacks constructed out of sheet metal and canvas, and which were referred to disparagingly as *ma'abarot* (transit camps), a term which soon became synonymous with slums.

Establishing the transit camps did not require exercise of expropriation powers, since most of the camps were on public land on the outskirts of existing towns. But the severe housing shortage led to a practice of apartment confiscation in urban settings as a means of providing temporary accommodation to immigrants and others.

The practice of apartment confiscation was prevalent from early 1949 until 1952, against the background of the acute housing shortage. However, immigration was not the only cause of this housing shortage. Severe conditions had existed in urban localities even before the influx of Jews from Eastern Europe and from North Africa.[12] This was a chronic problem which with respect to Tel-Aviv grew significantly after independence, in light of the Government's decision to locate its offices and to hold

---

12   In 1946, for example, the average population density was 4.6 persons per room in Tel-Aviv and 6.1 in Jerusalem. Rents in Tel-Aviv and Haifa were extremely high, reaching 25 to 30 percent of the average worker's wages. Back in 1940, the Mandate Government had promulgated a Rent Control Ordinance to combat escalating rents. But this measure had only served to bring to a halt private construction of badly needed apartment buildings intended for rental accommodation (Darin-Drabkin 1957, 24-8; Gonen 1995).

meetings of the Provisional State Council there rather than in Jerusalem, which at the time was under siege. In 1948 communications between Tel-Aviv and Jerusalem were unreliable, and government officials who lived outside Tel-Aviv needed to be relocated to the city. Initially, the Government believed that some 500 officials could be billeted one or two to a room in private apartments, and about 1,700 could be housed in large dormitory-style halls (Sharef 1962, 158-69). In practice, there were no free rooms at reasonable prices in Tel-Aviv before the surrender of the Arab neighborhood of Jaffa, so the Government resorted to confiscating scores of Jewish-owned apartments.

The confiscation of apartments was carried out pursuant to the provisions of several different items of emergency legislation. At first, the Government made use of the Defence Regulations of 1939 and the Defence (Emergency) Regulations of 1945, which Israel had inherited from the British. Then, in 1948, the Government promulgated the Emergency (Requisition of Property) Regulations which were transformed into the Emergency Land Requisition (Regulation) Law, 1949, still in force today.[13]

The language of the Emergency Land Requisition (Regulation) Law reflected the prevailing view that the very existence of the State depended on rapid Jewish population growth. In addition to incorporating clear-cut security considerations as factors to be taken into account at the discretion of the requisitioning authority, the law cited the goal of immigrant absorption as grounds justifying the issuance of confiscation orders. Section 3(b) provided that a non-elected administrative officer could take immediate possession of private property whenever it appeared to him that this action was necessary for the 'defence of the State, public security, the maintenance of essential supplies or essential public services, *absorption of immigrants* and rehabilitation of ex-soldiers and war invalids' (emphasis added).

The Emergency Land Requisition (Regulation) Law regulated two types of orders: land requisition and housing.[14] In the original version of the law, the legislature mandated that land that was properly requisitioned pursuant to this law could not be occupied for a period exceeding three years. Later, however, the initial period was extended to six years and subsequently to ten (Hofnung 1996, 109-112). As regards housing orders, the legislature did not specify an expiration date, but in practice such orders were generally issued as a means for providing temporary shelter only. Between 1949 and 1952, the Government made extensive use of the Emergency Land Requisition (Regulation) Law, issuing 1,255 housing and 1,124 land requisition orders. Of these, 952 were for the benefit of immigrants, 801 were intended for provision of essential public services, 82 for national security and defense and 544 for rehabilitation of discharged soldiers and war invalids.[15] Requisition orders as well as housing orders dramatically affected the value of private property. Their

---

13 4 L.S.I. 3 (1949).

14 The Law created an overlap between the definition of 'land' and 'house' According to Section 1, land included '[l]and of any category or tenure and any building, tree or other thing fixed in the land.' House meant 'building or other structure, whether permanent or temporary, which is fixed to the land and includes any part of such a building or structure.'

15 15 D.K. (1953) 366.

effect was to take over a vacated apartment before it could be rented out again and to give it to a 'benefited tenant,' instead of a tenant chosen by the apartment owner. A benefited tenant who entered an apartment under the terms of a housing order immediately gained the status of a statutory tenant. As such, the tenant only had to pay fixed minimal rent fees and was protected against eviction.

A large number of the issued orders were annulled by appeals committees shortly after their issuance, sometimes even before physical possession took place.[16] Interestingly, however, owners whose private property was physically seized did not hurry to bring their claims before the Court. Between 1948 and 1952 fewer than 15 cases concerning apartment confiscation reached the Supreme Court. Almost all involved confiscation orders issued for accommodation of government bureaucrats, as opposed to orders issued for accommodation of immigrants and the rehabilitation of ex-soldiers (Holzman-Gazit 2002a).

Apartment Confiscation Adjudication: Judicial Performance and Social Context

From a formalistic legal perspective, the case law of apartment confiscation does not touch directly on the subject matter of this study. Apartment confiscations were exercised under Mandatory and Israeli emergency legislation, whereas this study focuses on the Court's treatment of the exercise of expropriation powers under the 'normal' scheme of the AO of 1943 and the Planning Law of 1965. Yet this distinction, although important for a doctrinal analysis of the Court's record, should not lead us to ignore the fact that substantively it presented the Court at a very early date with the choice between competing interests that were very similar to the ones that arose in cases of expropriations under the above-mentioned laws. The Justices who handled challenges against expropriation powers in the early years were the same ones who sat in apartment confiscation cases, and in both situations they were faced with a legal practice that harmed the right of property owners for the sake of what the government defined as the public interest. The Court's pattern of adjudication in apartment confiscation cases thus serves to illuminate the political, social and cultural environment of the 1950s, in which providing housing to immigrants emerged as a central value.

Many of the cases of apartment confiscation that reached the Supreme Court involved the preferential treatment of government officials. In a period of severe shortage of housing, it was not uncommon for a civil servant to approach the Requisitioning Officer and to ask him to confiscate a particular apartment for the civil servant and for their family.[17] One such case was *Zeev v. Acting District Commissioner of the Urban Area of Tel-Aviv*, in which the Director of the Financial

---

16 Reporting to the Knesset, Minister of Justice, Pinchas Rosen stated that of the total number of approximately 2,500 requisitions and housing orders, about 850 were set aside by the appeals committees or by the requisitioning authority itself before the orders had been carried out. 15 D.K. (1953) 366.

17 H.C. 10/49, *A.S. Ltd. v. Acting District Commissioner of Tel-Aviv*, 2 P.D. 226; H.C. 82/49, *Schwartz v. Component Requisitioning Authority*, 2 P.D. 170; H.C. 29/49, *Sheinin v. Acting District Commissioner of Tel-Aviv*, 2 P.D. 654.

and Control Section of the Ministry of the Interior asked the requisitioning officer to confiscate a four-room apartment in Tel-Aviv for his and his family's use.[18] The facts of the case, as it turned out, were that prior to issuing the requisition order, the Director had been in lease negotiations with the owner of the apartment. When it seemed that the negotiations could not be concluded to the Director's satisfaction, he approached the Acting District Commissioner and asked to have the apartment requisitioned. Other ethically troubling cases involved requisition orders issued in order to prevent eviction proceedings commenced by the apartment owner.[19] Among those who benefited from such confiscatory proceedings were several judges and even the Attorney General, who had to move from Haifa to Tel-Aviv and could not find suitable accommodation.[20]

In reviewing challenges to apartment confiscations, the Supreme Court generally declined to interfere, and upheld the temporary confiscations. The Justices held that they were not authorized to consider the unreasonableness of the expropriation order unless the authorities had acted in bad faith. But although the Court deferred to the authorities in all such cases, it criticized the phenomenon itself.

> The confiscation of an apartment is not [to be] carried out for the benefit of the public servant but for the purpose of establishing essential services of the state, and on no account must the impression be left that matters concerning confiscations are decided in so light a fashion, so that a civil servant has only to discover a flat and to approach the competent authority and he will immediately receive a confiscation order in his favor.[21]

Any attempt to explain the Supreme Court's decision, taken time and again, to allow such confiscations to proceed despite the evident mismanagement and dubious ethics of the practice, must take several factors into account. First, the harm associated with apartment confiscation was of temporary duration. This may have swayed the Court in favor of upholding the orders. Another important factor was the political culture of the country. Israel of the 1950s strongly inclined toward collectivism. (Eisenstadt 1967, 17-8; Horowitz and Lissak 1978, 131-3). Ben-Gurion spoke repeatedly of the need for a pioneering spirit in lifting the heavy load of absorbing immigrants and developing the country. In a speech he gave in 1951 entitled 'The Call of Spirit in Israel,' the Prime Minister said:

> The State cannot depend entirely on the apparatus of the government, on members of the cabinet and the Knesset in fulfilling its missions of constructing farm buildings, houses,

---

18　H.C. 10/48, *Zeev v. Acting District Commissioner of the Urban Area of Tel-Aviv (Yehoshua Gubernik)*, 1 P.D 85; translated in 1 Selected Judgments of the Supreme Court of Israel (1948-53) 68.

19　H.C. 11/48, *Mizel v. Acting District Commissioner under the Terms of the Defence Regulations*, 1 P.D. 133; H.C. 38/49, *Zanbar v. Acting District Commissioner of Haifa*, 2 P.D. 794.

20　H.C. 5/48, *Leon v. Acting District Commissioner of Tel-Aviv*, 1 P.D. 58; translated in 1 Selected Judgments of the Supreme Court of Israel 41 (1948-1953).

21　H.C. 29/49, *Sheinin v. Acting District Commissioner of Tel-Aviv*, 2 P.D. 654 (upholding confiscation order for the personal use of low-ranking officer in the visa department of the Ministry of Immigrant Absorption).

schools, factories, hospitals, laboratories, railways and roads. We shall need them, but with them alone we can not harness completed the pioneer energy latent in us ... I do not mean only the few gifted individuals with special talents and unusual attributes. Within each man and woman are hidden tremendous powers: it is only a question of knowing how to reach their source, and reveal and exploit them. (State of Israel 1951, 9-11)

The pioneering image served to legitimize the belt-tightening measures that the Government imposed for the sake of immigrant absorption. Between 1949 and 1951 the Government applied an austerity program in an attempt to ease the severe shortage in essential commodities. The austerity program included price controls and the rationing of food, clothing, shoes, building materials and foreign currency. The success of the program depended on the willingness of the public to stand in line for hours in order to obtain, in exchange for coupons, frozen codfish and dehydrated eggs. In 1949, the expectations for self-sacrifice were met and most Israelis complied with the strict rationing program. Shortly after, however, an extensive black market in food, goods and foreign currency developed, signifying that the public was tired of complying with collective demands (Barkai 1990, 37-41; Gross 1997; Naor 1987).[22] Another example of the political atmosphere of self-sacrifice was Ben-Gurion's proposal to employ immigrants in a quasi-military system 'without private profit' and in this way to pursue 'national works' without needless expenditure. Although the proposal was never put in practice, its very elaboration points to the types of demands imposed on Israelis in the 1950s (Horowitz and Lissak 1989, 108-9; Segev 1986, 152-4).

As far as housing is concerned, the belief in the spirit of collectivism and the genuine shortage in housing may have made it socially acceptable to require apartment owners to temporarily give up their property in order to provide accommodation for those in need. 'We have no alternative,' Golda Meir, the Labor Minister, declared in justification of the government's policy of housing several thousand immigrants in wooden huts, often crammed four to a room. 'There is no harm if a family of three or even four lives in one single room ... We intended to provide a roof. Not a ceiling—[just] a roof. No plaster—only whitewash. The immigrant himself will in time plaster the walls and add a ceiling ...'(Segev 1986, 133).

It is striking indeed that although two-thirds of the requisition orders aimed to provide temporary housing for immigrants, the war-disabled and discharged soldiers, property owners by and large did not challenge the legality of the orders. Property owners were willing to tolerate the temporary loss of income. However, when government bureaucrats began to abuse the process at their expense, they resisted, taking them to court (Eisenstadt 1954, 125-31). In one case, an elderly woman was ordered to vacate her apartment and move to another apartment she owned, located on a higher floor of the same building, so that a civil servant who claimed to suffer from poor health could occupy the more desirable apartment.[23]

Such confiscations raised the ire of property owners. And still the Court refused to interfere. It is possible that in addition to the influence of the dominant collectivist

---

22   The austerity regime was officially repealed in 1951 before the election to the second Knesset.

23   H.C. 31/48, *Yechimovitz v. Acting District Commissioner*, 2 P.D. 198.

ideology of the period, two other factors contributed to the espousal of a hands-off approach. One was the uncertain political status of the Court, and the other was the fact that the purpose of confiscation orders was to enable government officials to facilitate the absorption of immigrants (Holzman-Gazit 2002a). The early Court needed to fight for institutional independence and therefore sought to avoid clashes with the politically dominant executive branch. Had it invalidated confiscation orders issued on behalf of bureaucrats, the Court could have expected a political fight on its hands with the government. Furthermore, ultimately the confiscations were not purely a matter of the personal comfort of government staff. One must remember that confiscation orders issued on behalf of government officials, including those involving preferential treatment, were intended to facilitate the provision of 'essential public services' (as the language of the emergency legislation required). The primary mission of the first Israeli Government was the absorption of immigrants. A judicial decision declaring confiscation of an apartment for a bureaucrat and their family as inappropriate acted against this effort. It meant that the officer would not be able to provide their 'essential public service' and the fulfillment of the national mission of immigrant absorption would be hindered.

After 1952 there was a dramatic drop in the number of properties requisitioned for the purpose of providing temporary accommodation. The transfer of the political capital from Tel-Aviv to Jerusalem at the end of 1949, the accelerated pace of construction of permanent housing and the improvement in transportation services combined to ease the housing pressure in Tel Aviv somewhat, and the practice was essentially discontinued. Still, the mission of absorbing mass immigration was not completed. It now focused on providing the newcomers with permanent housing.

Expropriations for Economic Development and Permanent Housing

While temporary solutions provided shelter for the huge wave of immigration in the 1950s, construction of permanent housing was already under way. Yet despite considerable investment of public funds in new housing, at the end of 1951 about 250,000 immigrants—20 percent of Israel's population and 40 percent of all recent immigrants—were still living in temporary transit camps. The poor living conditions in the camps underscored the urgency of the housing problem. The structures gave little protection, if any, against winter rains, and the huts were blazing hot in summer. Overcrowding was severe; the resultant lack of privacy had an inevitably deleterious effect on family life. There was no electricity or running water, and the sanitation facilities amounted to little more than open sewage pits (Bernstein 1981, 29-30). Furthermore, although the transit camps were located adjacent to main population centers in order to enable the immigrants to enter the labor market, local authorities refused to include the camps within their municipal boundaries, so the level of public services for residents of the transit camps was below average and unemployment remained high (Hacohen 1994, 298).

Since the vast majority of the immigrants of the 1950s did not have the economic resources to strike out on their own—only 15 percent of the newcomers had such means—public agencies were able to direct the hundreds of thousands of people searching for homes to geographic locations of the government's choice. As mentioned, the intensive program of housing construction and regional development in the first decade of statehood was geared towards the goal of geographic dispersal of the Jewish population. The government constructed affordable housing in the outlying regions and on the fringes of existing urban centers and directed immigrants to these areas (Brutzkus 1964). Expropriation was used to further the goals of housing construction and regional development in two ways. One, which will be discussed in the next chapter, involved massive expropriation of Arab-owned land defined under law as 'absentee property.' Most of the 400 new Jewish cooperative settlements and kibbutzim and the 35 'new towns' established between 1948 and 1964 were built on Arab absentee land, located in the geographic periphery of the country in the Galilee and in the Negev. The second was expropriation of Jewish-owned land undertaken for so-called 'everyday' public purposes. Expropriations of Jewish-owned land were typically pursued under the general statutory authority of the AO of 1943, which is not intended for emergency situations. Nonetheless, in its review of expropriation orders issued under the Ordinance's terms, the Supreme Court of the 1950s employed legal terms similar to those it used in cases involving the use of emergency powers for security reasons (Holzman-Gazit 2002a).

A good example of the Court's security mode of reasoning is the 1955 ruling in *Salomon v. Attorney General.*[24] The issue at stake was an expropriation pursuant to the AO for the purpose of constructing a small port on the Kishon River near the city of Haifa. The proposed port was intended to speed up the export of various goods (particularly citrus fruit) and to provide the necessary infrastructure for the establishment of a chemicals industry in the city of Haifa. The petitioner, who owned several tracts of land in the area, did not challenge the public purpose determination. Instead, he argued that his land could not be considered 'necessary or expedient' for the implementation of the public project, given that, despite the Ministry of Finance's expropriation order, the planning authorities had yet to prepare a complete plan for the development of the port. In the absence of an approved plan, the petitioner claimed, it was not certain that the land designated for expropriation would be necessary for the realization of the project.

As indicated in Chapter 1, when land was expropriated before final planning approval had been received, there tended to be delays in the implementation of the public purpose for which the expropriation occurred. In addition, such expropriations often resulted in more land being taken than was ultimately required for the intended project. Despite the arguments of the petitioner in *Salomon* highlighting these concerns, the Supreme Court dismissed the petition. It held that there was 'no doubt from the language of Section 3 of the AO that the Minister's discretion is absolute,' and therefore the Court would not evaluate the merits of the Minister's decision.[25]

In support of its holding, the Supreme Court cited the 1942 English case of *Liversidge v. Anderson,*[26] one of the most frequently cited precedents in Israeli case law of the 1950s in matters relating to infringement of civil rights for security

---

24 Application 33/55, *Salomon v. Attorney General*, 7 P.D. 1023.

25 *Id.* at 1027.

26 *Liversidge v. Anderson* (1942) A.C. 206.

Land Expropriation in Israel

reasons (Bracha 1991; Shetreet 1988). In *Liversidge*, the House of Lords was asked to review a decision of the State Secretary to use his powers under Regulation 18B of the British Defence Regulations of 1939. This Regulation empowered the State Secretary to issue an order holding a person in detention 'if he has reasonable cause to believe that the person is affiliated with a hostile association.' Relying on the broad language of Regulation 18B, the House of Lords held that it had no authority to review the considerations underlying the detention decision. Lord Atkin, in a minority opinion, held that the Court had jurisdiction to investigate whether the State Secretary had reasonable cause to believe that the detainee was affiliated with an enemy organization. Given the security context of the English precedent, it is interesting that the Israeli Supreme Court referred to it in *Salomon*. After all, the expropriation in *Salomon* dealt with construction of a port intended to be used for the export of commercial goods and did not touch directly on security matters. But in Israel of the 1950s, 'immigration was undoubtedly a question of housing and employment' and thus economic development that created jobs and expanded the capacity of the country to absorb immigration was of strategic importance (State of Israel 1951, 32).

In a recent article, Rachel Kallus and Hubert Law Yone have provided a critical review of public housing policy for immigrants in the early years of Israel. The authors claim that the waves of immigrant in the 1950s were used by the state as raw material to fulfill the strategic goal of expanding the Jewish presence throughout the national territory. 'Housing units were built not in accordance with the needs of the inhabitants, but in according to national aspirations ... Hence, the State which had presented itself as responsible provider for housing for the masses used this housing to build itself, while pursuing national and territorial goals' (Kallus and Law Yone 2002, 771). Kallus and Law Yone point to the hegemonic practice of the state in its formative years in which immigration, housing and regional development policies were carried out. The Supreme Court, while reviewing challenges against land expropriation, acted within this hegemonic practice. The embedded codes of the enterprise of immigrant absorption tied it to what was seen as Israel's security concerns. And while scholars acknowledge that during periods of national emergency courts should not take it upon themselves to decide what government policy should be (Gavison 1990), the same principle could be said to apply to the deferential stance that Israel's Supreme Court adopted in the early land expropriation adjudication. In light of the strategic importance of immigration, the Supreme Court was unwilling to scrutinize the reasonableness of the considerations of those responsible for creating the infrastructure necessary for developing the country. In *Salomon*, the role of the port in creating employment, speeding the export of local products and allowing for the establishment of a chemical industry influenced the Court in its refusal to second-guess the executive decision to proceed with the expropriation, even ahead of an approved plan.[27] In the 1949 case of *Savorai v. Minister of Labor and Construction*,

---

27 The same principle was upheld by the Court in H.C. 76/52, *Keren Zvi v. Minister of Finance*, 6 P.D. 1107. *Keren Zvi* involved an expropriation of land that was earmarked for the expansion of a hospital. The Court expressed its opinion that the mass immigration of 1949 justified immediate action to facilitate medical treatment for the immigrants.

on which I will further comment in Chapter 6 below, the Supreme Court expressed its opinion that road construction is required 'for public use and for security of the state.' This was one of the considerations taken into account by the Supreme Court in reaching the conclusion that the expropriation should be upheld despite the failure of the authority to issue an expropriation order before taking possession of the land and beginning the construction work.[28]

The emphasis on the strategic importance of immigration and economic development lasted for many decades. In the 1981 case of *Notzer*, the possibility of creating jobs for immigrant doctors apparently swayed the Court sufficiently for it to permit the construction of a health center despite the harm the project would cause to the neighborhood. 'Considerations regarding promotion of immigration are at the core of planning laws,' Justice Landau wrote for the Court. 'These are considerations of prime national priority that planners should take into account.' However, starting in the 1970s, immigrants were not the only beneficiaries of Israel's housing policy. New exigencies appeared in the housing market reflecting the existence of socioeconomic gaps among various strata of long-time Israelis.

Provision of Improved Housing for Immigrants and Long-Time Residents

By the early 1970s, the gap between the number of households and number of available housing units brought about by the mass influx of immigrants in the 1950 had been closed. Yet the high volume and rate of construction continued as Israeli society had to contend with new housing shortages. Shortly after the Six-Day War (June 5, 1967 to June 10, 1967), a third wave of some 250,000 immigrants arrived in Israel. About 37 percent of the newcomers came from Soviet Union, 20 percent from Western Europe, 12 percent from North America and the rest from Asian and North African countries (Friedlander and Goldscheider 1979, 100-14). The immigrants of the 1970s preferred residential locations offering proximity to economic, social and cultural opportunities in the city centers of Tel-Aviv, Haifa and Jerusalem. The Westerners among the newcomers also expected better housing conditions than those provided to the immigrants of the 1950s.[29]

Seeking to meet the expectations of the new immigrants from Western countries, the government in effect privatized the housing market, gradually withdrawing from its involvement in construction, reducing construction subsidies and switching to the provision of financial assistance to home-buyers. The change in the mechanism of public support enabled a wider role for private construction companies which began building large apartments in Tel-Aviv and in new suburban towns in the Central District.[30] The housing units that were built in the 1970s offered the Israeli population

---

28 H.C. 85/49, *Savorai v. Minister of Labor and Construction*, 2 P.D. 887, 889.

29 The architecture of the publicly constructed housing in the 1950s was 'architecture for the poor.' Public housing projects were standardized and the typical building was a small concrete block of two floors with tiny apartments of 40 square meters.

30 Figures show that over the period between 1948 and 1999, private construction dominated the market for large apartments and it located its activity in the urban network. Over the years, some 65 percent of all housing units constructed by private companies were

improved conditions not only in terms of geographic location but also in terms of the quality of the housing and of the standard of living. The size of the avergage apartment in public housing nearly doubled: from 40 square meters in the 1950s to 75 square meters in the 1970s. Apartment density decreased from 2.2 persons per room to 1.6, and the average number of rooms per apartment increased from two to three (Haber 1975, 46-8).

The relatively high quality of the housing offered to the immigrants of the 1970s and the high social and economic status of long-time citizens of European origin accentuated the low social standing of those citizens of North-African origin who had immigrated to Israel in the 1950s. Housing prices in desirable urban locations increased sharply in the early 1970s, making it impossible for those who did not own an apartment to acquire one. [31] The sense of deprivation among low-income citizens erupted in the early 1970s into social protest. Two groups of citizens made demands for improvement in housing. The first was a group of young people of North-African origin, second-generation immigrants, who called themselves the 'Black Panthers,' in conscious imitation of the American black social and political protest movement of that name. Drawn predominantly from the metropolitan slum areas, the Black Panthers demanded 'better housing conditions, slum clearance, more jobs, better education and an end to all ethnic discrimination.' Comparing themselves to new immigrants, the Black Panthers hung posters in the streets of Jerusalem that read 'New Immigrants Get Housing—We Get Nothing' (Cohen 1972). The other protest group was the 'Young Couples' movement. The main claim of this group, whose membership was also comprised largely of Israeli-born children of North African immigrants, was that housing had become unaffordable and that they lacked the financial means to become homeowners. Their repeatedly voiced demand was to have access to the same mortgage subsidies received by new immigrants (Etzioni-Halevy 1977).

The Government at first ignored the anger and frustration. Prime Minister Golda Meir stated publicly that if a choice had to be made between social equality and immigration, the latter came first. Attitudes, however, soon changed. Acknowledging the connection between ethnic protest, social turmoil and the threat to the established political order, and seeking to prevent downward mobility of long-time citizens, the Government widened its eligibility criteria for public housing assistance. It initiated a subsidy program aimed at young married couples of low socioeconomic

---

in Tel-Aviv and the Central District; 20-25 percent were in Jerusalem and Haifa districts; only 10 to 15 percent were in the periphery—the Galilee and the Negev. By contrast, 40 percent of public housing units were constructed in the peripheral districts in the north and south of Israel—areas that were reached by only a small minority of private projects (Carmon 2002, 184).

31   During the 1970s, housing prices in urban localities of high demand outstripped the Consumer Product Index in all but seven quarters of the decade. The opposite was true for public housing in outlying areas, which fell in relative terms throughout the decade, outpacing the CPI only in a single six-month period (Gabriel 1986, 231). Hence, families from the earlier wave of immigration who lived outside those areas, mostly Israelis of North-African origins, lost out in relative terms. They were forced to remain in the outlying regions of the country or on the fringes of existing cities which had gradually become slum areas.

status (Lithwick 1980; Ministry of Housing 1974). The Government also launched an extensive project of neighborhood rehabilitation directed at improving housing conditions, physical infrastructure and local social services in distressed neighborhoods throughout the country.[32]

Elimination of the slums and the provision of housing to the poor represented only one of the three national goals underlying the housing policy of the 1970s and early 1980s. A second goal was to create physical diversification of the housing projects as a means for enhancing social diversification of residents. By the 1970s, the Government was already aware of the negative results of the homogeneity in the public housing projects of the 1950s. The response was a change in the housing strategy of allocating designated areas to specific eligible groups such as young families. From the 1970s, the projects initiated by the Ministry of Housing attempted to engineer social integration by combining economically strong households with weaker ones (Carmi 1977; Wallfson 1976). The third national goal that shaped Israel's housing policy in the 1970s related to the geographical results of the Six-Day War. After the War, housing construction played a central role in establishing Jewish control, authority and domination in politically sensitive Jerusalem.

The new social codes embedded in the housing policy of the 1970s shed light on the Court's land expropriation record of the period. As recalled, the Court of the 1970s showed growing willingness to review government actions closely in order to protect civil rights. Yet in the case law of land expropriation, it tended to defer to the government and failed to render substantive protection to landowners. For example, in the 1974 case of *Spolansky*, the Court declined to intervene in an expropriation whose public purpose designation was originally intended for the construction of a new neighborhood for immigrants, but eventually part of the land was designated for the building of luxury housing.[33] Similarly in *Banin*, the Court dismissed the claims of the petitioners whose land in the Talpiyot neighborhood of Jerusalem was expropriated for the purpose of establishing a military base and afterwards the public use designation was changed for development of a residential project for low-income families.[34] Situating the outcomes of *Spolansky* and *Banin* in the context of the goals underlying the housing policy in the 1970s, the Court's rulings stand as a reflection and reinforcement of the strategic social and political significance granted to housing. Both cases concerned land located in Jerusalem and in both cases the purpose of the expropriation corresponded to the goals of enhancing social diversification and assistance for low-income groups.

In the discussion below, I would like to suggest that the same values that turned immigration and housing into national goals of the first order affected more than the Court's hands-off approach in reviewing the Minister's definition of public purpose. Another doctrine that was fashioned in light of these values was the judicial treatment of the no-compensation rule.

---

32   In the 1970s, renewal projects encompassed 70 neighborhoods. Ninety percent of them were public housing projects for houses built in the first 25 years of the State. About 70 to 90 percent of the population who lived in renewal project neighborhoods in the 1970s were of Asian and North-African origin. At that time, Oriental Jews constituted approximately 45 percent of the Jewish population in Israel (Alterman and Churchman 1991; Carmon 1988).

33   H.C. 147/74, *Spolansky v. Minister of Finance*, 29(1) P.D. 421, 429.

34   H.C. 282/71, *Banin v. Minister of Finance*, 25(2) P.D. 466.

Housing Subsidies and the No-Compensation Rule

As previously discussed in Chapter 2, the Court's ruling in the 1979 *Feitzer* case stands as a symbol for the disfavored status of landowners when it came to the right for full compensation.[35] In *Feitzer*, the Court held that the compensation paid to the owner of expropriated land could be reduced by up to 40 percent, regardless of the fact that the owner's land was expropriated in its entirety (and therefore the owner could not be said to benefit to the extent of their remaining property from the public use to which their expropriated land was put). Writing for the Court, Justice Landau offered a tax rationale for the decision. He explained that the no-compensation rule should not be interpreted as depending on the betterment of the owner's remaining property. Rather, the no-compensation rule should be viewed as a kind of general property tax. It could be collected from landowners without regard to betterment.

It is easy to criticize the expansion of the no-compensation rule in *Feitzer* and the tax rationale that the Court enunciated in support of its ruling. Nonetheless, normative arguments aside, the burden imposed on landowners as a result of the no-compensation rule is not totally out of line with the social mores manifested in Israel's housing policy. The social consensus on the role of housing as an instrument for attaining national goals led all Israeli governments to intervene in the housing market and to formulate subsidy programs (Borukhov 1980). During the 1950s and 1960s, public assistance took the form of public housing. In that period, the overwhelming majority of housing starts were constructed either directly by the Ministry of Housing or indirectly through quasi-public agencies such as the Histadrut (the national Trade Union Organization) and the Jewish Agency. The expenditure on housing imposed a considerable economic burden on the state. Public housing was already subsidized by direct subsidies granted to the price of the apartment itself or of the land on which was built. To this expenditure the government added from the mid-1960s home-buyer assistance of subsidized short- and long-term mortgages as well. Home buyers had to pay 10-20 percent of the total investment as a down payment, and the rest came from loans provided by the public sector (Roter and Shamai 1990). In 1964 and 1965, for instance, public housing starts averaged around 60 percent of the total new units, and expenditure on housing amounted to 17 percent of the Government's annual budget (Brutzkus 1964, 58).

Housing subsidy programs for immigrants also existed in the 1970s.[36] Their existence reflected the survival of the national importance of immigration. For old-timers, subsidy programs took a different form. The Government structured a progressive need-based mortgage subsidy system. Furthermore, the subsidized mortgage system also contained a geographic component. Buyers of homes in outlying regions of the country or in areas designated by the government as 'national priority zones' could receive mortgages on more advantageous terms and usually

---

35 C.A. 377/79, *Feitzer v. Ramat Gan Local Planning and Building Commission*, 35(3) P.D. 645.

36 In 1973, for example, state-subsidized mortgages bore an average interest rate of 7.62 percent against 15.6 percent, for privately financed mortgages (Haber 1975, 54).

also received a loan which was converted to a grant once the family had remained in the location for a certain number of years (Gabriel 1986; Lithwick 1980).

Israel's housing subsidy programs were sharply criticized by economists who blamed such policies for soaring house prices and for the heavy burden they placed on public finances (Lerman 1976; Lipow 1996). Yet, in the same manner that Israelis do not protest against tax increases to pay for national security, they by and large accepted the burden imposed on them as a result of Israel's housing subsidy programs.[37] The strategic significance attributed to land use programs produced a social consensus that regarded the imposition of a significant financial burden on the public for the purpose of providing adequate housing as legitimate and fair. In the context of the societal consensus on the need for redistribution of resources for housing, the no-compensation role which required landowners to dedicate land for community services did not appear out of line. Yet a serious question remains regarding the extent of the burden imposed on landowners. Why should landowners pay more than other citizens when, after all, like everyone else they already pay taxes that finance the housing subsidy programs?

A possible answer can be found by looking at the social values enshrined in Israel's property tax regime. Property tax applies to all segments of Israeli society. But for years, the Israeli legislature created a punitive system of property tax directed at owners of residential land who chose to leave it vacant. The expectation was that the punitive tax would cause landowners to build on their land, or that, at the very least, it would attenuate land speculation. The Israeli property tax regime, which lasted until 2000, fostered a societal perception that landowners were a special minority holding a valuable and limited resource which should be used for the public good, rather than for private benefit. Turning back to the legal reasoning in *Feitzer*, the tax rational carried problematic consequences for the application of the no-compensation rule in terms of inequality among landowners and the waiver of a requirement for any sort of nexus and proportionality between the burden imposed on the landowner and their share in the need for additional public facilities. Yet the tax rationale used by Justice Landau in *Feitzer* perfectly captures the Israeli values that legitimize punishment of landowners if they do not use their land for purposes valued by society. As opposed to owners of other types of property, landowners are required to make their property available for the general good either by building on the unused land or by dedicating portions of it for public facilities without receiving monetary compensation.

The prominent place of the absorption of immigration and the provision of housing assistance explains the Supreme Court's unwillingness to set barriers to the powers of expropriation and to narrow the statutory no-compensation provisions. Yet another important factor that affected, if somewhat ironically, the legal doctrine of expropriation to the extent that it was aimed at Jewish landowners was the Israeli-Arab land struggle. In the next two chapters I will focus on this component of the sociopolitical environment.

---

37 For example, in March 1990, in order to finance the expenditure on absorption of the immigrants from former Soviet Union, the Government raised the value-added tax by one percentage point to 16 percent and then in January 1991, the VAT was raised to 18 percent.

Chapter 5

Expropriation of Arab Land in the 1950s: Policy and Process

The previous chapters discussed two important phenomena in the sociopolitical environment within which Israel's Supreme Court reviewed challenges to land expropriation. One was the long-term impact of the ideology and culture of nation-building which held sway in Zionist society prior to independence, with its intellectual rejection of private property as the paradigm for Israel's tenure system. The other was the significance that was accorded in Israeli society to Jewish immigration, not only as the raison d'être of the Zionist enterprise generally, but, more urgently perhaps, as a strategy of state- and society-building. At various points in the discussion I have referred to the connection between, on the one hand, these two phenomena and, on the other, the nature of Israel as a society that contains within itself a fundamental division between two communities, Jews and Arabs. Israel's tenure system of public land ownership and its policy of encouraging Jewish immigration reinforced (and therefore to a certain degree also advanced) a worldview in which Israeli Arabs were seen as posing a demographic (and therefore ultimately political) threat to the existence of Israel as a Jewish state. In keeping with the Zionist ideology and experience, the strategy employed to counter this perceived danger was to encourage the demographic growth of the Jewish population and to disperse it geographically throughout the country, with particular emphasis on the regions in which Jewish presence was sparse compared to that of Arabs.

This chapter focuses on the ways in which the Jewish-Arab struggle for control of the land played out domestically in Israel's legal practices of land expropriation in the 1950s. Few issues have had a more immediate impact on the tensions between Arabs and Jews within Israel than the Israeli policy of expropriating Arab land. During the British Mandate, Jews and Arabs in Palestine had equal political and legal status, which to a certain extent held in check their mutually incompatible aspirations for control over the territory. After the establishment of Israel, however, the struggle for control of the land in the new Jewish state became a dispute between the rulers and the ruled. In the wake of the 1948 War, Israeli authorities expropriated large tracts of Arab land, and initiated widespread Jewish settlement programs aimed at controlling the growth and the spread of the Arab minority by securing a dominant Jewish presence in, and ownership of, all parts of the national territory. For this purpose, a special legal framework was created that institutionalized the transfer of land from private or collective Arab ownership to collective Jewish ownership, that is, to the state.

Territorial Control and National Security

The focus of national security policy tends to be external threats. Frequently, however, national security has a domestic dimension as well: the need to contain a perceived enemy within the national borders. This is the case in a plural society such as Israel, which employs an 'ethnic democracy' model to negotiate Jewish-Arab inter-communal relations (Smooha 1997).[1] Israel is a state created by and for Jews. Driven by ethnic nationalism, it identifies with the core national group, rather than with its citizens as such. The state acts, with varying degrees of consistency and success, to promote the language and culture of the Jewish majority, to increase its numbers and to strengthen its economic and political interests. And while the Arab minority in Israel enjoys citizenship and voting rights, it was for a long time (and in certain important respects still remains) excluded from the nation's power structure, and its members subjected to a policy of control and surveillance by the state (see, for example, Al-Haj 1996; Jiryis 1976; Kretzmer 1990; Lustick 1980; Rabinowitz, 1997; Rouhana and Ghanem, 1998; Saban 2004; Shafir and Peled 2002). This characterization of Israel as an ethnic democracy is a function not only of the definition of the state's collective identity, but also of the continuing Jewish-Arab conflict. Arabs in Israel maintain close ties with Arabs in neighboring countries, and especially with the Palestinians in the Occupied Territories. The protracted and often violent conflict between Israel and its neighbors has caused Jewish society in Israel to be highly suspicious of Arab Israelis and to question their loyalty to the state. In the domestic dimension of security, Arabs are suspected of potentially constituting a fifth column, and of actively supporting the hostile Arab states and Palestinian extremism.

The issue of security acquired early on the status of a cultural master-symbol in the Israeli system of societal beliefs (Arian 1995; Kimmerling 2001, 208-21; Saban 2002; Yaniv 1993). Not surprisingly, in the dimension of Israel's domestic policy it has covered primarily issues that are perceived critical for maintaining the dominance and supremacy of the Jewish majority (Al-Haj 2004; Barzilai 1998; Bar-Joseph 2000). In this regard, control of the land is a main area in which the Jewish-Arab demographic ratio and the theme of security have featured on the public agenda and have served as a reference in shaping governmental policies. From the establishment of the State of Israel, successive governments have acted on the basis of the strategic assessment that any area of the country that was exclusively populated by Arabs posed a threat to Israel's security and ultimately to its sovereignty. The preferred method of handling this perceived security threat has been to transfer Arab land to Jewish hands and to encourage Jews to settle in predominantly Arab regions. Change in the demographic balance between Jews and Arabs on the Jewish periphery was perceived as a way of both symbolically advertising the state's sovereignty and enhancing its effective control over its territory (Yiftachel 1998; Yiftachel 1997; Newman 1989; Kimmerling 1983; Jiryis 1976, 76-136).

---

1   In a model of ethnic democracy, the state is not a neutral arbiter standing above the fray, but rather identifies (and is identified by its citizens) as standing alongside one of the two (or more) rival communities.

Inevitably, these perceptions have affected the country's land regime. The tenure system of public ownership, for example, drew its legitimacy from the nature of inter-communal relations. The phenomenon of national ownership of undeveloped areas has enabled the Jewish State to control the extent and timing of land allocation to the two national communities. Similarly, as discussed in Chapter 3 above, the division of public landholdings between the state and the JNF also stemmed from the context of Israel's security policies toward the Arab minority. The JNF, formally a non-governmental institution, could (and still can) set limits on the use of land by Israeli Arabs which the state itself could not.[2] Another example is Israel's system of land use planning. Concerns over the strategic implications of excessive geographical concentration of the Jewish population in the coastal plain resulted in the establishment in 1965 of a hierarchical structure under which the Government and the National Board of Planning have the power (at least in theory) to oversee planning decisions at the regional and local levels (Alterman 2001; Evans 2006; Torgovnik 1990).

In the discussion below, I will focus on the link between security and territorial control in the historical context of Israel's legal practices of expropriation of Arab land in the wake of 1948. The transfer of the land of Arab refugees to Jewish ownership in the aftermath of the War of Independence laid the groundwork for the formation of Israel's current tenure system.

Israeli Policies toward Abandoned Arab Property

Until independence, the Zionist movement could acquire land in Palestine only through market transactions. Political independence and sovereignty over a national territory led to a dramatic change in the Zionist strategy for land acquisition. At the end of the War of Independence, which lasted from December 1947 until June 1949, the new State of Israel controlled an area of approximately 20.6 million dunams (roughly 77 percent of the territory of Mandatory Palestine); and the number of Palestinian inhabitants in the territory under Israeli control decreased from over 750,000 to roughly 160,000, compared to a Jewish population of 600,000 (Morris 1987, 297-98). The question of whether Jewish authorities actively expelled Palestinians or whether the Palestinians left of their own accord or under the orders of their leadership is a hotly debated issue which is not ultimately pertinent to the present discussion (Morris 2004; Shlaim 1999). What is clear is that shortly after the creation of the state, the Israeli government adopted a policy barring the return of the Palestinian refugees. Consequently, those Palestinians who fled to the West Bank, to the Gaza Strip, to Transjordan (as it was then known), to Syria or to Lebanon became permanently separated from their now-abandoned properties (Erzt 1997, 31-7). Land transactions between Jews and Arabs were for the first time relegated to a minor role, as state expropriation of land assumed center stage, rapidly developing into an official and institutionalized practice.

---

2   The status of the JNF and its long-standing policy of discriminating against Arab citizens have recently been called into doubt as a result of a series of legal challenges. These issues have not yet been fully resolved. See H.C. 9205/04, *Adalah v. Israel Lands Administration* (case pending). See also below in Chapter 9.

In the early stages of the war, Israeli policies towards abandoned Arab property reflected uncertainty about the future disposition of the refugee problem (Golan 1995; Golan 2001; Morris 2004). The transfer of Arab property to state hands and the appointment of a Custodian of Abandoned Areas were initially articulated as temporary measures to prevent the looting of abandoned movable property, and to end the process of *de facto* land expropriation carried out by Jewish agricultural communities. However, with the invasion of Israel by regular Arab armies and the accelerated rate of Arab flight in mid-1948, a political decision was taken to take advantage of the opportunity that had arisen and to prevent the return of the refugees. The decision was not presented openly for fear that an official expulsion policy would jeopardize the relations of the newly established state with those, such as the United Nations (UN), the United States and the Soviet Union, on whose good will it depended. Instead, the state initiated a complex mechanism of expropriation which provided a legal fig-leaf for the confiscation of absentee property, for the establishment of Jewish settlements on formerly Arab-owned land and, finally, for the permanent alienation of such land in favor of the Jewish State (Forman and Kedar 2004).

There is no agreed-upon estimate of the extent of the post-1948 expropriations. A 1951 study by the UN Conciliation Commission for Palestine mentions a figure of 16.3 million dunams, comprising both communal and privately owned land. In contrast, the 1964 UN Conciliation Commission for Palestine estimated that just over 7 million dunams of land were expropriated (Fischbach 2002).[3] The substantial discrepancy between these two figures is due largely to disagreements over legal classification of Arab land in the Negev desert.[4] More recently, Arab researchers and organizations have estimated the extent of expropriations at between 5.7 and 6.6. million dunams (1.2 and 1.4 million acres), while Israeli officials and researchers have provided estimates ranging from 4.2 to 6.5 million dunams (1 to 1.3 million acres) (Golan 2001; Granott 1956, 86-90; Kark 1995; Peretz 1958). Even the number of abandoned Arab villages is uncertain, because 'village' and 'abandoned' have not been defined consistently by various researchers.[5] Regardless of the accuracy of these conflicting assessments, it is beyond doubt that Arabs as a group lost large tracts of rural and urban land: farmland, houses, factories and shops. According to one estimate, of the 370 new Jewish agricultural settlements (moshavim and kibbutzim) founded in the

---

3   One reason for the difficulties in determining the scope of the property is that British Mandatory authorities never completed a thorough cadastral account of the land in Palestine. By the time that British rule came to an end in 1948, the process of creating a comprehensive land registry was completed for only about 20 percent of Palestine's total land area (Forman 2002; Sandberg 2000).

4   The Negev was not subject to the normal rural tax procedures found in the rest of Palestine that served as evidence for land rights. Compounding this difficulty of inadequate sources of documentation is the disagreement between Israelis and Arabs as to what types of property constitute abandoned Palestinian property. The Negev contained many semi-nomadic Bedouin tribes prior to 1948 (Fischbach 2003).

5   Jiryis (1976) identifies 374 abandoned communities that were destroyed by Israelis. Morris (1987) puts the figure at 369 abandoned localities. *See* also Flapan (1987, 83); Kimmerling (1983, 123).

first five years following independence, a full 350 were established on abandoned Arab land (Fischbach 2003, 72-3). As to abandoned homes, these were used to settle Jewish immigrants who arrived in Israel after 1948. By April 1949, leaders of the ruling Mapai party noted that a total of 75,000 new immigrants were living in the Arab quarters of the mixed towns of Haifa, Safed, Jaffa and Jerusalem, 16,000 in the formerly Arab towns of Ramla, Lydda and Acre and 18,000 in abandoned Arab villages (Stock 1988, 86). By 1954, approximately one-third of Israel's entire Jewish population was settled on former refugee property, including 250,000 new immigrants housed in formerly Arab-owned houses in urban areas (Fischbach 2003, 73; Zinger 1973, 57).

What was notable about this process of transferring a very large percentage of the national territory from Arab to Jewish hands was the effort and energy expended by the authorities to construct a legal regime that would legitimize the expropriation. As Prof. George Bisharat and others have observed, while justice and fairness were not present in the process of de-Arabization of the land, resort to law as a means for executing the negation of Arab ownership rights was a prime concern (Forman and Kedar 2004; see also Bisharat 1994).[6]

The Legal Basis for Expropriation

The 1948 war resulted in the Jewish state controlling a territory of approximately 20.6 million dunams. However, this military and political victory did not for the most part imply legal ownership of—as opposed to sovereignty over—the land, the exception being state-owned lands which came into the hands of the State of Israel as the political successor to the Mandatory government. By the end of the war, Jewish individuals and organizations, including the JNF, owned approximately 8.5 percent of the total area of the State of Israel. With the addition of state-owned land, land under Jewish ownership still accounted for only about 13.5 percent (2.8 million dunams) of Israeli territory (Kark 1995, 477-80).[7] In other words, the State of Israel was faced from its inception with the serious problem that the overwhelming majority of the national territory was legally owned by persons who could reasonably be regarded as hostile to the State and to the interests of the majority of its citizens.

The legal regime established in the early 1950s provided a basis for closing this gap between sovereignty and ownership of the land. Two legal routes were used. The first involved the systematic application of Ottoman and Mandate laws of settlement

---

6   The 'Judaization' of the land was accomplished not only by massive transfer of land to Jewish ownership. Additional components of the project involved physical destruction of most of the now-deserted Arab villages, towns and neighborhoods, geographic restrictions on Arab settlement and development, transforming Arab names into Hebrew ones, parallel development of Jewish urban and industrial centers, and the redrawing of municipal boundaries in ways that ensured all-encompassing Jewish control (Benvenisti 2000; Falah 1996).

7   While Jewish ownership reflected only a very small part of all the land of the State of Israel, it accounted for more than 30 percent of the total of 7.5 million dunams of cultivable land north of the Negev desert. The largest owner of agricultural land was the JNF (Granott 1956, 255-6; Weitz 1950, 21-42).

of title (Kedar 2001; Sandberg 2000).[8] The second, which is the focus of the present discussion, involved creating legal powers and administrative frameworks for expropriating and transferring Arab property to public Jewish ownership.

The confiscation of Arab land began in a haphazard, illegal manner during the early spring of 1948. In the confusion of war and the preoccupation of the provisional government with the military situation, some Jews began on their own initiative to move into abandoned Arab houses (Jiryis 1972, 83; Segev 1986, 68-72). In response, the Hagana (the Jewish community's pre-state military organization) set up ad hoc mechanisms to prevent the looting of Arab property. In March 1948, military committees were created to take formal (yet still not legally authorized) control of Arab abandoned land and to coordinate its use (Fischbach 2003, 14-19; Forman and Kedar 2004, 813).

The Abandoned Property Ordinance of June 21, 1948 was the first law enacted to provide a legal basis for the seizure of Arab land.[9] The purpose of the Ordinance was to stop the illegal seizures of Arab property described above and to restore a measure of state control over the situation. The Minister of Agriculture, Aharon Tsizling, who was responsible for the leasing of the abandoned Arab property, described the legislation's purpose as a way to:

> ...regularize the legal situation in the abandoned areas. So far there is no single central authority and no legal system by virtue of which action can be taken in regards to Arab property in the towns and in the dozens of villages which have been abandoned by the majority of their inhabitants. I permit myself to say that there is a degree of chaos in this field which can only do harm and prejudice to the general interests of the state and the interests of the Arab inhabitants, which must not be prejudiced.[10]

The Abandoned Property Ordinance provided for a Custodian of Abandoned Areas to take possession of the refugee land. On July 15, 1948 the Minister of Finance appointed the first Custodian. The Custodian's office was responsible both to the Ministry of Finance and to semiannual review by a subcommittee of the legislature. The Custodian's early policy was to lease refugee land to Jewish farmers for short periods, generally lasting one year. Profits from the annual leases were turned over to the Ministry of Finance. Two aspects of the Ordinance merit particular notice. First,

---

8   Settlement of title, also referred to as land settlement, is a legal process carried out by government authorities to create a comprehensive land registry and to strengthen ownership rights. The process involves defining an area with no comprehensive registry of indefeasible title, surveying and mapping it, dividing it into parcels and deciding who owns each one. In the late 1950s and 1960s, Israel took over millions of dunams in this manner mainly in the Negev and in the Galilee. Much of this land—precise figures are hard to come by—had been unregistered and indeed was probably state land to begin with, dating as such from the Ottoman period. However, some of this land was transferred to state ownership as a result of legally defining Bedouin lands in the Negev and Arab lands in the Galilee as *mewat* (dead land), and as a result of the crucial changes that the Israeli legislature made to the law of adverse possession.

9   1 L.S.I. 25 (1948).

10   Minutes of People's Council and Provisional Council of State (June 24, 1948) p. 25 in Fischbach (2003, 19).

the Ordinance granted far-reaching discretion to the authorities. Second, it was made retroactively valid as of May 16, 1948, two days after Israel declared independence. As will be shown below, these two measures subsequently became fixtures of the various items of legislation enacted by the Knesset to legalize the transfer of Arab land.

In October 1948 the government promulgated new regulations for expropriation, the Emergency Regulations (Cultivation of Waste Lands and Unexploited Water Sources) (hereinafter the Waste Lands Regulations).[11] Drafted by the Ministry of Agriculture, these regulations allowed the Minister to classify as 'waste land' any land with respect to which he was 'not satisfied that the owner of the land has begun or is about to begin to cultivate the land.' The effect of declaring land as 'waste land' was that it was immediately transferred into state hands. The decisions made by the Minister could not be challenged in court. The Regulations did provide for an Appeals Committee whose decisions were final, but the Committee served only to rubber-stamp the Minister's decisions (Nakkara 1985). Like the Abandoned Property Ordinance, the Waste Lands Regulations had retroactive effect, legitimizing earlier seizures of abandoned Arab property. The explanatory note to the law stated that:

> War conditions have resulted in land being abandoned by its owners and cultivators and left untilled, fields neglected and water resources unexploited. On the other hand, the interests of the State demand that, without prejudice to the right of ownership of land or other property, agricultural production should be maintained and expanded as much as possible and the deterioration of cultivated areas and farm installations prevented. For the attainment of these objectives it is necessary that the Minister of Agriculture should have certain emergency powers, which are conferred to him by these Regulations. (Fischbach 2003, 20)

The authorities typically applied the Waste Lands Regulations in conjunction with Section 125 of the DERs of 1945. This section was one of the most important tools of the local military authorities that were set up after independence in regions of the country that were predominantly Arab (Hofnung 1996, 89-95; Lustick 1980, 123-9).[12] Section 125 allowed local military commanders to close areas for security reasons. Closure prevented Arab cultivators from reaching their land, which as a result would eventually be declared 'waste land' and transferred to Jewish possession (Lustick 1980, 178; Nakkara 1985; Oded 1964).

Strictly speaking, the Waste Lands Regulations did not authorize the confiscation of uncultivated land, merely permitting its temporary use for a period of up to two years and eleven months. Any profits from the land were to be held in trust for the owners.[13] But the temporary transfer of rights legalized by the Waste Lands

---

11 *Official Gazette* No. 27, 3 (1948) (Hebrew). Extended in 2 L.S.I. 70 (1949).

12 In 1949, the areas under military rule contained over 90 percent of Israel's Arab population; in 1958, fully 85 percent of all Israeli Arabs still lived in areas under military rule. The regime of military government was abolished in 1966.

13 When the validity of the law was extended, the length of time that the Minister of Agriculture could keep uncultivated lands under his control was increased from two years and eleven months to five years. By the time this new law had been passed, in January 1949,

Regulations and the Abandoned Property Ordinance did not correspond to the actual activities of long-term cultivation and development that were carried out on abandoned land by Jewish individuals and groups. The first step in closing this gap was the promulgation of the Emergency Regulations (Absentees' Property) (hereinafter the Absentees' Property Regulations) in December 1948.[14]

Absentee Property Legislation

The Absentees' Property Regulations shifted the emphasis in the legal definition of what constituted abandoned land from the land to its owners. Henceforth, land was deemed abandoned if its owners were declared absentees whose property could be seized by the state. An absentee was anyone who, on or after 29 November 1947 (the date of the UN General Assembly resolution to partition Palestine), was either a citizen or subject of one of the Arab countries at war with Israel, physically present in any of these countries or in any part of Palestine outside Israeli territory, or, finally, a citizen of Mandatory Palestine who had abandoned their normal place of residence.[15]

The definition of 'absentee' made no legal distinctions between Arabs and Jews. In reality, of course, the law was never intended to apply to Jews who had abandoned their homes in the course of the War of Independence and who subsequently returned to Israel. The Absentees' Property Regulations contained mechanisms designed to exempt Jews from the status of 'absentees'. For example, Section 28 provided for the issuing of a confirmation of 'non-absentee' status to persons who otherwise came under the definition of absentees but 'who had left their place of residence out of fear of Israel's enemies … or who were capable of managing their property efficiently and will not in doing so be aiding Israel's enemies' (Kedar 2002, 424-5).[16] Needless to say, this provision was not applied to Arabs. Furthermore, the definition of absentee encompassed virtually all Arabs who fled their homes during the war, regardless of whether or not they had left Israeli territory. The result was that over 75,000 Arab residents of Mandatory Palestine who fled their homes during the war but who remained in Israel and subsequently became Israeli citizens, were nevertheless classified as absentees, in the process falling into the absurd legal-bureaucratic category of 'present absentees' (Cohen 2000; Kretzmer 1990, 57; Lustick 1980, 173-4). In addition to these internal refugees, Arab residents of areas that lay beyond the prospective borders of Israel before the war but that were subsequently annexed

---

some 500,000 dunams of 'waste land' were already under cultivation by Jews (Jiryis 1972, 97; Peretz 1958, 141-64).

14 *Official Gazette* No. 37, Supp. II, 59 (1948) (Hebrew).

15 The definition of 'absentee' applied not only to individuals, but also to any company or other legal entity, half or more of whose owners had been declared absentees. The definition also covered *waqf* property under the administration of absentees.

16 Additional conditions for release of absentee property are prescribed in sections 29 and 30 of the Absentees' Property Regulations.

to Israel pursuant to the armistice agreements, also fell into the legal category of absentees, in this case without having to leave their homes.[17]

The Absentees' Property Regulations provided for the appointment of a Custodian of Absentee Property who took over from the former Custodian of Abandoned Areas. The new Custodian was granted far-reaching powers.[18] They could expropriate any property at their personal discretion, the sole condition being that they certified in writing that either the property or its owners met the definition of 'absentee'. Written certification of such status automatically transferred the property into the possession of the office of the Custodian. The burden of proof then shifted to the presumed absentee to show that they (or it) were not in fact an absentee under the law. But the Regulations made it extremely difficult for anyone to challenge the facts stated in such a certificate. Typically, the Custodian was shielded from even having to reveal the factual basis for their classification of a person as an absentee.[19]

After the certificate was issued, the Custodian had full control over the land, except that he was not allowed to sell it or to lease it for a period exceeding five years. The Regulations thus reflected the initial uncertainty of the new Israeli authorities regarding the long-term future of abandoned property. However, the Government was forced to confront the issue once the UN General Assembly voted in favor of Resolution 194 in December 1948, calling for the speedy return of 'refugees wishing to ... live in peace with their neighbors.' Both the Government and military officials were unanimous in their assessment that the return of Arab refugees and the establishment of all-Arab regions in the country threatened the security and the sovereignty of Israel. Military officials urged the government to resolve the issue immediately, and to shift from leasing refugee land to settling it permanently, so as to prevent 'a serious danger that these villagers will re-establish themselves in their villages deep behind our lines ... There is no time to be lost in taking a decision.' The Foreign Ministry echoed these concerns. '[The] infiltration of individual Arabs, ostensibly for reaping and threshing, alone, could in time bring with it the re-establishment [of the refugees] in the villages, something which could seriously endanger many of our achievements during the six months of the war' (Morris 1993, 116).

Against these concerns, and given the inconsistency between the legal status of absentee land and its de facto expropriation, Israeli authorities decided in early 1949 to move from a regime of temporary land seizures to a regime of title transfer and permanent alienation of refugees' land. The piece of legislation that made possible

---

17   The most notorious case was that of the residents of an area know as the 'Triangle', a 30-kilometer strip bordering the West Bank. The 1949 Rhodes Armistice Agreement between Jordan and Israel determined that the area would be turned over to Israel. The residents of the Triangle thus acquired Israeli citizenship. Nevertheless, they were considered absentees with regard to their property inside pre-1949 Israel, since at the time the Absentees' Property Regulations were published in December 1948 they were Jordanian residents (Cohen 2000; Hofnung 1996, 105-6).

18   The Custodian was entitled to appoint inspectors of absentees' property and to delegate to the inspectors any of their powers.

19   Section 32 of the Absentees' Property Regulations and Section 30 of the Absentees' Property Law.

the implementation of this new strategy was the Absentees' Property Law, which was enacted in March 1950.[20]

The Absentees' Property Law was an expanded version of the Emergency Regulations. The law defined absentee in terms similar to those used in the earlier Regulations, and again placed absentees' property in the hands of the Custodian, who was now authorized to lease the land under their control for up to six years at a time. Significantly however, the Custodian was also empowered to sell the land to a 'development authority'. Such a body was in fact established pursuant to a separate law, the Development Authority (Transfer of Property) Law, which was also passed in 1950.[21] This was the only exception to the rule that the Custodian could not sell land under their control. The Development Authority was in essence a 'land laundering' agency whose *raison d'être* was to distance the Government from direct involvement in the unilateral action of expropriating absentee land. The law empowered the Development Authority to 'buy, rent, take or lease in exchange or otherwise acquire property' from the Custodian, and 'sell or otherwise dispose of, grant leases of, and mortgage property' to the State, to the JNF or to local authorities. Together, the Absentees' Property and Development Authority Laws allowed for the sale of absentee property permanently while establishing a bureaucratic mechanism that concealed, if barely, the involvement of the Israeli Government (Fischbach 2003, 53-8).

In advocating the move to a regime of permanent expropriation of Arab land, Zalman Lifshitz, the Prime Minister's Advisor on Land and Border Demarcation, emphasized both financial and legal considerations. In a 1949 report submitted to the Prime Minister and to the Foreign, Justice and Finance Ministers, he wrote that 'investments that have already been made and that will be made in the future must be safeguarded. Legally unauthorized actions that have already been taken must be given legal force, in order to prevent complications and legal claims against the government or against possessors of the absentees' property' (Forman and Kedar 2004, 816). Lifshitz adduced relevant precedents, noting that other countries in similar situations, such as Turkey, Greece, Bulgaria and Czechoslovakia, had assumed vast powers in order to liquidate refugee property for the benefit of the state. Later, presenting the Absentees' Property Law to the Knesset in 1949, the Finance Minister, Eliezer Kaplan, told the Knesset that the drafters of the law had in mind the British legislation passed during the Second World War that had created a Custodian for Enemy Property. The Trading with the Enemy Act of 1939 allowed this Custodian to sequester land in Palestine which belonged to citizens of Germany and of nations and territories that were either allied with, or occupied by, Germany. The

---

20   4 L.S.I. 68 (1950). Another purpose of the law was to tighten the Custodian's control over refugee land and prevent any attempts by the refugees to liquidate their property in exile. The law required all persons in possession of absentee property to notify the Custodian, and forbade anyone from acquiring absentee property. The law also specifically outlawed the sale by refugees of their land to someone remaining in Israel and then arranging for the money to be sent outside the country. Likewise, it sought to stop refugees from giving their land to relatives who had remained behind (Fischbach 2003, 25).

21   4 L.S.I. 151 (1950).

Absentees' Property Law also drew on the recent example of the statute enacted by Pakistan two years earlier to deal with the issue of land permanently abandoned by Hindu refugees fleeing to India. Pakistan had established a Rehabilitation Authority to which the Custodian of Evacuee Property transferred the appropriated refugee land. The Rehabilitation Authority was allowed to reallocate the land in order to resettle Muslim refugees from India (Fischbach 2003, 22).

The Absentees' Property Law was greeted with dismay and hostility by a variety of circles. Within Israel, liberals decried the law for confiscating the land of Arabs who until quite recently had been fellow citizens of Palestine, not enemy aliens.[22] Internationally, the United States also opposed the new law because it prejudiced the rights of refugees. All this, however, had little impact on the application of the Absentees' Property Law. All abandoned land outside urban areas was eventually transferred by the Custodian to the Development Authority, which in turn transferred it to the JNF or leased it to cooperative agricultural settlements.[23] The Development Authority also acquired from the Custodian the majority of the absentees' improved land in urban areas. By the end of the 1950s, only 30 to 40 percent of the urban properties remained on the Custodian's books, consisting mainly of old buildings of lesser economic value (Cattan 1969, 82).[24]

The Land Acquisition Law of 1953

In addition to the million of dunams of absentee property, a considerable amount of land was seized during and after the War of Independence without any legal basis at all, or on the problematic legal basis of laws permitting temporary seizure of land. This situation was resolved by the Land Acquisition (Validation of Acts and Compensation) Law of 1953 (hereinafter the Land Acquisition Law), the final piece of legislation in the machinery through which Israel institutionalized its legal possession of formerly Arab-owned lands.[25]

In late 1950, dispossessed Arab landowners who were not absentees began submitting claims through the courts for the return of their land. The authorities were frequently unwilling to release the property, which in many cases was already in use

---

22   Knesset member, Klebanoff, of the General Zionists urged his fellow legislators to consider the impact of legislation that essentially relegated the refugees to the status of enemy whose land can be seized: 'we are not dealing with enemy property, but with property of substantial part of the population of our country, who must have very important rights ...' D.K. (1949) 911-12 in Fischbach (2003), 23.

23   The Absentees' Property Law empowered the Custodian to sell the land at a price that was not less than its official value, that is, its declared valuation for tax purposes. Such prices therefore bore no relation to its real market value. According to Arab researchers, the official value formula produced a value which was sometimes less than 5 percent and never more than 10 percent of the real value of the property (Hadawi 1963, 62-6).

24   To the extent that these properties were not sold to the Development Authority at a later date, they are still being managed by the Custodian in accordance with the provisions of the Absentees' Property Law, which is still in effect today.

25   7 L.S.I. 43 (1953).

by others. Officials initially discussed the status of such seized property along with present absentees' property. Despite the legal basis for defining Arabs as present absentees, the dispossession of Arab citizens was perceived politically problematic and requiring a solution. Hence a special committee began releasing some urban property, but no rural land was released, as this would have harmed both Jewish agricultural communities and the military (Forman and Kedar 2004, 819).

In August 1951, Foreign Minister Sharett appointed a subcommittee composed of senior land and Arab affairs officials to resolve the outstanding issues of illegal dispossessions and rural land owned by present absentees. The subcommittee made several recommendations, only one of which was accepted: to enact retroactive legalization that would legitimize all past seizures of land, regardless of whether or not the former owners were absentees. This proposal was the basis of what became the Land Acquisition Law. The introductory note to the law explained that because of 'needs of security and essential development, the land in question could not be returned to its owners.' The aim of the law was 'to establish a legal basis for the acquisition of this land and to provide its owners with the right to compensation.' Implementation was to be supervised by the Minister of Finance, as in the case of all prior legislation regarding expropriation of Arab land.

The law was retroactive, facilitating the expropriation of all land that met the following three conditions: (1) had been used for essential development, settlement, or security purposes until April 1952, (2) was still needed for these purposes, and (3) was not in its owner's possession on 1 April 1952. By issuing a certificate stating that these conditions had been met, the Minister of Finance could automatically transfer title to the land to the Development Authority. Moreover, there was no legal requirement to notify the affected property owner of the expropriation of their land. Notably, the law contained a sunset provision: the powers granted to the Finance Minister were to lapse automatically one year after the law came into effect, that is, in March 1954.

In the year between March 1953 and March 1954, the Land Acquisition Law was used extensively. The Minister of Finance issued 465 certificates expropriating some 1.2 million dunams.[26] Israeli Arabs waged an unrelenting political struggle against the law and congresses, conferences and protest meetings were held throughout the country. Despite all this, the authorities still refused to return the land.

The law provided two alternative methods of compensation: cash payments and the granting of alternative lands. However, few of the Arab citizens affected by the Land Acquisition Law claimed rights under the compensation scheme. Compensation was regarded within the Arab community as a legal and moral recognition of the expropriation. In addition, the monetary compensation that was offered was derisory.[27] By 1959, compensation had been awarded with respect to only 64,500

---

26   The estimate of 1.2 million dunams includes state-owned lands and Bedouin lands in the Negev (Cohen 2000, 84-9). If these are subtracted from the total, the number stands at 325,000 dunams of private land (mostly belonging to Arabs) that were expropriated by virtue of the Land Acquisition Law (Kislev 1976, 27; Israel Lands Administration 2003, 137).

27   Compensation was offered on the basis of the assessed value of the expropriated property in Israeli pounds as of 1 January 1950, plus an additional 3 percent per year thereafter.

dunams of expropriated land, 170,000 dunams of land by 1970—approximately half of the total area expropriated under the Land Acquisition Law (Forman and Kedar 2004, 822; Kimmerling, 1983, 138). Compensation in the form of land amounted to 55,629 dunams (Israel Lands Administration 2003, 138).[28]

The enactment of the Land Acquisition Law marked the end of legislative efforts to provide a legal basis for the seizure and reallocation of expropriated Arab land. After the enactment of this law in 1953, no new legislation was passed. This is not to say, of course, that after 1953 Israel ceased expropriating Arab land. As will be discussed in the next chapter, in addition to utilizing the expropriation laws enacted in the 1950s, the authorities also fell back on what was in effect the default takings law of the country—the Mandatory 1943 AO.

This is the place to emphasize that it was not only the legislature and the executive that institutionalized and legalized the appropriation and transfer of ownership of Arab land in the wake of independence. The judicial system played an important role, as well. There is a similarity between the way Israel attempted to base Arab land expropriation on legal foundations and the way other ethnocratic states acted to legitimate their construction of domestic power relationships (Kedar 2002; Russell 1998; Shamir 1996; Singer 1991). The creation of an array of statutory tools facilitated the transfer of Arab lands to Jewish control, and at the same time concealed under the guise of neutrality the discrimination and oppression embedded in the policy of dispossession. In setting up this land regime, the legislature was acting at the behest of the executive branch, as is typically the case in parliamentary democracies. And in its implementation of such laws, the executive branch was generally supported by the Supreme Court, which issued decisions interpreting the expropriation laws and reviewing their implementation.

Patterns of Adjudication of Arab Dispossession Cases

Relative to the extent of land that was expropriated, the number of cases brought before the Supreme Court under the new laws of the 1950s was extremely small. There were two reasons for this. First, most of those who were legally categorized as 'absentees' were in fact refugees who were physically outside of the country, living in countries that were at war with Israel. As a practical matter, therefore, they were unable to petition the High Court, file a law suit or appear in person before an Israeli judge. The cases

---

In 1950, the value of Israeli pound was equal to that of the British pound sterling. Three years later, at the time of the enactment of the Land Acquisition Law, inflation had decreased its value relative to the British pound by 80 percent. In 1973, the Land Acquisition Law was amended to provide more realistic rates of compensation. Further changes to the formula of monetary compensation were introduced in 1979 and 1989 (Bisharat 1994, 519-21; Kislev 1976, 24).

28   The law imposed severe restrictions on compensation through grants of alternate land. Compensation in land was accorded only when the owners themselves, as opposed to their sons or other close family members, had worked the land and supported the family primarily from agriculture (Oded 1964, 18). Moreover, in cases where alternate land was offered, it often belonged to other Arab absentees, sometimes even members of the same family, which made accepting the new land impossible for social reasons.

that reached the Supreme Court thus related primarily to persons who came under the definition of 'present absentees'. Second, many of the dispossessed refused to apply to the Israeli judicial system for reasons similar to those that stopped them from applying for compensation from the state (Kedar 2002, 427).

In adjudicating Arab expropriation cases, the Supreme Court had limited authority. Since Israel adopted the British model of parliamentary democracy, the Court lacked the power of judicial review over statutes. Consequently, the Court could not invalidate the absentee legislation, even if had wanted to (which was far from being the case). However, like certain common law courts, the Israeli Supreme Court enjoyed broad powers of interpretation and classification that potentially gave it substantial leeway. Accordingly, litigants approaching the Court tended not to contest the absentee legislation directly and as a matter of principle, but attempted instead to persuade the Court to review the decisions of the Custodian with a critical eye.

A limited number of Arab petitioners succeeded in persuading the Supreme Court that the Custodian had incorrectly classified them as absentees—the first step toward regaining their land. For example, in one 1950 case, the Custodian failed to issue the appropriate written certificate required under the legislation. The Court agreed with the petitioner, a Christian Arab, that the Custodian had, for this technical reason, failed to make a *prima facie* case that the petitioner was an absentee. In the same breath, however, the Court reminded the Custodian that they enjoyed wide evidentiary powers. In other words, provided the Custodian issued the written certification stating that the owner of the property came under the legal definition of 'absentee', they could expropriate practically any property they deemed fit. The Justices stressed in their opinion that their decision in favor of the petitioner did not prevent the Custodian from issuing such a certificate at a later date.[29] In a separate subsequent case, the Court even allowed the Custodian to issue a certificate while the judicial proceedings were still pending. Once the certificate was issued, the burden of proof automatically shifted to the petitioner to show that he was not legally an absentee. In this case, the petitioner failed to meet the burden of proof and the Court dismissed his petition.[30] In another case, however, the Court decided that the Arab landowner had met the burden of proof, successfully refuting the presumption created by the issuance of the certificate.[31]

Another line of cases before the Supreme Court involved petitioners who asked to be reclassified as non-absentees. These were people who admitted that they had left their places of residence and who therefore formally met the requirements of the 'absentee' definition. However, they argued, they were entitled to receive a non-absentee certificate, as they had left their homes not 'because of military operations, nor for fear of them or for fear of Israel's enemies.' In a number of cases, the Court in fact compelled the Custodian to grant the desired exemption. It is noteworthy that the few individuals who reached the Supreme Court requesting to be exempted from the status of absentee were not the typical expropriated Arab landowners. They

29 H.C. 91/50, *Yoseph v. Inspector of Absentee Property*, 5(1) P.D. 154.
30 H.C. 137/50, *El Marti v. Custodian of Absentee Property*, 5(1) P.D. 645.
31 A.C. 216/58, *Custodian of Absentee Property v. Habib Hana*, 13(1) P.D. 740.

tended to be either Christian Arabs,[32] or persons who could prove a special link to Israel, such as one petitioner who had left Palestine on a spying mission for the State of Israel, but who was classified as an absentee upon his return.[33]

The Supreme Court intervened in the Custodian's actions in a number of individual cases in the years immediately following the War of Independence. But these cases were the exception and not the rule. By 1958, of the tens of thousands of cases of Israeli Arabs classified as present absentees, only 209 persons were issued with certificates releasing their property back to them, and not even all of these changes of heart by the Custodian can be chalked up to the efforts of the Supreme Court (Jiryis 1976, 88; Peretz 1958, 155).[34] Evidently, except when pressed to intervene, the Court preferred to remain above the fray.

The Court's general non-interventionist stance was also evident in its review of the application of the Land Acquisition Law. In the leading case, *Younis v. Minister of Finance*, the Court broadly interpreted the consequences of issuing a certificate under Section 2 of the law.[35] Younis was a resident of an Arab village that was declared as a closed military area. A portion of his land lay outside the closed area, but he could not cultivate it, since without a permit he was unable to leave his village. Soon after the enactment of the Land Acquisition Law, the Finance Minister issued a 'Section 2 Certificate,' which stated that Younis' land was not in his possession, as a result of which it was formally transferred to the Development Authority. Younis appealed to the High Court, claiming that he was entitled to present his version to the Minister before the certificate was issued, and that, furthermore, the certificate was factually incorrect. Younis argued that as long as nobody else had taken possession of his land (which was the case), he remained its sole possessor. The Court, however, held that under the law, issuance of the certificate by the Minister of Finance constituted irrefutable evidence that the conditions of the statute had been fulfilled. By adopting this interpretation, the Court deferred to the authorities and went far beyond the written words of the statute. It increased the evidentiary power granted in the statute, by transforming the certificate into an irrefutable presumption. The law, the Court concluded, should be interpreted as denying the right to a hearing, and as 'precluding any practical possibility to appeal the facts mentioned in the certificate.'

Dr. Kedar has suggested that in adjudicating Arab dispossession cases, the Supreme Court acted in concert with the state in order to minimize Arab landholdings, and

---

32 H.C. 43/49, *Ashkar v. Inspector of Absentee Property*, 2 P.D. 926; H.C. 3/50, *Kauer v. Custodian of Absentee Property*, 4 P.D. 654. As a group, Christian Arabs enjoyed a marginally less hostile treatment than Moslems.

33 H.C. 99/52, *Palmoni v. Custodian of Absentee Property*, 7(2) P.D. 83.

34 Under an amendment to the Absentees' Property Law from 1965, some of the *waqf* land which had passed to the Custodian was released to the Moslem community in towns in which 'trust committees' were appointed by the government. Absentees Property (Amendment No. 3) (Release and Use of Trustee Property) Law, 1965 (Kretzmer 1990, 167-8). Section 29 of the Law states that these committees are to be appointed by the government, with no express obligation to consult with the Moslem community itself. Therefore, the potential for self-government rights related to the *waqf* has been eroded (Dumper 1994, 30-35, 44-51, 125-7).

35 H.C. 5/54, *Younis v. Minister of Finance*, 8(1) P.D. 314.

that as a result of its claim to be an independent institution, it contributed through its rulings to the legitimization of the new land regime by which Israel gained ownership and control of Arab-owned land (Kedar 2002). I tend to agree. Like supreme courts in other societies with ethnocratic agendas, Israel's Supreme Court played a central role in the institutionalization and legitimization of the power relationship between Jews and Arabs. The judicial construction and application of rules of evidence, such as burdens of proof, and procedural rules, such as the denial of a right to a hearing, facilitated the transfer of land from Arabs to Jews and simultaneously legitimated the new land regime by imaging it as technical, neutral and devoid of political biases.

But there were also structural grounds for the Court's weakness in its relations with the executive branch. Even if the Court had wanted to strike out morally on its own, which was not the case, it would have been very difficult—if not impossible— to enforce any decision requiring the authorities to return illegally seized Arab land to its owners. The Justices knew this from experience. The few decisions that were favorable to Arab landowners were ignored by both the civil and military authorities. The most notorious case in this regard was that of the Christian Arab villages of Iqrit and Bir'im.

Iqrit and Bir'im were located on Israel's northern border with Lebanon. The two villages surrendered to Israeli forces during the 1948 War without putting up any resistance, and their inhabitants did not flee. About a week after the surrender, the 600 Catholic inhabitants of Iqrit were instructed by the military commander of the Galilee to leave their homes on the understanding that they would be allowed to return as soon as the border was secured. The 800 Maronite Christian residents of Bir'im were also evacuated, and the same promise was made to them. These promises were not kept. When the fighting subsided, the military government declared the villages closed military zones, pursuant to the existing Emergency Regulations.[36] In July 1951, the villagers appealed to the High Court of Justice, which upheld their right to return to their homes, a decision based on the grounds that, first, the villagers were permanent residents (in other words, they were not absentees) and, second, the evacuation order was technically invalid, as it had not been published in the *Official Gazette*.[37] However, the Court's decision was never implemented. In an attempt to stop the villagers from returning, the military commanders corrected the defect in the original evacuation order by issuing new evacuation orders in September 1951. The villagers again petitioned the High Court, but before the Court had the opportunity to hear the case, the Israeli air force blew up all the residential buildings in Iqrit and Bir'im. At the second hearing, the Court dismissed the petition on the ground that the eviction order was legally valid since it was published as required.[38] The Court's second decision could not but have been affected by the army's chosen path of action. The destruction of the villages while a petition was pending—a blatant act of

---

36 3 L.S.I 56 (1949). The Emergency Regulations (Security Zones) empowered the Minister of Defense to declare a 'security zone' within 10 kilometers of Israel's border in the northern half of the country and within 25 kilometers of the borders of the southern half. Entry into or exit from the area was thereafter impossible without permit.

37 H.C. 64/51, *Daud v. Minister of Security*, 5(2) P.D. 1117.

38 H.C. 239/51, *Daud v. Appeal Committee for Security Zones, Galilee*, 6(1) P.D. 229.

disrespect for the authority of the Supreme Court, to say the least—left the Justices with little option as a practical matter but to dismiss the petition. The Justices realized that the issue of Arab land expropriation had the potential to bring about a major confrontation with the Government. Any attempt by the Court to force the military and civilian authorities to act within the law would at best be ignored. The land of the two Arab villages was transferred to the state, and was subsequently divided among a number of kibbutzim and moshavim in the areas, including Bar'am, Sasa, Shomra and Dolev (Kimmerling 1977).[39]

In the first years following independence, therefore, the Justices were clearly aware that they and their office enjoyed only limited autonomy—that is, the Supreme Court was autonomous only to the extent that it did not attempt to impinge on the interests of the hegemonic powers (Barzilai 2004; Stone 1985). Its freedom of action was circumscribed not only by the objective political realities—its unclear status, a consequence of the absence of a written constitution, the lack of tenure for Justices in the early years, the overwhelming power of the dominant political party in the country, which controlled not only the unicameral parliament but the executive branch, and whose influence extended to other key sectors of society, such as the military—but also by the Justices' subjective assessment of the limits of their ability to act independently within the political system, and their need to husband their limited political resources and to choose their battles wisely.

The more interesting question, to my mind, is whether and to what extent the Court's decisions in Arab land expropriation cases affected the judicial view of property rights in general as they were reflected in cases of expropriation of Jewish-owned land. The patterns of adjudication in the first decade of statehood provide support for the assumption that judicial standards employed in early Arab dispossession cases shaped the Court's overall approach to property rights. This issue is discussed in the next chapter.

---

39   Iqrit and Bir'im were not the only villages that were treated in this way in the early 1950s. The military also ignored a Court decision in the case of Khirbat Jalama, a hamlet situated in the eastern Sharon region and inhabited, until their eviction, by the members of two extended families, Nadaf and Daqqa. The expulsion of the families was unquestionably illegal, and upon their petition, the High Court of Justice granted an *order nisi*. The situation was complicated by the fact that Kibbutz Lehavot Haviva had already taken over the land. The government did not respond to the *order nisi*, and instead, while the appeal was still pending, caused the Land Acquisition Law to be enacted, retroactively granting legitimacy to both the expulsion and the expropriation. H.C. 36/52, *Al-Nadaf v. Minister of Security*, 6(1) P.D. 750; H.C. 14/55, *Al-Nadaf v. Minister of Finance*, 11(1) P.D. 785. See also (Benvenisti 2000, 157-161).

Chapter 6

Expropriation of Arab Land as the Basis for a General Legal Practice

The overwhelming majority of land expropriated by the Israeli authorities in the 1950s was Arab-owned, and expropriations of Jewish-owned land were of limited scope by comparison. Obviously, one of the major effects of expropriations, and clearly the most immediate one, was the direct economic and emotional impact of expropriation on the affected individuals and families. The policy of expropriation of land from Israeli Arabs also severely affected their identity and status as a community within Israeli society.

In this chapter, I wish to discuss another effect of the land expropriations in the 1950s, one that in the legal context is often overlooked, namely, the way in which the legal practice of land expropriation from Arabs in the 1950s became the legal norm of land expropriation in general, not only from Arabs and but from Jews as well, and not only in the 1950s but for many decades to come.

Israel used the legal powers of expropriation to prevent the return of the Arab refugees after 1948 and to maintain the subordinate status of those Arabs who chose to stay in Israel as a minority. None of these considerations was relevant to Jewish landowners. Although the legal machinery enacted in the 1950s to address the territorial and demographic consequences of the War of Independence was carefully drafted to avoid any explicit reference to Arabs, significant *de facto* discrimination characterized its enforcement. The Absentees' Property Law, for example, was almost never employed to confiscate land owned by Jews. Selective enforcement also characterized the application of the Waste Lands Regulations and the 1953 Land Acquisition Law (Kretzmer 1990). There is, therefore, an element of irony in the fact that ultimately the Supreme Court treated Arabs and Jews in similar fashion when it came to expropriating their land. The first section of the chapter points at the similarities that exist between the legal principles that governed the practice of expropriation from Arabs and Jews. The second section offers explanations for the emergence of a unified regime of expropriation.

Similarities between the Regimes of Expropriation

As may be recalled, alongside the statutory machinery that Israel established for expropriation of Arab-owned land in the 1950s, Israeli law incorporated the AO as part of its Mandatory legacy. The AO served as the general takings law of the country, applied not only to Arab-owned land but to Jewish-owned land as well. Nonetheless, as shown below, the main principles that the Supreme Court developed in the 1950s for the application of the AO resembled the features of the special legislation that was enacted to enable the taking of Arab-owned land. This similarity suggests that, in addition to Mandatory precedents that prepared the ground for the interpretation of the AO, the legal practice of expropriation from Arabs played an important role in shaping the interpretation of this law.

First, there was the free rein that the Minister of Finance enjoyed, an all-but-unfettered authority in matters pertaining to the choice of the land to be expropriated and the identification of the public purpose for which such land would be used. The AO is silent about whether the Minister's determination of public use is subject to review. However, the Court ruled early on that the wording of Section 2 of the AO tied its hands as far as its ability to review the merits of the definition of 'public use.' Section 2, it will be remembered, was amended by the Mandatory government in 1946 by deleting the requirement that the public use should be of a 'public nature.' Focusing on the wording of this change to the law, the Court concluded that the AO granted the Minister of Finance considerable freedom to decide what satisfied the public use requirement. Publication of the notice of expropriation in the *Official Gazette* was deemed to be proof of the lawfulness of the public use. The burden was then on the landowner to prove otherwise. Even when the Minister simply indicated that the land was required for 'public use' without providing any details, the Court accepted such statement as sufficient for all legal purposes. The Court also ruled that the existence of an actual plan for implementing the public purpose was not a prerequisite for expropriation.[1]

Furthermore, there was no automatic right to a hearing under the AO. The Supreme Court held that the Minister of Finance was not obliged to give the affected party an opportunity to contest the expropriation prior to making his final decision. This was obviously a very serious matter, as decisions on expropriations were occasionally based on erroneous information—whether the mistakes were innocently introduced or otherwise. And given the speed at which expropriations tended to be executed and new, irreversible facts established on the ground, the absence of a right to a hearing had grave practical consequences.

It is important to note that these principles of interpretation were not supported by Mandatory case law. The Mandatory precedents concerning expropriations in the period close to the establishment of the State of Israel dealt by and large with expropriations pursuant to the Defence (Emergency) Regulations (DERs), 1945.[2] At the same time, the doctrines that the Supreme Court evolved for applying the AO mirrored the norms embedded in the legislation passed in the early 1950s to legalize expropriations from Arabs. As will be recalled, the absentee property legislation had also granted far-reaching powers to the Custodian to expropriate land, essentially

---

1   See the discussion in Chapters 1 and 2 above and the cases: H.C. 240/51, *Cohen v. Minister of Finance*, 6(1) P.D. 363; H.C. 124/55, *Dwiak v. Ministry of Finance*, 10(1) P.D. 753; H.C. 76/52, *Keren Zvi v. Minister of Finance*, 6 P.D. 1107; Application 33/55, *Salomon v. Attorney General*, 7 P.D. 1023.

2   See for example, H.C. 24/46, *Sakai v. District Commissioner* (1946) 13 P.L.R. 216. Interestingly, Israel's Supreme Court did not look at these precedents for guidance while interpreting the AO.

at his discretion. A certificate issued by the Custodian stating that the person came under the status of 'absentee' shifted the burden of proof to the owner to convince the Custodian they were not in fact an absentee as defined by law. Likewise, the 1953 Land Acquisition Law gave wide discretionary powers of expropriation to the state, as well giving it as the advantage of highly favorable evidentiary presumptions. A declaration by the Minister of Finance that the original seizure of the land was required for security reasons and that such reasons were still in effect was sufficient to transfer ownership of the land to the Development Authority, which in turn was authorized to sell the land to the state, to the JNF, or to local authorities.[3] As explained in the previous chapter, the absentee legislation made it extremely difficult for anyone to challenge the facts stipulated in the certificate. The Custodian was not required to grant the landowner a hearing in which he could refute the evidence purporting to support his classification as absentee. Nor was the Custodian required to reveal the factual basis on which his decision rested. With regard to the Land Acquisition Law, the law did not impose an obligation on the state to notify the property owner on the issuance of 'Section 2 certificate' and Supreme Court treated the expropriation order as conclusive as regards the factual basis of the expropriation.[4]

The similarity between the two regimes of expropriation is evident in another troubling principle which was sanctioned in the case law of the 1950s: the right accorded to the Minister of Finance retroactively to correct technical illegalities in the expropriation process. In *Savorai*, for example, the Supreme Court allowed the expropriation to proceed even though the expropriating authority had failed to issue the requisite expropriation order.[5] In *Feldman*, the Court ignored the authority's failure to post a notice in the manner required by law, although in this case the Court may have been swayed by the fact that the petitioner admitted that despite the absence of formal notification he had actual knowledge of the state's intention to expropriate his land.[6] In *Biala* and *Dwiak*, the Court dismissed a petition to set aside an expropriation order that was issued without first obtaining funding for compensation, as required by law.[7] All these cases involved application of the general law of expropriation to Jewish-owned land.[8] As may be recalled from the discussion in Chapter 2, in the early years of the Supreme Court's existence, the Justices tended to insist on strict adherence to legal formalities, and even though they were generally loathe to intervene on behalf of individual petitioners against state interests, they were nonetheless willing to do so when technical, formal requirements set by law were not complied with by the state. The Supreme Court's tolerance of irregularities

---

3   The Waste Lands Regulations also granted far-reaching powers to the Minister of Agriculture to take possession of any land that, as determined by him alone, was uncultivated. A certificate declaring the land as fallow shifted the burden to the affected owner to refute it.

4   H.C. 5/54, *Younis v. Minister of Finance*, 8(1) P.D. 314.

5   H.C. 85/49, *Savorai v. Minister of Labor and Construction*, 2 P.D. 887.

6   H.C. 136/50, *Feldman v. Minister of Finance*, 5(1) P.D. 432.

7   H.C. 120/52, *Biala v. Jerusalem Municipality*, 7 P.D. 91; H.C. 124/55, *Dwiak v. Ministry of Finance*, 10(1) P.D. 753.

8   In *Dwiak*, the expropriation was issued under the terms of the AO, while in *Savorai*, the legislation involved was the Roads and Railways (Defence and Development) Ordinance 1943.

in the expropriation process from the mid-1950s onward was thus a new departure. Furthermore, when viewed from the wider perspective of the development of the legal philosophy of the Court over the decades, it stands in clear opposition to the Court's general trend of systematically expanding its protection of individual rights.

This newly found tolerance of irregularities was likely influenced by the newly legislated authorization to correct illegalities when Arab land was involved. All the land expropriation laws and regulations that were passed in the 1950s contained provisions permitting the state to retroactively legalize extra-legal seizures of Arab land.[9] The Court's failure to treat technical illegalities as fatal to expropriations under the AO are thus another example of how the legal practice pursuant to which land was expropriated from Arabs became the general legal norm.

There was also the issue of compensation for expropriated owners. The Supreme Court held that prior agreement on the amount of compensation was not a prerequisite for expropriating land. In *Salomon*, the Court interpreted the AO as allowing the transfer of property to the state regardless of the existence of an agreement to compensate.[10] Agreement in the matter of compensation, the Court held, was a separate issue from any claims regarding the legality of the expropriation itself, and it could not be raised as an argument against the validity of the expropriation.[11] This holding, while not at odds, strictly speaking, with the AO (which provided for situations where the state is allowed to make less than full payment for the land), appears to have been influenced by the fact that the principle of less than full compensation was already standard practice in the overwhelming majority of expropriations of Arab land. Both the absentee legislation and the Land Acquisition Law permitted the transfer of the property to the state, whether or not compensation to the interested parties had been paid.

Finally, another legal doctrine under the AO that was established in the context of the expropriation of land from Arabs was the denial of a right to a hearing. This principle was established in the 1954 case of *Younis*.[12] Few commentators, however, have referred to the fact that *Younis* did not involve expropriation under the terms of the AO but rather under the 1953 Land Acquisition Law. As may be recalled, the Land Acquisition Law was the legislation that provided the basis for permanent alienation of Arab-owned land. The law authorized the Minister of Finance to issue a certificate for each tract of land in question, confirming that it was used at some point after 29 November 1947 'for security or essential development purposes,' that it was 'still needed for one of these purposes' and that it was not currently in the landowner's possession. The petitioner in *Younis* claimed that he was entitled to present his version to the Minister of Finance before the certificate was issued, and that, furthermore, the certificate was factually incorrect. Technically, his claim to the

---

9   See Chapter 5 above.

10   Application 33/55, *Salomon v. Attorney General*, 7 P.D. 1023; see also H.C. 120/52, *Biala v. Jerusalem Municipality*, 7 P.D. 91

11   Section 9A of the Acquisition for Public Purposes (Amendment of Provisions) Law 1964 provides that the expropriating authority will pay the amount of compensation that is uncontroversial within 90 days after taking possession of the land.

12   H.C. 5/54, *Younis v. Minister of Finance*, 8(1) P.D. 314.

right to a hearing rested on the argument that issuance of a Section 2 certificate was a quasi-judicial act, and therefore one that could not be carried out without granting the affected individual a prior hearing.[13] The Court, however, decided that the Minister's certificate should be regarded not as a quasi-judicial act but as written testimony, and that issuance of a certificate constituted 'conclusive evidence' that the conditions laid down in the statute had been fulfilled. The Court consequently found no basis for granting a hearing as a matter of right under the terms of Land Acquisition Law. In reaching this conclusion, the Court revisited the AO, and ruled that it too did not require the Minister to grant a hearing. *Younis'* harming principle of interpretation that originated in the particular context of expropriation from an Arab survived as a general norm attached to the AO. In subsequent cases, it weakened the ability of Arabs and Jews alike to defend themselves against expropriations.

So far, I have noted certain similarities between the body of case law that the Supreme Court developed in the context of the AO and the principles that had been formalized in the special laws that enabled expropriation from Arabs. Another important factor that suggests that the special laws may have influenced the general application law is that the AO in fact was occasionally applied in the Arab sector as well. Indeed, some of the principles of interpretation relating to the AO originated in cases involving Arab-owned land. For example, one of the early cases that stands for the principle that the Minister of Finance has complete autonomy in defining public purpose is *Dor*, discussed above in Chapter 2. The petitioners in *Dor* were Arabs whose land was expropriated in order to provide housing for immigrants. The facts of the case revealed that the authorities employed the AO to confiscate the land after an attempt to use the absentee legislation for this purpose failed. Initially, the state believed that the petitioners' land came under the legal definition of 'absentee property'. But after the land was seized and when construction was already under way, it turned out that the petitioners were not 'absentees'. At that point, the state resorted to the AO in order to retroactively provide a legal basis for the expropriation. For reasons that will be elaborated below, the Court's interpretation of the AO in *Dor* did not remain confined to the Arab sector but was subsequently applied to the Jewish sector as well.

On other occasions, the authorities resorted directly to the AO because of their concerns regarding Arab organized protests against the biased enforcement of the absentee legislation. This was the case in the mid-1950s and in the 1960s with expropriation of Arab-owned land in the Galilee.[14] A leading case in this regard

---

13   Under English law doctrines, incorporated into Israeli law upon independence, an administrative body pursuing a quasi-judicial function is subject to principles of natural justice. 'Natural justice' boils down to two rules. The first is that whoever conducts the quasi-judicial proceedings must be free of bias. The second is that both sides to a dispute should be heard. Natural justice does not apply to decisions of an administrative nature.

14   Joseph Weitz, a senior JNF official and the first director of Israel's Lands Administration, recalled that when the authorities sought to expropriate large tracts of Arab land in the Galilee they often preferred to apply the AO rather than the absentee legislation (Weitz 1965, 26; Yiftachel 1992). See also the discussion in Chapter 7 below.

was *Committee for the Defense of Expropriated Land in Nazareth*.[15] In this case, the Minister of Finance used his power under the AO to expropriate 1200 dunams of Arab land in and around the Arab city of Nazareth for the construction of government offices. The petitioners, an organization of Israeli Arabs who were residents of Nazareth, challenged the discretion of the Minister to expropriate a particular plot of land situated on the highest hill of the city. The Court rejected their petition, ruling that the AO granted considerable autonomy to the Minister to choose which land to expropriate, and that the Court would not intervene unless the decision was tainted by extraneous considerations such as political discrimination.[16]

To a certain extent, therefore, the doctrines enunciated against the background of the Israeli-Arab conflict developed into standard rules for the country as a whole, and were applied to expropriations of Jewish land as well. Indeed, when these principles were applied to support expropriations in the Jewish sector, this was done without pausing to consider—at least to the extent reflected in the written decisions of the Court—whether this was indeed the intent of the legislator. This seamless application of legal principles requires an explanation. All the principles embedded in the special expropriation laws enacted by the Knesset in the 1950s reflected the belief that the Arab population of Israel constituted a real threat to the security of the country, one that needed to be demographically and strategically contained. Some of these laws were developed as part of emergency legislation subsequently incorporated into regular law. Ostensibly, these principles were not intended to be applicable in the Jewish sector. Why, then, did the Supreme Court treat these principles as applicable to the country as a whole?

Broadly speaking, there are two categories of possible explanations. First, there are what might be termed systemic explanations, relating to the structure of the laws set up to expropriate Jewish and Arab property as well as to the status of the Supreme Court and its inherent political weakness *vis-à-vis* the other branches of government. The second category is the web of ideological imperatives that fashioned the views and beliefs of the Justices of the Israeli Supreme Court and guided them (to a greater or lesser extent) in their decisions.

Structural and Ideological Explanations

A central factor that contributed to the emergence of a single system of justice in the case law of the 1950s was the technical relationship between the laws used to expropriate land from Arabs and from Jews. While Arab property tended to be expropriated under new and purposely enacted legal categories such as 'waste land,' 'absentee property'

---

15 H.C. 30/55, *Committee for the Defense of Expropriated Land in Nazareth v. Minister of Finance*, 9(2) P.D. 1261.

16 It later emerged that only 80 to 100 dunams of the expropriated land were intended for government offices. The remainder was earmarked for the construction of several thousand residential units which subsequently formed the core of Jewish town of Upper Nazareth. See, H.C. 181/57, *Qasam v. Minister of Finance*, 12(3) P.D. 1986. On the events surrounding the expropriation and the relations of the state with the Arab city of Nazareth in the 1950s, see (Forman 2006).

and 'abandoned property' that were not applicable, by and large, to Jewish property, the AO was enforced indiscriminately in both sectors (Kretzmer 1990. 51-60).

It is important to note that the AO served as a secondary route taken by the Government to expropriate land from Arabs, the preferred course of action, at least in the first decade after independence, being application of the Absentees' Property Law and the 1953 Land Acquisition Law that were tailored to the specific needs of the state in this regard. However, as occurred in *Dor* and *Committee for the Defense of Expropriated Land in Nazareth*, once the special laws were inapplicable, there remained the AO under which Arab land could still be expropriated.

The application of the AO in the Arab sector must have had a profound impact on the principles developed by the Supreme Court to interpret that law. First, differentiating between Jewish land and Arab land in the context of the AO contradicted the legal ideology of formalism. As both the Mandatory regime and subsequently the Israeli Knesset chose not to distinguish formally between the two national communities for purposes of the AO, the Justices were unwilling to introduce blatant discriminatory jurisprudence where no legal grounds for it existed.

Interestingly, in other areas of the law where the legislature provided for the selective use of different mechanisms for the Jewish and Arab sectors, a dual system of justice did develop (Kimmerling 2002; Saban 2004). For example, there were two different censorship laws: the 1933 Press Ordinance and Regulation 94 of the 1945 DERs. The government typically applied the former to Jewish newspapers and the latter to Arab publications. Censorship case law reveals that the Supreme Court developed a separate jurisprudence for each of these laws. It applied free-speech principles under the Press Ordinance for the Hebrew press, but declined to limit the censor's power under the 1945 DERs with respect to Arab newspapers. Nonetheless, the image of the Court in the political world, as well as in legal circles, as objective and impartial was not tarnished because such cases were adjudicated under distinct legal regimes and it was therefore reasonable—from a blinkered formalistic perspective, at least—to expect that these distinct legal regimes would yield different outcomes (Shamir 1991).

However, the same could not be said regarding the jurisprudence of land expropriation. Discrimination in the judicial interpretation of the AO based on the ethnicity of the landowner would have harmed the interest of the Court in projecting an image of professionalism, objectivity and impartiality. In the context of the land expropriation cases of the 1950s, the Supreme Court's commitment to upholding its professional image may have led it to apply its own precedents across the board to Jews and Arabs alike.

Another explanation is what can only be termed the degree of intellectual confusion regarding the various items of legislation on the basis of which land was expropriated. As mentioned above, the structure of the special laws aimed at Arab landowners was similar to that of the AO. Not only did the two bodies of laws grant considerable autonomy to the expropriating authority, but they employed similar procedures to so do. Unlike the 1945 DERs, which allowed for expropriation by the military, both the AO and the special laws that enabled expropriation of Arab property were implemented by civilian authorities, and disputes were adjudicated in the regular court system. Furthermore, in both bodies of laws, the Minister of Finance was the final authority for expropriation decisions. The Minister of Finance served (and still serves) as the expropriating authority under the AO as well as under the 1953 Land Acquisition Law and he also was in charge of appointing the Custodian of Absentee Property and supervising the Custodian's actions.

These similarities may have led the special and general regimes to be conflated over time, causing them in effect to be regarded, both by the executive branch and by the judiciary, as two sides of a coin. Evidence of this conflation can be found in *Younis*, where the Court moved seamlessly from an analysis of the 1953 Land Acquisition Law to one of the AO, without even a brief mention of whether the context, principles and legislative intent underlying the latter were pertinent to a jurisprudentially correct interpretation of the former.

What happened in subsequent cases, and in particular once the special laws were no longer applicable, was that the precedents set in the context of the 1950s legislation were used to support and interpret the AO.[17] For instance, in the 1955 case of *Dwiak*, decided one year after *Younis*, the Supreme Court followed its own precedents for applying the AO in the Arab sector in order to adjudicate a case involving Jewish-owned land.[18] A similar process can be seen in the cases of *Avivim, Shmuelson, Banin, Spolansky* and *Schwartz*.[19] In all these cases, decided in the late 1960s and 1970s, precedents from the first decade that had been crystallized in the context of expropriations from Arabs survived as attached to the AO as the body of case law interpreting that law.

The explanations mentioned to this point all relate to the formal structure of the various expropriation laws and the pattern of their application. Another category of factors that has to do with the emergence of a unified regime of judicial deference in cases of expropriation in the 1950s relates to the weak status of the Court *vis-à-vis* the executive branch. As noted in Chapter 2, the Supreme Court was created four months after the establishment of the State of Israel, and the law granting tenure to Justices and judges was only passed in 1953. This was much more than a mere technical issue. It had tremendous political and symbolic implications. Whether intentional or purely the consequence of the exigencies of the time—the need to create a state and simultaneously fight for independence—delaying the establishment of the Supreme Court sent an unmistakable message to the legal establishment that the Supreme Court was, in certain fundamental aspects, the junior of the three branches of government, which indeed it remained for many years.

The political and structural imbalance between the judiciary and the other branches of government was exacerbated by two other factors. First, alone among democratic nations, the Israeli judiciary operated up until the early 1990s in a

---

17 As recalled, the Land Acquisition Law of 1953 had a limited application period of one year. The Absentees' Property Law of 1950, while still formally on the books, was rarely applied after the mid-1950s.

18 H.C. 124/55, *Dwiak v. Ministry of Finance*, 10(1) P.D. 753.

19 F.H. 26/69, *Avivim Ltd. v. Minister of Finance*, 24(2) P.D. 397; H.C. 67/79, *Shmuelson v. State of Israel*, 34(1) P.D. 281; H.C. 282/71, *Banin v. Minister of Finance*, 25(2) P.D. 466; H.C. 147/74, *Spolansky v. Minister of Finance*, 29(1) P.D. 421; H.C. 114/77, *Schwartz v. Minister of Finance*, 31(2) P.D. 800.

constitutional void. In terms of the question at issue here—namely, assessing the status of the Supreme Court and the extent to which it was permitted (and regarded itself as permitted) to oversee the work of the legislature in any meaningful way, and to put a halt to its excesses and those of the executive—the constitutional void was crucial in limiting judicial interference. The second reason for the imbalance was a purely political one, and that was the centralized nature of Israeli politics. Israeli political, economic and administrative systems in the 1950s and 1960s—in fact until the political upheaval of the 1977 elections—were dominated by one political grouping commonly referred to as the Labour Party, which, despite its internal divisions and differences, was able to control both the executive and the legislative branches of government. The ability of the Labour establishment to do so was in no small part the consequence of the parliamentary regime that was put in place after independence, again following the example of the British House of Commons. Furthermore, the Justices themselves came from the Labour establishment and maintained close ties with it, a factor which, when combined with the absence of a constitution, no doubt contributed to the Court's restraint (Barzilai 1999). If the Supreme Court required a lesson in the futility of trying to rein in the authorities, it received one in the case of the Christian Arab villages of Iqrit and Bir'im. There, the Israel Defense Forces (IDF) blew up all the residential buildings in the villages in order to render impossible compliance with the Justices' ruling permitting the residents of the villages to return to their homes. The military authorities were never sanctioned for this blatant obstructionism.[20]

Finally, there are what might be termed ideological considerations that underscored the unified approach of judicial restraint in land expropriation cases in the 1950s. One was the tradition of legal formalism that shaped the scope of judicial intervention. As explained in Chapter 2, legal formalism dominated Israeli jurisprudence in the first decades. In part, it was the legal inheritance from the British Mandate, an early twentieth-century legalism. In the case of some Justices (and, more generally, numerous members of the Israeli legal profession), the formalism of their pre-Second World War legal education in Germany also influenced their legal approach (Mautner 1993; Salzberger, and Oz-Salzberger 2000). Formalism took the form of an emphasis on the letter of the law. Therefore, even if in specific instances the Justices were troubled by the outcomes that they reached, as in the case of *Younis* concerning the absence of a right to a hearing, they did not regard it as falling within their powers to do more than criticize the legislature in the hope that it would revisit certain items of legislation.[21]

There were also ideological explanations of a different kind. The expropriations in the 1950s were viewed as strategic and of national importance, requiring, in the eyes of the state, the taking of land from Arabs. Similarly, there were often pressing

---

20   The issue underlying Iqrit and Bir'im has over the years repeatedly returned before the courts in various guises. See the discussion in Chapter 9 below.

21   The Court in *Younis* conceded that 'it would have been more appropriate if the system that permitted issuance of certificated under the terms of the Land Acquisition Law provided the harmed parties the opportunity to challenge such orders.' H.C. 5/54, *Younis v. Minister of Finance*, 8(1) P.D. 314, 317.

needs of prime strategic importance justifying expropriation of land from Jews. The main such recurring need was immigration. And if one looks at the case law of land expropriation not from the perspective of the individual dispossessed landowner, whether Arab or Jewish, but from the perspective of the national authorities, whether those involved in taking the land or in adjudicating the legitimacy of the expropriation, the bundle of expropriation laws can be seen to a certain extent as unified. In that sense, whenever land was needed in the 1950s for national-strategic reasons, be they related to the perceived dangers of Arab demographic growth or military reasons or reasons of encouraging and developing the economic development of the country, or finding housing solutions for large numbers of Jewish immigrants, the needs of the state were always equally pressing, and therefore the Court was willing to apply the same laws in the same manner to promote and protect those interests.

With the developments that took place between the 1950s and 1970s in the Court's sensitivity to its role as a guarantor of civil rights, the harming principles of expropriation that were upheld in the 1950s under the guise of the state's needs could not so easily escape judicial intervention in the second cycle of expropriation following the Six-Day War. Still, the practice of Arab land expropriation and the security-territorial emphasis continued to influence the Court's approach to property rights, as the next chapter illustrates.

Chapter 7

The Politics of Land
Expropriation after 1967

The post-1967 period witnessed an expansion of Israel's expropriation and settlement policy to the Occupied Territories. The first part of this chapter looks at the policy and the legal measures applied by Israel to obtain control over Arab land in the Occupied Territories, and, in particular, in the West Bank. It should be noted, however, that Israel and the West Bank are subject to different legal regimes. One consequence of this is that the legal mechanisms of expropriation in the Occupied Territories are not, strictly speaking, relevant to the present study, whose focus is the Supreme Court's approach to property rights of Arabs and Jews in Israel proper. Rather, to the extent that the examination of the legal machinery of expropriation in the Occupied Territories is pertinent to the issue under consideration here, this is in order to understand the political context in which property rights have been adjudicated in Israel since 1967. As is argued below, Israel's policy of expropriation in the Galilee and East Jerusalem has been heavily affected by strategic concerns that have a lot to do with the ongoing occupation of the Territories.

The second part of the chapter addresses the land expropriation case law of the 1970s and 1980s with respect to Jerusalem and the Galilee. Since that time, Israel's goal has been to maintain a Jewish majority in the unified Jerusalem. After providing some background for understanding the policy of land expropriation in East Jerusalem and the Galilee, I will turn to the case law. The patterns of land expropriation adjudication after 1967 reveal the dominance of the security-territorial discourse which equates sovereignty with land control. Despite the separation of the West Bank from Israel and from Jerusalem, the ongoing occupation strengthened the security discourse within Israeli society, advocating expansion of Jewish presence in the Galilee and East Jerusalem. The dominance of the territorial-security discourse resulted in different legal doctrines being developed by the Supreme Court compared to those of the 1950s. In practice, however, the development of new legal doctrines was by no means a guarantee of different results. Where in the past, the arguments made by expropriated landowners were rejected by the Supreme Court on grounds of formalism, they were now brushed aside by a Court swayed by the state's substantive arguments of strategic necessity.

The Six-Day War and the Occupied Territories

The 1967 War transformed the map of the Middle East and the political agendas of the various parties to the Arab-Israeli conflict. Over the course of six days (June 6 to June 11, 1967) Israel defeated three neighboring Arab countries, Egypt, Syria and Jordan, gaining control over the Sinai Peninsula, the Gaza Strip, the West Bank of the Jordan river (including East Jerusalem) and the Golan Heights, a total area of 65,400 square kilometers of which the single largest component, comprising some 57,900 square kilometers, was the Sinai Desert (Parker 1996; Segev 2005).[1] The territories conquered by Israel in 1967 presented a variety of new challenges (as well as some partial answers) to Israel's existing security doctrine. The territory which became the main focus of controversy in the context of Israel's land politics was the West Bank, where substantial Jewish settlement activity went hand-in-hand with outright expropriation and other forms of alienation of Arab land.

The conquest of the West Bank, an area of 5,860 square kilometers, resulted in Israel controlling a population of more than a half a million Palestinians (*CIA World Fact book*, n.d.; Kimmerling 1983, 147-8).[2] During the first decade of occupation, the Labour governments operated on the basis of the Alon Plan, which advocated the establishment of settlements in areas perceived as being important for Israel's security and where the Palestinian population was relatively sparse (the Jordan Valley, parts of the Hebron Hills and greater Jerusalem). However, after the Likud came to power in 1977, the settlement policy changed. Influenced by the fundamentalist ideology of the Greater Land of Israel Movement and by the security argument which pointed to the involvement of Palestinians in terrorist organizations and the consequent danger to Jewish civilians, the Government began to establish settlements along the densely populated mountainous ridge of the West Bank. The Likud Government's first settlement plan, submitted in 1978, stated quite clearly that the objectives of establishing such settlements were to 'reduce to a minimum the possibility of establishing another Arab state in the region' and to make it difficult for the local Palestinian population to create territorial continuity and to achieve political unity (Benvenisti 1984, 49-63; Gazit 1999, 217-49; Kretzmer 2002, 76; Peleg 1995, 22-81; Peretz, 1986, 57-78).

It is estimated that by the mid-1980s Israel had seized 35-40 percent of the territory of the West Bank, and 50 percent by 2002 (Benvenisti 1984; Lein 2002, 47).[3] Some of this land was taken for military purposes, such as army bases and other facilities. But on the vast majority of the expropriated land, the state established civilian Jewish settlements. In the course of 20 years (1972-91), the number of Jewish settlements in the West Bank rose from 9 to 119, and the size of the Jewish population swelled from 1,000 to 90,000 strong (CBS 1992). By the end of 2002, there were 212,000 Jewish

---

1   Israel withdrew from the Sinai in 1979, following the signing of an Israeli-Egyptian peace treaty, and from the Gaza Strip in August 2005.

2   About 250,000 Palestinians fled from Judea and Samaria as a result of the conquest. Some later returned. The census of 1967-68 reported 600,000 inhabitants in the West Bank, 356,261 in the Gaza Strip and in the Northern Sinai, and 66,857 in East Jerusalem. Today, the estimates on the number of Palestinians living in the West Bank (not including East Jerusalem) range from 1.4 to 2.8 million. Aluf Benn, Demographic Politics, *Ha'aretz* (Hebrew Daily) February 2, 2005.

3   Land that was already owned by Jews in the West Bank prior to the 1967 war is estimated at about 1 to 2 percent.

settlers living in the West Bank (not including East Jerusalem), compared to fewer than 9,000 in the Gaza Strip (CBS 2003).[4]

From a legal perspective, the methods employed for land expropriation in the West Bank differ substantially from those applied within Israel's pre-1967 borders. This is due to the fact that Israel, as a belligerent occupier, cannot apply its law to the citizens of the Occupied Territories. After the Six-Day War, Israel left largely intact the mixture of Ottoman, Mandate and Jordanian land laws of the West Bank (Drori 1982, 44-80; Shehadeh 1988, 17-59). At the same time, however, Israel created a military authority for the Territories, and conferred on it full legislative and executive powers. Furthermore, unlike expropriations within Israel itself, the legality of expropriations and settlements in the Occupied Territories is subject to the international law of belligerent occupation. Since Israel did not annex the Territories, the Territories remained legally 'occupied' (or 'administrated') areas in which the international laws of war apply.[5]

The various layers of law that apply to the West Bank—pre-1967 Ottoman, Mandate and Jordanian law, post-1967 Israeli military law and customary international law of war—created complex legal and bureaucratic mechanisms for land expropriation (Lein 2002). In the first decade after the Six-Day War, the Labour government emphasized the taking of land for security and military purposes only. On this basis, Israeli military commanders issued dozens of orders for the requisition of private land in the West Bank, on the grounds that it was required for 'essential and urgent military needs.' Although such lands remained theoretically under private ownership, the Palestinian owners lost their rights of possession and use, and eventually Jewish settlements were established on such lands. The total area seized for 'military use' under Labour governments (1968-77) is estimated at between 35,000 and 50,000 dunams (Peleg 1995, 29).

In several instances, Palestinian residents petitioned the High Court of Justice against the seizure of their land, claiming that the establishment of Jewish settlements on land taken for military purpose was contrary to international law. However, until the *Elon Moreh* decision (see below), the High Court rejected all such petitions, and

---

4   In August 2005, Israel completed its disengagement from the Gaza Strip, ending 38 years of military rule there.

5   The official Israeli position views the West Bank and the Gaza Strip as 'disputed' and not 'occupied' areas. Nevertheless, Israel concurred with the interpretation that the Hague Regulations for occupied lands are applicable to these areas. Other elements of international law of war such as the Fourth Geneva Convention that would apply were Israel the temporary ruler of the Territories are not acknowledged by Israel as binding. The Israeli position holds that Israel is not bound under international law to apply the Geneva Convention IV to the West Bank and the Gaza Strip, for the reason that the recognized governments (Jordan and Egypt) that ruled the Territories before they were displaced by Israel in the Six-Day War, were themselves occupiers who had seized control of the territory in 1948 before the final status of these territories could legally be determined in a manner that was internationally recognized. In this light, Israel is the 'administrator' but not the 'occupier' of the Territories, whose legal status is *sui generis*, and any application of rights pursuant to the Geneva Convention IV is a matter of humanitarian choice on the part of the Israeli authorities (Shamgar 1971). The international community, however, has never accepted this interpretation (Kretzmer 2002, 31-56).

accepted the state's argument that the land seizure was legal because the settlements performed key defense and military functions. In the words of Justice Vitkon: 'In terms of purely security-based considerations, there can be no question that the presence in the administrated territory of settlements—even 'civilian' settlements—of the citizens of the administrating power makes a significant contribution to the security situation in that territory, and facilitates the army's performance of its functions …'.[6]

All this changed dramatically in the wake of the 1979 case of *Elon Moreh*.[7] The petition in *Elon Moreh* was submitted by several West Bankers who asked the High Court to nullify an order issued by the local IDF commander expropriating some 5,000 dunams of land. The land affected was slated for the establishment of a settlement which was to be named Elon Moreh. Work on the infrastructure for the settlement began on the same day the order was issued. The state's response to the petition was by then the customary one: the decision to establish the settlement was taken for military-strategic reasons, and therefore the expropriation order was lawful. However, unlike previous cases, the factual record revealed that it was the government, not the military authorities, that had initiated the establishment of the settlement, and this under pressure from the politically powerful *Gush Emunim* settlers' movement. The dominant consideration was therefore clearly political (Kretzmer 2002, 85-9). Given that the factual record undermined the argument of military necessity, the Court ordered the IDF to dismantle the settlement and return the land to its owners. Writing for the Court, Justice Landau defined the term 'military needs' narrowly as referring strictly to interests that are based on a rational, military-strategic analysis of the potential dangers facing the state, but excluding interests based on ideological goals and political views. In the political context of Israel, in which ideological positions and security considerations *stricto sensu* are often conflated, this was a significant statement (Naor 1999).

The immediate (and in a sense trivial) consequence of *Elon Moreh* was that the government found an alternative site for the new settlement. Beyond this, however, the ruling was a landmark case. After *Elon Moreh*, successive governments avoided direct confiscation of Palestinian land through military requisition orders, preferring instead to take possession of land by declaring it 'state land'.[8]

This method built upon the historical fact that when Israel conquered the West Bank, only one third of the land there had been registered. Following the *Elon Moreh* decision, the Knesset decided that *all* uncultivated unregistered rural land would be declared state land. The legal framework for this decision was found in the 1858 Ottoman Land Law, still then in effect in the West Bank, and which

---

6   H.C. 606,610/79, *Ayyub v. Minister of Defense*, 33(2) P.D. 113, 119. See also H.C. 302, 306/72, *Abu Khelou v. Government of Israel*, 27(2) P.D. 169; H.C. 834/78, *Salame v. Minister of Defense*, 33(1) P.D. 971.

7   H.C. 390/79, *Dweikat v. Government of Israel*, 34(1) P.D. 1 (*Elon Moreh* case).

8   However, outright expropriation was reintroduced in 1994 and applied widely to build bypass roads. This occurred as part of the plans for preparing the redeployment of IDF forces from the Occupied Territories following the signing of the Oslo Accords in 1993 (Lein 2002, 50).

provided that any uncultivated land 'beyond shouting range' of the closest village or town was the sultan's property (Shehadeh 1988; Zamir, 1985). And while, to the dispossessed Palestinian landowner, the difference between the two forms of expropriation may have seemed a technicality, this was hardly the case. The switch from expropriation of private land to its recategorization as 'state land' gave the state substantial advantages in terms of the legal process. First, it shifted the burden of proof regarding ownership of the land to the Palestinian claimant, who now needed to provide proof of possession, as determined by Israel, in order to exclude their land from being considered 'state land'. Furthermore, appeals of certification of land as 'state land' were heard by special committees rather than by courts of law. These committees were (and are) composed of three members, typically officials of the military government, and only one of them was required to be a legal professional. They were not subject to customary rules of evidence and procedure, and their decisions were not binding on the military commander in the region (Kretzmer 2002, 90-4; Lein 2002, 51-8; Peleg 1995, 29-35). According to Pliya Albeck, former head of the Civil Department in the State Attorney's Office, by 1985 approximately 90 percent of the settlements were established on land that had been declared 'state land.' In September 2004, *Ha'aretz* reported that in the year 2003 alone, Israel had used the Ottoman Land Law of 1858 to expropriate 2,000 dunams of land in the West Bank for the expansion of existing Jewish civilian settlements.[9]

Given the fact that expropriations in the Occupied Territories are pursued under a different legal framework than the one pertaining to Israel proper, the relevance of the former to the present discussion is limited.[10] Nevertheless, it is misleading in my view to treat Israel and the West Bank as entirely separate issues in the context of land expropriation (*cf.* Kretzmer 2005), as the state policy of expropriation in the Galilee and East Jerusalem after 1967 was shaped to a large extent by the experience in the West Bank. The geographic proximity to Israel of 1.5 million Palestinians under occupation fuelled the demographic fears of the Jewish majority that it would soon become a minority in its own state. This perception has been, in part, the motive for the ambitious national project of Judaizing the Galilee (Naor 1999).

Interestingly, the patterns of adjudication of land expropriation cases in the Occupied Territories constituted another factor that strengthened the security motive underlying expropriation of Arab land within Israel proper. Shortly after the Six-Day War, the Supreme Court, sitting as a High Court of Justice, extended its jurisdiction to actions carried out by the military government in the Occupied Territories (Kretzmer 2002, 19-29; Shamgar 1982). This landmark decision provided Palestinian residents

---

9   Aluf Ben, 'Israel Still Expropriating Land to Expand Settlements Under the Guise of 'State Lands', *Ha'aretz* (Hebrew Daily) September 29, 2004.

10   The creation of a separate system of justice for the Occupied Territories has permitted wide-scale human rights violations there. Palestinian residents of the Territories have been governed by the Israeli military and its orders, and Israeli law and justice do not apply to them (Sheleff 1996, 97-127). Israeli law does however apply to the Jewish residents in the Territories and their settlements, as well as to local Jewish authorities, an arrangement providing a form of personal jurisdiction that accompanies settlers wherever they go (Benvenisti 1989; Shehadeh 1993).

access to Israeli civilian legal fora where they could (and occasionally do) challenge land expropriations issued pursuant to military orders.

The jurisdiction of the Supreme Court over land expropriation in the Territories reinforced the perceived link between national security inside Israel proper and encouraging Jewish population growth in areas of the country where Israeli Arabs predominated. As mentioned above, this link was strengthened by the geographic proximity of the Territories to Israel and by the ties—personal, familial and cultural—between Israeli Arabs and Palestinians. In addition, as international law requires an occupying power to refrain from making any substantial changes in the status of occupied territory except for reasons of security, the concept of security was repeatedly addressed by the Court on the various occasions in which it had to review the legality of Jewish civilian settlements in the West Bank. Even in the landmark decision of *Elon Moreh*, the Court did not challenge the premise that Jewish settlements under certain circumstances could be considered as legitimate security measures. The Court's acceptance of settlements in the Territories as fulfilling a prime security role paved the way for its acceptance of similar reasoning in the case of expropriations of Arab land in East Jerusalem and the Galilee.

Israel's settlement policy in the West Bank and the treatment this policy received at the hands of the Supreme Court are important for understanding the sociopolitical context in which property rights have been adjudicated in Israel after 1967. The West Bank aside, the two principal regions in which expropriations of Arab land continued through the 1970s and 1980s were the Galilee and East Jerusalem, which, following its annexation in 1967, was considered part of Israel under Israeli law.

Expropriations in East Jerusalem and the Galilee

Following the 1967 War, the Israeli government annexed the Old City of Jerusalem and the surrounding area (collectively referred to as East Jerusalem), incorporating these areas within the existing municipality of (West) Jerusalem.[11] With the expansion of the municipal boundary, legal distinctions were made between Jerusalem Arabs and West Bank Palestinians. At the time of the census that was conducted after the city boundaries were changed, Arab residents of the newly expanded Jerusalem were given the option to accept Israeli citizenship provided they were willing to forfeit their Jordanian citizenship.[12] Unlike the rest of the West Bank, therefore, Israeli law

---

11　Since 1948, Jerusalem has been usually been discussed in terms of a threefold division: the Old City (an area of six sq. km); East Jerusalem (an area of 64 sq. km, which includes 28 villages in the West Bank and reaches the municipal boundaries of Bethlehem and Beit Jalla) and West Jerusalem (an area of 38 sq. km). The Old City and East Jerusalem were under Jordanian rule between 1948 and 1967 (Efrat 2000). In 1992, Jerusalem was again enlarged, this time by the addition of roughly 15,000 dunams, largely to the west of the city. This move was made in order to provide reserves for immediate and future growth.

12　Few Palestinians accepted this offer, and of those who did many later renounced it. As of 1992, approximately 1,500 Palestinian residents of Jerusalem held Israeli citizenship, less than 1 percent of the 221,800 Palestinians who were legally permanent residents in the city.

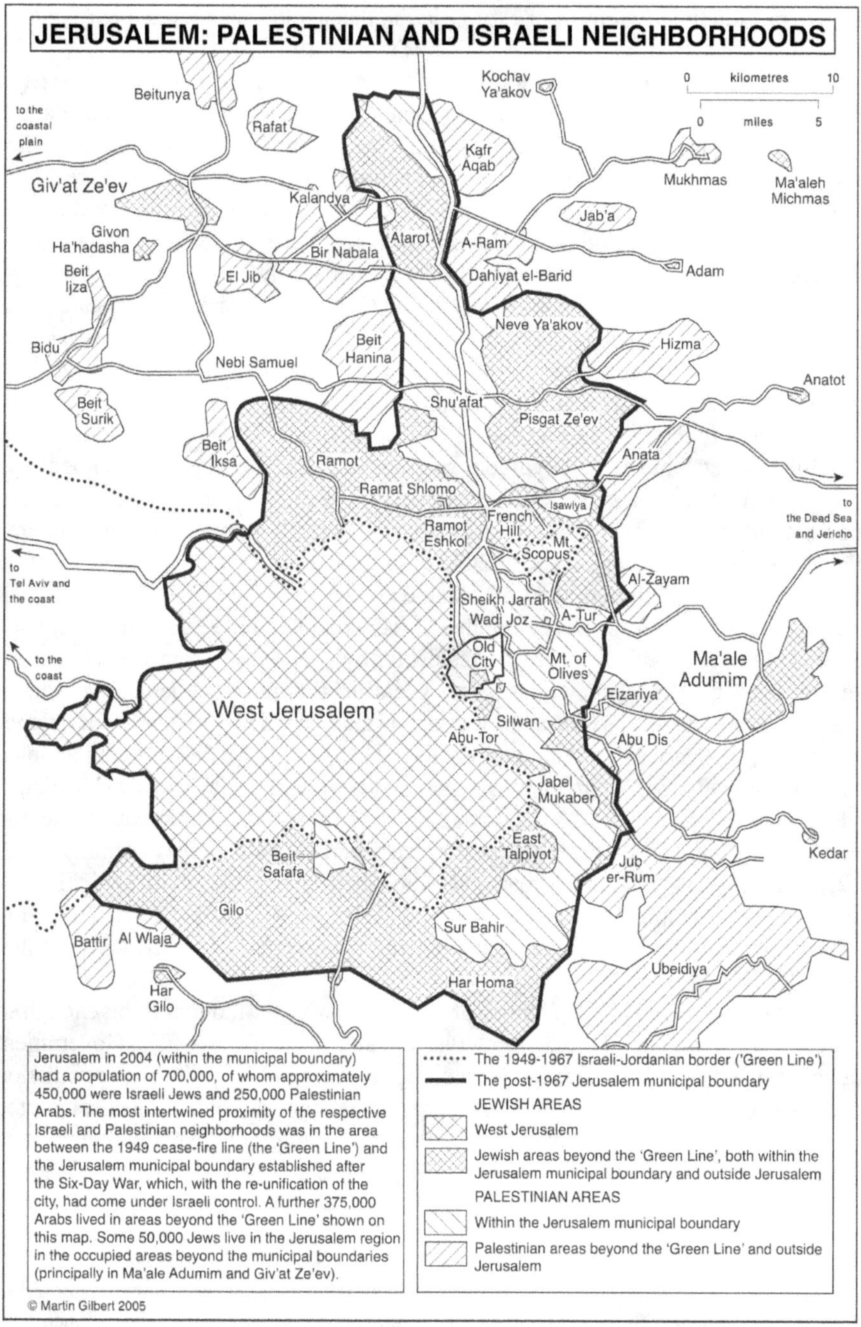

JERUSALEM: PALESTINIAN AND ISRAELI NEIGHBORHOODS

Beitunya

Kochav Ya'akov

to the coastal plain

Rafat

Kafr Aqab

0 kilometres 10

0 miles 5

Giv'at Ze'ev

Kalandya

Mukhmas

Ma'aleh Michmas

Givon Ha'hadasha

Atarot

Jab'a

Beit Ijza

Bir Nabala

A-Ram

El Jib

Dahiyat el-Barid

Adam

Bidu

Nebi Samuel

Beit Hanina

Neve Ya'akov

Hizma

Anatot

Beit Surik

Shu'afat

Pisgat Ze'ev

Beit Iksa

Ramot

Anata

Ramat Shlomo

to Tel Aviv and the coast

Ramot Eshkol

French Hill

Isawiya

Mt. Scopus

Al-Zayam

to the Dead Sea and Jericho

Sheikh Jarrah

Wadi Joz

A-Tur

to the coast

Old City

Mt. of Olives

Ma'ale Adumim

West Jerusalem

Silwan

Elzariya

Abu-Tor

Abu Dis

Jabel Mukaber

East Talpiyot

Beit Safafa

Jub er-Rum

Kedar

Gilo

Sur Bahir

Battir

Al Wlaja

Har Homa

Ubeidiya

Har Gilo

Jerusalem in 2004 (within the municipal boundary) had a population of 700,000, of whom approximately 450,000 were Israeli Jews and 250,000 Palestinian Arabs. The most intertwined proximity of the respective Israeli and Palestinian neighborhoods was in the area between the 1949 cease-fire line (the 'Green Line') and the Jerusalem municipal boundary established after the Six-Day War, which, with the re-unification of the city, had come under Israeli control. A further 375,000 Arabs lived in areas beyond the 'Green Line' shown on this map. Some 50,000 Jews live in the Jerusalem region in the occupied areas beyond the municipal boundaries (principally in Ma'ale Adumim and Giv'at Ze'ev).

······· The 1949-1967 Israeli-Jordanian border ('Green Line')
—— The post-1967 Jerusalem municipal boundary

JEWISH AREAS

West Jerusalem

Jewish areas beyond the 'Green Line', both within the Jerusalem municipal boundary and outside Jerusalem

PALESTINIAN AREAS

Within the Jerusalem municipal boundary

Palestinian areas beyond the 'Green Line' and outside Jerusalem

© Martin Gilbert 2005

Map 7.1   Jerusalem: Palestinian and Israeli Neighborhoods
Adapted with permission from: *Routledge Atlas of the Arab Israeli Conflict*, 8th Edn by Martin Gilbert, ISBN 0415359015 (HB) and 0415359007 (PB). Published by Routledge 2005.

in general, and the framework of expropriation that applies within pre-1967 Israel in particular, are also valid in East Jerusalem (Dumper 1997, 38-52).

The annexation of East Jerusalem and the encouragement of Jews to settle there enjoy a wide consensus in Jewish Israeli society. Soon after the annexation, the Government undertook numerous actions to strengthen its sovereignty in East Jerusalem and to ensure that the city remained unified. Hebrew names were added to (or replaced) Arabic street signs, the city's infrastructure was unified, and certain government offices (including the Justice Ministry) were moved to East Jerusalem (Benvenisti 1976, 251-3; Kroyanker 1988).[13] In the political sphere, in 1980, the Knesset enacted the Basic Law: Jerusalem, Capital of Israel, which stated that 'complete and united Jerusalem is the capital of Israel [...] the seat of the presidents of the state, the Knesset, the government and the Supreme Court.' The Basic Law did not mandate any new changes. Its main purpose was to unequivocally express Israel's claim to the right to exercise its sovereignty over the unified capital.[14]

But legal statements and symbolic acts alone could not alter the demographic reality in the city after 1967. The Israeli census in September 1967 placed the total population of the unified city, which was approximately three times larger in area than pre-1967 Jewish Jerusalem, at 267,800 inhabitants – 196,800 Jews and 71,000 Palestinian Arabs (Schmelz 1987, 72). In the first years following annexation, Israeli authorities set a target for increasing the Jewish population of Jerusalem to between 80 and 90 percent of all the city's residents, by providing incentives to Jews to live in the city. However, within a few years it became clear that the growth of the Jewish population in Jerusalem was lower than hoped for, while the city's non-Jewish population was growing at a higher rate. In 1973, the Government adopted the recommendation of an inter-ministerial committee, which determined that a 'demographic balance of Jews and Arabs must be maintained as it was at the end of 1972,' that is, at 73.5 percent Jews and 26.5 percent Palestinians (Amirav 1992, 12; Felner 1995, 43). Over the years, all Israeli governments have affirmed this ratio as a guiding principle of municipal planning policy, and it has been the foundation of most demographic and urban plans prepared by government ministries since that time.

Increasing the Jewish population of Jerusalem was not thought to be enough to prevent any future attempt to divide Jerusalem after its unification. The Government believed that it was also necessary to encourage the development of Jewish population centers in Arab East Jerusalem. The Jerusalem Master Plan, which was completed in 1968, called for implementation of a three-step policy of Jewish neighborhood construction (Benvenisti 1996; Dumper 1997, 86-127; Kroyanker 1988).[15] The first

---

13   Plans were made to transfer the Supreme Court to Mount Scopus as well, but they were ultimately not carried out.

14   The law was introduced as a private member's bill by Knesset members opposed to the peace agreement with Egypt. Following its ratification as a Basic Law, 13 states, including Egypt, removed their embassies from Jerusalem to Tel-Aviv.

15   In addition to strategically situating the new Jewish neighborhoods to cut off Palestinian neighborhoods, the government used afforestation as a political tool. Since 1967, afforestation sites in Jerusalem have frequently been selected on the basis of their strategic value (Cohen 1993).

phase of the Plan was implemented immediately after the war. The construction of three new Jewish neighborhoods—Ramot Eshkol, the French Hill and Givat Hamivtar—closed the gap in the north of the city, combining to create what was referred to as the 'northern lock' (see map 7.1). The second stage began in the 1970s and continued until the early 1980s. Its main feature was the establishment of four large urban settlements in the four corners of the annexed areas: two in the north (Ramot and Neve Ya'akov) and two in the south (Gilo and East Talpiyot) (see map 7.1).[16] The third stage of Jewish growth in Jerusalem included the building of Pisgat Ze'ev in 1980, located between French Hill and Neve Ya'akov, and the creation of an outer security belt by placing the Jewish settlements of Ma'ale Adumim (1977), Givon (1981) and Efrat (1983) on ridges and crests, and beside strategic roads in the Palestinian territory (Dumper 1997, 109-27; Kallus 2004). The third stage is still in play today, with the construction of the Har Homa neighborhood in southern Jerusalem and the attempts to achieve a link between this neighborhood and Ma'ale Adumim in what has come to be known as the 'Greater Jerusalem' plan.[17]

The policy of strategic planning in unified Jerusalem resulted in an increase in the number of Jews living in urban and suburban neighborhoods in East Jerusalem. Between 1967 and 2001, some 44,000 new housing units were constructed in the annexed areas of Jerusalem and sold to Israelis at special terms. Virtually all of these new housing projects were for Jews (Dumper 1997, 119).[18] During these years, only two small-scale Arab housing projects, comprising some 550 housing units in all, received state subsidies. At the end of 2002, 45 percent of the residents who lived on annexed areas were Jews and 55 percent were Palestinians (B'Tselem, n.d., *Statistics on Land Expropriation in East Jerusalem*; Cheshin et al. 1999, 65-6)[19] However, all

---

16   Each of these urban settlements has a clear military strategic value. Neve Ya'akov is situated on the main route heading north to Ramalla and Nablus. Gilo, an extensive Jewish settlement for approximately 35,000 residents, overlooks the road south to Bethlehem and Hebron, and separates the only Palestinian neighborhood on the southern perimeter of Jerusalem, Beit Safafa, from the closest large Arab population centers of Bethlehem and Beit Jalla. Ramot and East Talpiyot, planned for 30,000 and 15,000 residents respectively, are also similarly strategically located.

17   In 1994, the Rabin government declared the expansion of Ma'ale Adumim on 3110 acres of Palestinian land, but did not implement the plan. Called the E-1 Plan, the Government proposed to construct new residential areas that would create geographical contiguity between Jerusalem and Ma'ale Adumim as part of the comprehensive 'Greater Jerusalem' plan. The objectives of the plan were to establish a break between eastern Jerusalem and Bethlehem, to strengthen the Jewish majority in metropolitan Jerusalem and to ensure that Ma'ale Adumim would remain part of Israel under any future territorial deal with the Palestinians.

18   Atypically, the benefits were made available also to those who had not served in the military, provided they had a close male relative who had served. This expansion of the entitlement was clearly intended to attract orthodox Jews, while still excluding the vast majority of Israeli Arabs.

19   Housing construction in Arab neighborhoods of Jerusalem is thus pursued privately, with no government assistance and often illegally, due to the absence of town planning schemes (which are a precondition for obtaining legal building permits). Since 1967, Israel has used planning laws to control expansion of Palestinian localities by denying them building permits (Perry 2003). Only in the mid-1980s did the municipality of Jerusalem begin to

this did not solve the demographic dilemma facing successive Israeli governments. From 1967 to 2002, the Jewish population of Jerusalem increased from 198,000 to 458,000. At the same time, however, the Palestinian population in Jerusalem had a higher growth rate, increasing from 69,000 to 221,800, constituting 33 percent of the residents of the city (B'Tselem, n.d., *Statistics on Land Expropriation in East Jerusalem*).

In terms of the legal tools used to acquire land for the new Jewish settlements, the title settlement procedure was too slow for achieving the goals of rapid construction and population growth (Sandberg 2004). Hence, in the post-1967 period, expropriation became the Government's preferred method for acquiring land in Jerusalem. Between 1967 and 1992, a total of 23,378 dunams—over one-third of the area annexed to the city—was expropriated in favor of Jewish housing projects (Felner 1995, 52-3). The French Hill, Ramot, Gilo, Pisgat Ze'ev and most recently Har Homa are some of the Jewish neighborhoods built on expropriated land. The land acquired by these expropriations was owned mostly by Arabs, although some was owned by Jews. The legal tool used by the authorities to acquire land in East Jerusalem was the AO, the general expropriation law.

Another region in which the outcome of the 1967 war drove the Government to intensify its efforts to contain the Arab population through land expropriation was the Galilee. Although the Galilee had been under Israeli sovereignty since independence, unlike other regions of Israel, it remained overwhelmingly Arab. The fighting in the Galilee in 1948 took place mostly at the later stages of the war, at a time when Arab flight had largely come to an end. Consequently, the residents of only five villages, with a combined population of less than 5,000, abandoned their homes in the central and upper Galilee. The vast majority of the local population, nearly 20,000 Arabs, remained in the area (Koren 1998; Yiftachel 1992, 119-121). Given the assessment of both political and military authorities that an exclusively Arab region posed a potentially serious security threat, efforts to Judaize the Galilee got underway as early as the mid-1950s (Yiftachel 1997a). As mentioned in Chapter 6 above, 1200 dunams of land in and around Nazareth were expropriated by the Minister of Finance under the terms of the AO in 1954. A small portion of the land (about 100 dunams) served for construction of government offices, while the rest was used for the building of a new Jewish township, Upper Nazareth (Forman 2006).[20] A few years later, in 1962, the Minister of Finance ordered the expropriation of a further 5,100 dunams from the Arab villages of Deir el-Assad, Binah, Nahaf and Majd al-Krum in the upper Galilee. On these new lands, the Jewish development town of Carmi'el was built (Yiftachel 1998, 50-62).

---

prepare outline plans for all the Palestinian neighborhoods. Most plans have been completed, while others are in various stages of planning and approval. Palestinians nevertheless claim that the plans, instead of contributing to the development of Arab neighborhoods and easing housing shortages there, restrict the building percentages on the lots and declare broad swaths of land as green areas reserved for future planting and where construction is not permitted.

20   H.C. 30/55, *Committee for the Defense of Expropriated Land in Nazareth v. Minister of Finance*, 9 P.D. 1261; H.C. 181/57, *Qasam v. Minister of Finance*, 12(3) P.D. 1986.

Aside from these expropriations, during the first two decades of independence, Israel did not pursue extensive settlement programs in the densely populated central Galilee. There were two reasons for this. First, the most urgent national priority was to invest such resources as were available in establishing Jewish settlements along the international borders, in order to secure the armistice lines. Between 1949 and 1952, 22 kibbutzim and moshavim were established along the international border. Second, and more importantly, control of Arab territorial expansion within Israel was, until 1966, accomplished primarily by virtue of the regime of military government. Between 1948 and 1966, military administrators governed areas of dense Arab population such as the Galilee.[21] In areas under their control, military authorities had wide discretional authority over security issues, including the ability to detain, try, convict and sentence anyone suspected of having committed hostile acts or of spreading hostile propaganda. They could restrict the movement of activists, ban political organizations and declare areas as closed, prohibiting civilians from traveling through them. The military government enabled Israel to closely supervise the movements of its Arab citizens and to prevent the creation of geographic contiguity between Arab villages (Amitai 1998; Hofnung 1996, 73-123).[22]

In 1963, the Arab population of the Galilee was roughly 120,000, compared to a Jewish population of only 10,000 (Kimmerling 1983, 141-2). Concerns that the Galilee was not yet Jewish took on urgency after the abolition of military government for the region in 1966. And particularly after the Six-Day War, Israeli officials became alarmed at the prospect of the Israeli Arabs in the Galilee demanding annexation of the majority-Arab Galilee to a new Palestinian state, should one come into being in the West Bank. Public officials noted also that the Galilee had not been included in the territory of the Jewish state according to the 1947 Partition Plan, and that there might be legal justification for holding a public referendum in the Galilee, an area where Arabs still constituted 92 percent of the population. In 1972, in response to the perceived threat of an all-Arab Galilee, the Government initiated a national demographic plan, one of whose specific goals was the promotion of Jewish settlement in the Galilee (Yiftachel 1992, 97-8). In 1975, the Prime Minister's Office issued its New Development Plan for the Galilee which sought to create a 'massive increase in the Jewish population, far above the targets of the 1972 National Plan,

---

21 Other areas subject to military rule were the Negev desert and the area known as the 'Triangle', a cluster of Arab villages bordering the West Bank.

22 The legal basis for the regime of military government was the DERs enacted by the British in 1945. The official reason given to justify the military government was considerations of national security. The argument was that the loyalty of the Arab citizens to the newly established Jewish state was questionable, and that they might collaborate with hostile elements outside Israel, particularly the Palestinians living in the West Bank and the Gaza Strip, to undermine Israel's security. Without minimizing the importance of security considerations, the military government clearly also served as an efficient mechanism for control. It institutionalized Arab dependence on state institutions and on the Jewish economy, and it legitimized discrimination in the allocation of resources for economic, municipal and educational development. The military government and its policy of restricting freedom of movement increased the social distance between Jews and Arabs, and fostered mutual negative images and fear (which exist to this day) (Lustick 1980).

aiming for 300,000 Jews in the hills of the Galilee by 1990' (Yiftachel 1992, 138-9; see also Falah 1991). The central component of the 1975 plan was the expropriation of roughly 1900 dunams of privately owned Arab land for the expansion of the Jewish town of Carmi'el. The government also designated a new type of settlement, known as a *mitzpe* (plural *mitzpim*), or lookout settlement. Such mitzpim, each comprising fewer than 20 families, were to be established in the central Galilee in strategically located sites near Arab villages. The locations were carefully selected to create Jewish wedges between clusters of Arab villages. The plan called for the establishment of 50 mitzpim between 1977 and 1981 (Yiftachel 1992, 142-4, 169-74; see also Carmon et al. 1990). Overall, some 20,000 dunams (approximately 5500 acres) were included in the development plan. Of these, about 30 percent were to be expropriated from Arabs and 15 percent from Jews, while the rest was state-owned land (Yiftachel 1992).

In view of the Government's intention to expropriate their land, Arabs in the Galilee organized rallies and mass demonstrations. The protests culminated in a general strike on March 30, 1976, in what was known as 'Land Day,' in the course of which six Arabs were killed in clashes with Israeli authorities (Reches 1977). Despite vigorous Arab protest, Israel carried out the 1975 plan. By 1981, there were 26 mitzpim in existence, and 52 by 1988 (Carmon et al. 1990). The entire project and the establishment of the so-called development towns of Upper Nazareth, Ma'alot, Migdal Ha'emek and Carmi'el changed the demographic composition of the Galilee. By the end of 1994, the population of the Galilee was 680,000, of which 72 percent were Arabs (compared to 92 percent in the first years of statehood) and 28 percent were Jewish residents of development towns, rural and exurban kibbutzim, moshavim and mitzpim (Yiftachel 1997). Since the 1980s, successive governments have refrained from further wide-scale land expropriations in the Galilee.

Changes in the Legal Setting

The 1970s witnessed some important changes in the legal framework of expropriation compared to the 1950s. One was the decline in the use of special expropriation laws against the Arab population. The mass expropriations of 'absentee' property had all but ended by the mid-1950s, and expropriations under the Land Acquisition Law (which included a one-year sunset provision), ended in March 1954. By the 1970s, outright expropriation of Arab-owned land was undertaken pursuant to the general expropriation law, the AO.[23]

This was not a mere technicality. As I suggested in the previous chapter, the extensive use of special expropriation laws against the Arab population in the 1950s shaped the judicial doctrines employed in regard to the land rights of Jews, as well. The legislative encroachment on principles of equity and justice that was codified in the absentee legislation and the Land Acquisition Law—the inequitable burden of proof, the retroactive approval of illegal expropriation, the absence of a right to a

---

23 Similarly, after 1954 the state speeded up the process of settling title in the Galilee (Forman 2002).

hearing—were a central element of the legal culture of expropriation in the 1950s. But by the 1970s, this was no longer the case.

Another change in the statutory framework of expropriation was the enactment of the Planning Law in 1965. The importance of this law for our purposes is that the law established an alternative way to expropriate land. As may be recalled, although the Planning Law permitted uncompensated expropriation of up to 40 percent of a plot (compared to the 25 percent limit under the AO), it also contained other, more democratically acceptable norms.[24] For example, it provided for the first time a list of acceptable public purposes, thus removing the definition of 'public use' from the hands of the expropriating authorities. It also provided a right to a hearing before a final decision to approve a plan could be reached, and granted landowners protection against post-expropriation changes in the public use designation of the land. Nonetheless, it is important to note that although the Planning Law introduced new norms of behavior, the state continued to resort exclusively to the AO with respect to land in Jerusalem and the Galilee. Due to its time-consuming requirement of planning approval as a prerequisite for expropriation, the Planning Law was employed in the 1970s and 1980s mainly in urban locations in central Israel.

In addition to the changes in the legal practice of expropriation, the growing sensitivity of the Supreme Court to its role as a social guarantor of civil rights also formed a basis for change in the standard of judicial review. As discussed in Chapter 2, throughout the 1970s and 1980s the Court gradually transformed its procedural authority into a moral one. It developed new standards against which it reviewed the state's compliance with substantive liberal values, compared to its earlier focus on legal formalities. For instance, in its 1982 decision in *Lubianker* (see more below), the Court severely criticized the norms of behavior by which expropriations were executed without granting landowners a right to a hearing and without stating a precise designated public use. For the first time, the Court called on the Knesset to amend the AO to reflect new standards of procedures for expropriation.[25] The Knesset did not amend the Ordinance. However, the Attorney General issued guidelines requiring the Minister of Finance to hear landowners before expropriation and specify the public use for which the land was designated.

While these developments suggest a trend toward an increased judicial protection of property rights, the politically sensitive nature of the expropriations that reached the Court in the 1970s and early 1980s dampened any awakening instinct in favor of judicial activism. Many of the post-1967 expropriation cases that came before the Court, relating to land both in Israel proper and in East Jerusalem, involved Jewish-owned land. The petitions in *Spolansky*, *Shmuelson*, *Lubianker* and *Makor* (on all of which see below) were all submitted by Jews who held parcels of land in East Jerusalem and in the Galilee that were part of larger tracts of land owned by both Jews and Arabs, and which had been designated for expropriation. All these cases were therefore complicated by wider security and strategic considerations that were at least partially extraneous to the legal issues but were nonetheless impossible to ignore. From the perspective of state officials (as well as of the Court), the crucial point

24 See Chapter 1 above.
25 H.C. 307/82, *Lubianker v. Minister of Finance*, 37(2) P.D. 141.

was to expropriate the entire area required for the establishment of large-scale Jewish residential developments and in this regard the identity of the expropriated owner was of secondary importance.

Demography, Security and the Expropriation of Jewish-owned Land

The circumstances surrounding expropriations in the 1970s in Arab East Jerusalem often raised the issue of whether land was expropriated for a legitimate public use. In *Spolansky*, for example, the petitioner owned seven and half dunams which constituted a small part of an expropriation of about 2,240 dunams in southern Jerusalem.[26] After the land was expropriated, Spolansky discovered that the expropriated land was intended in part for the construction of luxury homes. She petitioned the High Court of Justice to nullify that part of the expropriation on the grounds that it was an improper public use. In the alternative, she requested to be allowed to construct and sell the luxury homes herself.

The order at issue in *Spolansky* was issued in August 1970 as one of a series of eight expropriation orders covering 12,280 dunams of land. It was the largest expropriation carried out after 1967, covering about half of the total area of land that was expropriated in East Jerusalem between 1967 and 1991. Its purpose was to enable construction of 25,000 housing units in the city within a five-year period. Of the total area of 12,280 dunams expropriated, 10,000 belonged to Arabs, 1405 were owned by Jews and the rest were owned by the state (Felner 1995, 52-3).

Spolansky's land was located in an area on which the state planned to construct 5,000 housing units as part of a new Jewish neighborhood to be called East Talpiyot (see map 7.1) For the Government's strategic housing policy in Jerusalem to succeed in attracting Jews, it was held important to provide a high standard of living in the new neighborhood. As explained in an internal report prepared by the Jerusalem municipality:

> Growth in the Jewish population in Jerusalem stems from three factors: natural increase, the balance of migration between the city and other settlements in the country and the proportion of immigration which Jerusalem receives and its proportion of emigration. It is difficult to have any impact on natural increase, but some impact can be had on the balance of migration and the ability to attract new immigrants in three ways: first, the creation of housing sources to supply the needs of the forecast population, second, the creation of work places for the population in question and, three, assuring high quality of life by preserving the quality of the surrounding and providing superior services ... (Cited in Dumper 1997, 73)

Although the Court in *Spolansky* did not explicitly mention this report, the authorities' official policy could not but have an impact on its Court's ruling. Addressing the petitioner's claim that luxury housing was an abuse of expropriation powers, the Court held that the integration of a higher income population into a new neighborhood in which 80 percent of the housing units were intended for immigrants, young couples

26   H.C. 147/74, *Spolansky v. Minister of Finance*, 29(1) P.D. 421.

and low income groups was an appropriate public use. This broad reading of the public use requirement enabled the government to execute its strategic housing policy of attracting Jews to the annexed areas of Jerusalem.

The broad judicial interpretation adopted in *Spolansky* and subsequently in *Lubianker* and *Nusseibeh*[27] demonstrates the impact of the Jewish-Arab conflict in shaping Israel's expropriation jurisprudence. *Spolansky* and *Lubianker* involved expropriations from Jews who owned land in East Jerusalem, while *Nusseibeh* involved an Israeli Arab whose land was expropriated for a commercial center to be built in a Jewish neighborhood. In all three cases, the Court ignored the natural meaning of 'public use' in two respects. First, by approving Jewish residential housing as a lawful public use, the Court legitimated a policy which benefited the Jewish sector exclusively. Second, the Court's ruling in each case constituted an invitation to the government to trample private property rights whenever it believed it could identify a better use (whether public or private) for property currently held in private hands. In this second respect, the Court did not distinguish between Arabs and Jews. The issue of strategic planning in post-1967 Jerusalem usurped the owners' power to make decisions about the future of their property regardless of their identity.

Another effect of the broad reading of the concept of 'public use' was to prevent private landowners from developing their properties as an alternative to expropriation. The key decision on this point was the 1982 *Lubianker* case.[28] The land in question, 70 dunams in northeast Jerusalem near the Arab neighborhoods of Beit Hanina and Shuafat, was part of an expropriation order covering an area of 4,400 dunams. The purpose of this expropriation was to build the Jewish neighborhood of Pisgat Ze'ev, consisting of 12,000 residential units. In strategic terms, Pisgat Ze'ev allowed Israel to complete a continuous line of Jewish settlement in northeast Jerusalem from Neveh Ya'akov to the French Hill (see map 7.1).

The petitioners, a Jewish-owned construction company and certain Jewish individuals who also owned land in the region, claimed that the Minister of Finance had failed to carefully review the public worthiness of the expropriation. Writing for the Court, Chief Justice Shamgar took this opportunity to call upon the Knesset to amend the AO to provide a right to a hearing. The Court also reversed the existing legal precedents exempting the Minister from identifying with any degree of precision the designated public use, and that treated publication in the *Official Gazette* of the public use—no matter how vague and insubstantial—as conclusive evidence of the lawfulness of the Minister's decision. 'Like any other decision made by a governmental authority,' Justice Shamgar wrote, 'the Finance Minister's discretionary judgment must be reconcilable with the principles of administrative law [... It] should not be construed from the language of the AO that the Court will not examine, as is its wont, whether the Minister's considerations, including granting approval regarding the existence of a public purpose, are not tainted by a fundamental flaw, such as lack of good faith or arbitrariness.'[29] The AO, Chief

---

27 F.H. 4466/94, *Nusseibeh v. Finance Minister*, 49(4) P.D. 68. On this case see the discussion in Chapter 8 below.

28 H.C. 307/82, *Lubianker v. Minister of Finance*, 37(2) P.D. 141.

29 *Id.* at 145-7.

Justice Shamgar clarified, did indeed grant considerable autonomy to the Minister in determining the public use, but precisely because of this reason it was imperative that the public use should be stated publicly with a considerable degree of precision, so as to prevent abuse of power and to allow effective review by the courts.

While this language suggested that the Court might be willing to apply a higher standard of judicial review and possibly also to restrict the permissible scope of what constituted 'public use,' this was not the case. Chief Justice Shamgar stated that the objective of building 12,000 residential units for the Jewish population of Jerusalem was clearly a legitimate public purpose. The possibility that the public use, so defined, might be fundamentally flawed (in that it involved elements of private profit and was discriminatory with respect to the Arab population of Jerusalem) was not considered.[30]

The petitioners in *Lubianker* requested the Court to allow them to develop the housing project themselves. Their claim was that, given the harm to their property rights caused by the expropriation, a lesser measure of harm should be preferred to the extent possible. As may be recalled, this argument had previously been raised in *Spolansky* without success. However, the situation in *Lubianker* was different, as the main petitioner, the Lubianker Company, was a construction company. Furthermore, the facts of the case revealed the lack of good faith on the part of the authorities. For years it was Lubianker that had invested efforts in developing programs for the residential project on the area it owned. After it succeeded in getting the cooperation of the authorities, and particularly that of the ILA which managed state lands in the area, the project was approved, but Lubianker received an expropriation order requiring it to transfer its 70 dunams to the ownership of the state.

On the face of it, the Court's approval of the expropriation in *Lubianker* seems a simple question of balancing the needs of the state and the private entrepreneur. The state argued in court that it had no choice but to expropriate the land in order to carry out the large-scale development of 12,000 housing units. The argument was a reasonable one. The area of 4,400 dunams earmarked for the new neighborhood of Pisgat Ze'ev was divided among some 3,500 owners. It would obviously be impossible for so many owners to agree on a joint building project. Yet reading between the lines, the Court's refusal to allow Lubianker to undertake the construction on its 70 dunams appears to have been grounded in concerns relating to the fact that, of the 3,500 property owners affected by the expropriation, 2,872 were Arabs and only 630 were Jews. Chief Justice Shamgar did not refer explicitly to this fact, but justified the State's insistence on expropriating the area as a single unit:

> The state had to decide whether it can treat the 70 dunams of the petitioners [i.e., Lubianker] in a different manner than it would treat the rest of the 4,330 dunams included in the expropriation. The state answered the question negatively, and one cannot say that the answer is unreasonable or unfair, since obviously the authority can not discriminate between owners and prefer one over the other.[31]

---

30 *Id.* at 148. Before his appointment to the Supreme Court, Justice Shamgar had been the Attorney General (1968-75). In this capacity, he was in charge of the first cycle of expropriation in East Jerusalem (Cheshin et al. 1999, 41-4).

31 H.C. 307/82. *Lubianker v. Minister of Finance*, 37(2) P.D. 141, 151.

Granting all property owners (including the Arabs among them) the right to build on their land as part of the wider project would have undermined the goal of the expropriation, namely the creation of a new Jewish neighborhood as a means for ensuring Jewish demographic superiority in eastern Jerusalem. Furthermore, the political underpinnings of the housing project made timely completion a prime concern. Had the Court allowed Lubianker and the other petitioners to undertake the construction of the project themselves, this would have slowed down the development of the neighborhood considerably. It also entailed the risk that the project would not be completed due to financial problems of the individual owners, as often happens in the private sector.[32]

The centrality of Jewish-Arab demographic concerns in shaping the judicial approach toward Jewish landowners' claims to revoke the expropriation and pursue the housing project themselves was further illustrated in the extreme circumstances of the Har Homa affair. The neighborhood of Har Homa lies in southern Jerusalem between the Jerusalem Arab neighborhood of Beit Sahur, the West Bank village of Sur Bahir, and Bethlehem (see map 7.1). Unusually, most of the land expropriated in Har Homa was owned by a Jewish company, Makor Issues and Rights Ltd. Of the total area of 1,850 dunams expropriated, only 420 dunams were Arab owned.[33] In 1971, Makor acquired an area of 568 dunams of land on Har Homa. Makor prepared several plans for the development of the Har Homa residential neighborhood. According to the first plan submitted by Makor to the Jerusalem Development Authority, Har Homa was supposed to cover an area of 1,228 dunams. In 1990, in accordance with a directive of then Finance Minister Shimon Peres, requiring that the development of the neighborhood should be undertaken in collaboration with the JNF (which also owned a parcel of land in the area), Makor submitted a second plan. This time, the area designated for the Har Homa project was expanded to 1500 dunams. But the government ultimately preferred to expropriate the land, which it did in April 1991, at the same time further increasing the size of the neighborhood to 1,850 dunams.

---

32 While the Court in *Lubianker* treated Arabs and Jews equally in terms of approving the expropriation and not allowing the petitioners to develop the project themselves, the principle of equality was not maintained with respect to compensation. Subsequent litigation revealed that Lubianker itself, along with the other affected Jewish owners, had all reached a compensation agreement with the ILA, by which they received alternative land. The affected Arabs owners were not granted similar terms. C.A. 4541/91, *Lubianker v. Minister of Finance*, 48(3) P.D. 397.

33 H.C. 5601/94, *Abu Tir v. Prime Minister*, Takdin Supreme Court Precedents 1994(4) 246. It is ironic that the claim of discrimination in the practice of expropriation in Jerusalem reached the Supreme Court only in this case concerning the petition of Arab owners against the expropriation of their land in Har Homa. The Court rejected the claim, based on the fact that 'out of 1,850 dunams of expropriated land, only about 420 were under Arab ownership.' It concluded that 'expropriation is more damaging to Jewish than Arab landowners.' To the limited extent of the facts before it (and excluding, of course, the intended use of the expropriated land), this was true.

In 1992 Makor filed a petition to the High Court of Justice asking for revocation of the expropriation order and for permission to develop the Har Homa neighborhood.[34] Early in the adjudication process, the Court proposed that the landowners and the authorities reach a compromise. When negotiations between the parties broke down, the Court ruled in favor of the government, approving the Har Homa expropriation.

Because most of the land was already under Jewish ownership, the identity of the landowners was not a significant issue in the refusal of the government to allow Makor to undertake the project. What, then, were the reasons for the government's insistence on expropriating Har Homa and why did the Court approve this decision?

One plausible reason, mentioned above, may have been the concern that a private company, though eager to pursue the project, might encounter financial difficulties which, if they were to halt the project, could undermine the strategic goal of strengthening Jewish presence in Jerusalem and maintaining control of all of the city. Alternatively, a private construction company might decide for economic reasons to wait several years before actually developing the area.

A related question is why 1,850 dunams were expropriated instead of the 1,500 dunams originally earmarked for expropriation. Amir Cheshin, senior adviser on Arab community affairs and assistant to former Jerusalem mayor Teddy Kollek, has revealed that the extent of the expropriation was never a function simply of planning considerations. Rather, the motivation was to expropriate as much undeveloped land as possible in order to prevent Palestinian construction in the area. Publicly, Israel portrayed Har Homa as a typical development project of the kind any city in the world might carry out in order to guarantee housing supply for its residents.[35] Privately, however, Israeli officials made it clear that the goal of the Har Homa project was to contain Palestinian geographical expansion within the city limits In a letter dated April 4, 1992 from a senior municipal official to then Housing Minister Ariel Sharon, the writer explained that the expropriation of 1,850 dunams included several hundred dunams that could not even be developed. But this decision was reached 'in order to "straighten the line" of the Jerusalem municipal border ...' (Cheshin et al. 1999, 58-9).

The expropriation in Har Homa was intended, therefore, not only for the new neighborhood, but also to prevent Palestinian development. In this regard, the businesslike approach of the landowners did not fit the politics of the expropriation. A businessman would not acquire land he could not develop. Had the Court allowed private construction of the Har Homa project, this would not have enabled the Government to accomplish the real purpose underlying the expropriation, namely to ensure Jewish ownership over strategically located land as a means of preventing one

---

34 H.C. 3956/92, *Makor Issues and Rights Ltd. v. Prime Minister*, Takdin Supreme Court Precedents (1994)(4) 479.

35 The website of the Ministry of Foreign Affairs states the following: 'Jerusalem is a vibrant, growing city. The purpose of the Har Homa project is to alleviate the housing shortage of both Jewish and Arab residents of Jerusalem. As such it constitutes part of the overall municipal plan to construct 20,000 new housing units for the Jewish sector and 8,500 for the Arab sector—a ratio comparable that of the Arab populations in the city.' 'Building in Jerusalem', February 24, 1997 www.mfa.gov.il. The promise to build housing units for Arabs was never kept.

of Jerusalem's outlying Arab neighborhoods, Sur Bahir, from creating a contiguous demographic strip with Beit Sahur, a West Bank village.

Har Homa revealed yet another aspect of Israel's strategic policy of land expropriation, the taking of large tracts of land especially (but not exclusively) from Arabs as a means of ensuring Jewish territorial contiguity and the creation of land reserves for future development. The strategic importance of this policy was spelled out by a former Director for the Jerusalem District at the Minister of Housing:

> We have made enormous efforts to locate state lands near Jerusalem and we decided to seize them before... the Arabs have a hold there ... What is wrong with trying to get there before them? I know this policy is harmful to Jerusalem in the short run, but it guarantees living space for the future generation. If we don't do it today our children and grandchildren will travel to Jerusalem through a hostile Arab environment. (Cited in Dumper 1997, 117)

This policy posed a clear legal challenge. Delays between the stage of expropriation and the stage of implementation of a development are inherent to Israel's expropriation policy. Such delays were viewed by landowners as indicative of the fact that the expropriation did not have a substantive purpose in terms of its purported public use. The argument was that if construction was delayed, the state should return the land to its owner and should expropriate it only when development plans ripen. Return of the land to its owner would confer two benefits on the landowner. First, there was always a possibility that planning priorities would change and that the land would not ultimately be re-expropriated. Second, if the land was indeed re-expropriated, compensation would then be calculated on the basis of its value on the date of the re-expropriation. This was a point of considerable importance, given that Israeli real estate values have traditionally risen at higher rates than inflation.

The argument calling for return of the land because of delays in implementation of the public purpose for which the land was expropriated reached the Court in the 1979 *Shmuelson* case. The petitioner's land, located near the city of Safed in the Galilee, was expropriated in 1976 as part of the planned expansion of the city's Jewish population from 13,000 to 70,000 (a goal that has not been achieved to this day).[36] This planned expansion was one element of the 1975 New Development Plan for the Galilee, which was aimed at increasing the Jewish population in the region to 300,000 Jews by 1990. Three years after the expropriation, the landowner petitioned the Court to rescind the expropriation on the grounds that there was no government plan in existence for realizing the declared public purpose.

Addressing the petitioner's claim, the Court asserted the principle that if there was a delay in realizing the purpose for which the expropriation was carried out, or if the purpose itself was abandoned, the expropriation should be rescinded. Nevertheless, the Court did not intervene on behalf of the petitioner even though the planning authorities were unable to tell the Court when a plan for the development of Safed would be finalized. Justice Barak explained that:

---

36 According to the Central Bureau of Statistics, by the end of 2002 there were 26,400 inhabitants in the city of Safed, of whom 97 percent were Jews.

An expropriation undertaken in accordance with the [Land Acquisition] Ordinance should not be struck merely because at the time of its announcement an urban plan enabling its realization has not yet been filed. Occasionally it is impossible to avoid drawing up plans to determine the intended purpose of the various plots of land after the expropriation, when it is possible to lay out the plan for the entire [tract of] land. Nonetheless, an unreasonable delay in taking action after the expropriation on the part of the expropriating authority may under certain conditions result in the cancellation of the expropriation.[37]

Here again, the legal reasoning reflects the effect of Israeli land politics in shaping the outcome of the case involving land rights of Jews. Since Israeli expropriation policy is designed not only for building homes for Jews, but also for preventing Arabs from building *their* homes, as well as for preserving the land for future Jewish construction needs, delays in implementation of the public purpose are considered a public purpose in and of themselves, regardless of the identity, Arab or otherwise, of the affected owner.

Indeed, the plan prepared by Mayor Teddy Kollek in 1970 to settle East Jerusalem with Jewish families, which became the basis for Israeli housing policy in the city in the 1980s (and to a certain extent remains so to this day), heavily relied precisely on this element of expropriation as a tool in creating land reserves. Kollek proposed that the Government should hold a reserve of suitable land that could be used to respond to the housing, public building and industrial needs of the (Jewish) city for the next 10 to 12 years (Cheshin et al. 1999, 38). Following this proposal, the 2,240 dunams of land that were expropriated in East Talpiyot in 1970 resulted in the construction of a neighborhood which by 1995 covered only 1,800 dunams. The rest of the land was held in reserve. Similarly, 4,840 dunams were expropriated for the construction of Neve Ya'akov in 1968, but only 3,200 were used; in Pisgat Ze'ev only 7,500 housing units out of the total capacity of 12,000 were built by 1995, with an additional 4,000 built by 2002 (Cheshin et al. 1999, 60; B'Tselem, n.d., *Statistics on Land Expropriation in East Jerusalem*).[38] The unused land remained as open space, often forested, until such time as a need there would arise for additional construction in those Jewish neighborhoods (Cohen 1993).[39] The Court understood this rationale very well, as shown in *Nusseibeh*, which will be discussed in the next chapter.

Just as in the expanded interpretation of the public use requirement, the Court's rulings on the issues of development of the land by its current owners and delays in the public use realization have become general precedents. Because of the extensive expropriation policy in Jerusalem, which frequently reached the Supreme Court, the legal precedents that were created in this context guided the judiciary as a whole in the adjudication of cases that had no connection to Jerusalem or the Galilee, such as

---

37   H.C. 67/79, *Shmuelson v. State of Israel*, 34(1) P.D. 281, 285.

38   The Har Homa neighborhood was also planned to encompass some 6,500 housing units, with only 2,500 to be build on the first stage. As of the end 2002, there was no data as to the number of units built.

39   For an attempt to challenge the afforestation activity in East Jerusalem as an unlawful public use see, H.C. 704/85, *Aton v. Ministry of Finance*, Takdin – Supreme Court Precedents 1986(3) 14.

in the expansion of Ben-Gurion International Airport and a recreational project in Herzliya.[40] Land as a key element in Jewish-Arab relations in Israel thus had a broad impact on Israel's land expropriation jurisprudence. The Jewish-Arab land struggle shaped the Court's approach to property rights, not only in areas of high political and national tension such as Jerusalem and the Galilee, but created the pattern for expropriation adjudication throughout the country. The politics of land expropriation in Israel are, indeed, to a great extent a mirror of the politics of the Jewish-Arab struggle over land.

---

40 H.C. 3028/94, *Mehadrin Ltd. v. Minister of Finance*, 51(3) P.D. 85; H.C. 465/93 1135/93, *Tridet S.A., A Foreign Company Ltd. v. Local Planning and Building Commission of Herzliya*, 48(2) P.D. 622.

Chapter 8

The 1992 Constitutional Revolution: Continuity and Change

In 1992 Israeli law underwent a fundamental change. The Knesset enacted two Basic Laws which had the consequence of opening the door for judicial review. One of these two laws, Basic Law: Human Dignity and Liberty, guarantees property rights. The law states that there shall be no violation of rights under this Basic Law except by a law that befits the values of the State of Israel, enacted for a proper purpose, and to an extent no greater than is required.

Given the Basic Law's constitutional recognition of property rights, there was an expectation that the Supreme Court would increase the protection that it provided to landowners, and would place restrictions on expropriations. This, however, happened only to a limited extent—lip service rather than substance. Since 1992, land expropriation case law has contained repeated mention of ownership of private property as a newly established fundamental right under Israeli law. But this is as far as it goes. In the first decade following the enactment of the Basic Law, the Court intervened only once in an expropriation order. Even this unprecedented move was soon reversed in a subsequent hearing.[1]

This chapter assesses the impact of what is often referred to as Israel's constitutional revolution on the state's land expropriation jurisprudence. The chapter is composed of four sections. The first looks at the basics of the constitutional change that occurred in 1992. The second section examines the political and social context that shaped public discourse on private property and expropriations in the first years following the constitutional change. The third and fourth sections offer a sociolegal analysis of the Supreme Court's record in the first post-1992 decade.

The 1992 Constitutional Change

From independence until 1992, Israel's legal system operated without a constitution. This state of affairs was the result of political compromise. When the State of Israel was established, it seemed self-evident to all concerned that a constitution would soon be adopted. Indeed, the very first official document of the new state, the Declaration of Independence, expressly provided that the first elected parliament (referred to in the document as the Elected Constituent Assembly) would be elected under the

---

1   More recently, however, the Court has delivered two decisions which may be viewed as an important step toward strengthening the legal protection of property ownership, see Chapter 9 below.

provisions of the newly enacted constitution. A draft constitution was in fact drawn up and circulated, but political debate over its content made broad agreement on a single text impossible (Gavison 1985; Yanai 1990). The eventual compromise that was reached, known as the Harari Resolution, was that the Knesset would enact a constitution piecemeal, enacting Basic Laws from time to time. The idea was to initiate a process that would permit addressing constitutional issues one at a time, and whenever agreement on a particular issue was reached, it would be formalized and enacted as a Basic Law. Taken together, these Basic Laws would form the constitution. The nine Basic Laws that were passed prior to 1992 dealt mostly with the structure of government.[2] Procedurally, they were passed in the same manner as all other items of legislation, and for the most part, these Basic Laws do not enjoy any normative supremacy over regular laws.[3] None contains a bill of rights.

Basic Law: Human Dignity and Liberty and Basic Law: Freedom of Occupation were enacted in 1992. Together they covered some elements of what one would expect to find in a bill of rights. However, the 1992 Basic Laws did not explicitly provide for judicial review. Nevertheless, they did contain a section stating that all governmental authorities are bound to respect the rights enumerated in the Basic Laws. Both Basic Laws also include a general Limitation Clause that permits restricting such protected rights by a law that befits the values of the state, which is enacted for a worthy purpose, and which does not affect the protected rights disproportionately. The Limitation Clause states that human rights are to be protected according to the values of Israel as a 'Jewish and democratic state.'[4]

Soon after the enactment of the 1992 Basic Laws, scholars began describing their impact in terms of a constitutional revolution. Notable among these commentators was Justice Aharon Barak, who subsequently became the President of the Supreme Court in 1995 (Barak 1992). In writings and public speeches, Justice Barak expressed his view that the 1992 legislation granted human rights a preferred constitutional status and established the principle of judicial review.[5] Others, however, argued that

---

2   The nine Basic Laws are: Basic Law: The Knesset (1958, amended in 1985); Basic Law, Israel Lands (1960); Basic Law: The President of the State (1964); Basic Law: The Government (1968, replaced by a new version in 2001); Basic Law: The State Economy (1975); Basic Law: The Army (1976); Basic Law: Jerusalem, the Capital of Israel (1980); Basic Law: The Judiciary (1984); Basic Law: The State Comptroller (1988). English versions of the Basic Laws can be found at www.knesset.gov.il/laws.

3   One notable exception was Section 4 of Basic Law: Knesset, which provided that elections for the Knesset shall be 'general, national, direct, equal, secret and proportional' and that this Section can 'be changed only by a majority of the members of the Knesset', instead of a regular majority. In the 1969 case of *Berman v. Minister of Finance* (H.C. 231/73, 27(2) P.D. 758), the Court for the first time ruled that a law violating the equality of the elections (by not funding new parties) could only be enacted by special majority. Any law not enjoying this majority was invalid.

4   Section 8 of Basic Law: Human Dignity and Liberty; translated in www.knesset.gov.il/laws.

5   'Similar to the United States, Canada, France, Germany, Italy, Japan, and other Western countries, we now have constitutional protection of human rights. We too have the central chapter in any written constitution, the subject-matter of which is human rights ... we

the Knesset did not make a decision concerning the adoption of a constitution. Such a decision, including the desired form and scope of judicial review, still needed to be made (Gavison 1997; Gavison 2005; Landau 1996; see also Dorner 1999; Hofnung 1996a).

In a 1995 decision involving the interaction between a certain debtor relief law and Basic Law: Human Dignity and Liberty, the Supreme Court declared that the Basic Law had established the necessary constitutional framework for judicial review.[6] While holding that the statute in question was constitutional, the Supreme Court established the principle that a statute passed by the Knesset could be invalidated if it infringed upon property rights in a manner inconsistent with the Limitation Clause. To date, the Supreme Court has invalidated legislation only three times.

Basic Law: Human Dignity and Liberty states in Section 3 that 'there shall be no violation of the property of a person.' On its face, this provision would appear to affect the validity of numerous land expropriation decisions. However, Section 10 of the Basic Law grandfathers pre-existing legislation. This is crucial, as both the AO, which dates from 1943, and the 1965 Planning Law—the legal bases for almost all expropriations[7]—were, of course, enacted prior to 1992. Judicial review does not therefore apply to the provisions of these laws, which curtail property rights in ways that are otherwise unacceptable. What then is the relevance of the preferred constitutional status of private property in the context of land expropriation?

In the jurisprudence of rights that has developed since 1992, the Supreme Court has interpreted the grandfathering provision narrowly. In one of the leading cases on this issue, Chief Justice Barak held that, despite the fact that Basic Law: Human Dignity and Liberty explicitly exempts prior legislation from review, the application and interpretation of such legislation should be reconsidered to ensure that they are compatible with the new Basic Law to the extent possible.[8]

All in all, therefore, one could have expected Basic Law: Human Dignity and Liberty to improve the protection granted to property owners and to serve as a shield against violations of property rights. However, the Court has been slow to move in this direction. In the decade following the enactment of the Basic Law, the most noticeable change was in the Court's rhetoric, while its decisions continued to exhibit the old familiar deference to the executive branch. Explanations for this phenomenon should be sought in the social and political context of the 1990s that defined the margin of freedom enjoyed by the Supreme Court.

---

too have judicial review of statutes which unlawfully infringe upon constitutionally protected human rights' (Barak 1997).

6   C.A. 6821/93, *Bank Hamizrachi United Ltd. v. Migdal Communal Village*, 49(4) P.D. 221. The statute in question barred creditors of moshavim from applying to the courts to enforce repayment of debt, establishing instead a special entity with the authority to substantially reduce the amount of the outstanding debt.

7   See Chapter 1 above.

8   Cr. A. 2136/95, *Ganimat v. State of Israel*, 49(4) P.D. 589.

The Margin of Freedom of the Court

The legal and sociopolitical environment in which the Court exercises its authority defines the 'margin of appreciation' within which it functions.[9] This environment is dynamic, and the Court is not only affected by the changes to it but is also an agent of change itself. In this respect, there is no doubt that the passing of Basic Law: Human Dignity and Liberty granted the Supreme Court greater liberty to improve the lot of landowners. Yet in the years immediately following the enactment of the Basic Law, critical events in Jewish-Palestinian relations acted in an opposing direction, restricting the ability of the Court to exercise this new freedom.

Probably the most critical events for understanding the Court's record in the first decade of constitutional reform are the experience of the 1987 Palestinian uprising and the failure of the 1993 Oslo Accords. These experiences stoked the prevalent view that land was a qualitatively different form of property, one that should not be regarded purely from business or individualistic perspectives. In highly populated Arab areas such as the Galilee, and even more so in East Jerusalem, control of the land remained in the eyes of many a key component of the objective of ensuring the Jewish character of Israel and, indeed, the physical security of Jews in their land (Evans 2006; Kam 2003; Newman 2002).

The domestic security aspect of control over the land gained particular relevance in the early 1990s, when distinctions between Palestinian Arabs in the Occupied Territories and Israeli Arabs within Israel's pre-1967 borders became blurred in the popular mind (Bartal and Teichman 2004). The intifada, which started in December 1987 in a refugee camp in the Gaza Strip, quickly engulfed the whole Strip and the West Bank as well, and within ten days had reached Jerusalem, spreading rapidly through the Arab neighborhoods in the outer reaches of the city. Hundreds of Palestinian youths took to the streets, blocking roads, burning tires and waving Palestine Liberation Organization (PLO) flags.

Terror and unrest were not new in Jerusalem.[10] The intifada, however, was different. Before it erupted, rioting had tended to be localized, and involved relatively small groups of Palestinians protesters. During the intifada it spread over a wide area, and, in one form or another, involved a large proportion of the Palestinian population, particularly the young. The intifada effectively divided East and West Jerusalem for the first time since 1967. The old border between the two parts of the city was reestablished de facto as a result of the violence. Israelis living in West Jerusalem avoided Arab East Jerusalem. Their vehicles were regularly pelted with stones, bottles and firebombs when they ventured into Arab neighborhoods. Teddy

---

9   The 'margin of appreciation', a term often used by the Supreme Court (and by other Israeli courts) in their review of the actions of the other branches of government, refers to the degree of deference that the judiciary must exercise in reviewing the performance of state institutions. The margin of appreciation varies according to the relevant institution, its functions and its status. For example, the Israeli Supreme Court has marked the Knesset, in its legislative function, for special deference (Saban 2007).

10   In the 20 years following the 1967 war, 75 persons were killed and 880 were wounded in Palestinian terror attacks in Jerusalem. Most of the victims were Jews; a handful were tourists (Cheshin et al.1999, 160).

Kollek, the long-time Mayor of Jerusalem, believed that calm could be restored to the city. He believed that the violence that had broken out in Jerusalem as part of the intifada in the Territories was the direct result of the lack of government investment in improving the living conditions of the Arabs of East Jerusalem. 'If residents had better schools, bigger homes and more jobs, the conflict could have been avoided, or at least toned down considerably.' His efforts to convince the government to invest in the city's Arab neighborhoods were unsuccessful (Cheshin et al. 1999, 158-86). According to government officials, and particularly the security establishment, the uprising in Jerusalem had blurred the distinction between Israeli Arabs and Palestinians. It reinforced the widespread belief that Israeli Arabs constituted a security risk (Arian 1991; Bartal and Teichman 2004). As a result, the Government forged ahead in its policy of controlling the geographic limits of Arab neighborhoods and expanding the Jewish presence in the Arab areas of the city. But unlike previous years, after the intifada ended, no new expropriations were carried out, with the exception of Har Homa. Aware of the high external political cost of such action, the government pursued its demographic policies by less direct methods.

One such method was made public when a commission of inquiry appointed in 1993 under the pressure of Teddy Kollek revealed that during the 1980s and early 1990s, the Likud government had illegally transferred state funds to settlers in East Jerusalem. From Silwan and the Old City to the Mount of Olives and Wadi Joz, millions of dollars of state funds had been used to acquire Arab homes for Jewish settlers. In other cases, the settlement activists, with the support of state officials, took advantage of the outdated legislation (the Absentees' Property Law of 1950) to take over Arab homes in East Jerusalem and to evict their Arab residents.[11]

Another effect of the intifada was that it threatened to erase the so-called 'Green Line' separating Israel (and Israeli Arabs) from West Bank Palestinians. Although Israeli Arabs were, on the whole, careful not to be drawn into the violence, there were nonetheless a number of violent incidents inside Israel proper.[12] Furthermore, Arab Israelis identified explicitly and vocally with the uprising. Acts of solidarity included financial aid and the shipment of food and medical supplies, as well as demonstrations and strikes. The initial reaction of Israeli society, leaders and public alike, was shock and panic. A large part of the mainstream Israeli press reported that the intifada had already crossed, or was about to cross, the Green Line. Articles on the isolated violent incidents that occurred in which Israeli Arabs were involved warned that the intifada had reached Tel-Aviv, or Haifa, or that 'Nazareth [had become] like Gaza' (Al-Haj 2005, 192).

---

11 *Id.* at 211-24. In 1985, Israel spent some $12 million restoring Arab homes taken over by settlers. In 1987 the Israeli Housing Ministry paid approximately $800,000 to restore Arab buildings occupied by Jewish settlers in the Old City, and in 1991, over four years into the intifada, another allocation of approximately $1.1 million was approved for similar purposes. Overall, the inquiry committee traced some $8.2 million in state funds which were allocated to Jewish settlers in East Jerusalem.

12 Including clashes with the police in such central locations as Jaffa, Lod and Nazareth (Schiff and Ya'ari 1990).

The intifada was also a new experience in terms of its duration. Prior to the intifada, unrest would last at most a day or two and then die down. By contrast, the violence of the intifada lasted unabated for five years, during which 160 Israeli Jews (three quarters of whom were civilians) and more than 1,100 Palestinians died in clashes or other incidents both in the Occupied Territories (including East Jerusalem) and within the Green Line (B'Tselem, n.d., Statistics: Fatalities in the First Intifada).

The intifada subsided when peace negotiations between Israel and the Palestinians began at the Madrid Conference of 1991. It came to an official end with the signing of the Oslo Accords in September 1993, which required both sides to the conflict to recognize the other side and to reassess the territorial component of the conflict. On the Israeli side, the peace process called for a change in the perception of the role of territory as the ultimate safeguard.[13] Israel was asked to make territorial compromises. On the Palestinian side, the Oslo Accords required the relinquishment of their position with respect to the 1948 Arab refugees and of claims to a right to return to land under Israeli sovereignty (Ben-Ami 2005; Zureik 1996).

The Oslo Accords aroused the antagonism of extremists on both sides, who tried to derail the possibility of an agreement through violence. The massacre in Hebron of 29 Palestinians at prayer by Baruch Goldstein in February 1994 and a spate of Hamas suicide bombings in major Israeli cities epitomized the determination of hard-line Jews and Palestinians alike to halt the peace process. Despite the violence, Israel and the Palestinian Authority signed a second agreement, known as Oslo II in September 1995, under which Israel agreed to transfer major Arab cities in the West Bank (except for the Jewish enclave in Hebron) to the full responsibility of the Palestinian Authority.[14]

A month later, on November 4, 1995, Prime Minister Yitzhak Rabin was assassinated by a Jewish extremist. Rabin's assassination made the public realize that a deep division existed among Jewish Israelis as to whether a resolution to the Arab-Israeli conflict could be achieved. The 1996 election was won by the Likud candidate, Benjamin Netanyahu, who reverted to a traditional security doctrine in

---

13   Under the Oslo Accords, the interim arrangements were supposed to last for five years, during which time a permanent agreement was to be negotiated on issues such as Jerusalem, refugees, Israeli settlements, security and borders. Together with the general principles, the two sides signed Letters of Mutual Recognition. The Israeli government recognized the PLO as the legitimate representative of the Palestinian people and the PLO recognized the right of the State of Israel to exist and renounced terrorism, violence and its desire for the destruction of Israel.

14   The issue of control over land was dealt with in Oslo II by dividing the West Bank into three zones referred to as A, B and C. Zone A, which included the towns of Jenin, Nablus, Tulkarim, Kalkilya, Ramallah, Hebron and Bethlehem, would be under complete Palestinian control. In Zone B, which comprised 450 Palestinian towns and villages, Palestinians would control civilian matters, while Israel would retain control over security. Zone C, which encompassed the rest of the West Bank, accounting for approximately 70 percent of the land area of the West Bank, came under complete Israeli jurisdiction. It included uninhabited areas, Jewish settlements and military installations. The future status of the settlements and military installations was not dealt with in Oslo II.

which land figured largely as a geopolitical strategic asset. It was during Benjamin Netanyahu's tenure as Prime Minister that the decision was taken, in the face of considerable international opposition, to create the new Jewish neighborhood of Har Homa in Jerusalem.

When Labour won the 1999 elections, the Oslo process was put back on track. Labour, under the leadership of Ehud Barak, promised to press ahead with peace negotiations as a continuation of Rabin's legacy. In July 2000, Barak and Arafat met to negotiate a permanent status agreement at Camp David. But the summit ended in failure, and three months later, on September 29, 2000, the Palestinian leadership initiated the second intifada (also known as the El-Aqsa Intifada). The collapse of the peace negotiations and the renewed violence brought down the government of Ehud Barak (Rynhold and Steinberg 2004). Israelis once again turned to the defense paradigm, which emphasized territorial control as the solution to their security concerns.

In addition to the events relating to the Israeli-Palestinian conflict, another characteristic that defined the sociopolitical environment in which the Court exercised its authority in land expropriation cases after 1992 was the sudden increase in immigration. Starting at the end of 1989, a wave of immigrants from the former Soviet Union began to arrive to Israel. By the end of 1999, some 900,000 had arrived (Yaffe and Tal, 2001).[15] The timing of this wave of immigration was opportune from an Israeli perspective. The tension and hostility between Jews and Arabs that resulted from the first intifada highlighted the importance of immigration, which was seen as a means of alleviating demographic concerns and accelerating economic growth (Razin and Sadka).[16] Israeli leaders spoke of the 1990 wave of immigration enthusiastically. As Prime Minister Yitzhak Shamir put it to a Likud gathering in Tel-Aviv on 14 January 1990:

> Just when many among us were saying that time is working against us, time has brought us this aliya and has solved everything. In five years we won't be able to recognize the country. Everything will change—the people, the way they live—everything will be bigger, stronger. The Arabs around us are in a state of disarray and panic. A feeling of defeat shrouds them, because they see that the intifada does not help. They cannot stop the natural streaming of the Jewish people to their homeland. (Cited in Jones 1996, 57)

With similar enthusiasm, then Housing Minister Ariel Sharon declared that '[we] must use this mass aliya to solve a number of national problems. We have the opportunity to change the demographic situation in Israel, not only numerically, but also in terms of presence in the field.' The need to provide assistance to the immigrants and to

---

15   Soviet immigrants form the largest immigrant community in Israel. At the beginning of 2000, this community was estimated at 1.1 million persons, and it constituted 18 percent of the total population of Israel. It is thought that about 40 percent of the immigrants from the former Soviet Union who arrived in the 1990s are not Jews. On the social and cultural implications of this phenomenon, which to a certain extent is turning Israel into a multi-national country, see Lustick (1999); Weiss (2001).

16   The intifada had led to a decline in Arab employment in Israel and losses to Israel's economy.

help them settle gave rise to the formulation of various policies (Dominitz 1997). A particular challenge was dealing with the acute housing shortage. Urban and regional planners were directed to authorize and facilitate the construction of hundreds of thousands of additional housing units, as well as to expand physical infrastructure and the public services as necessary. The massive influx of immigrants who arrived in 1990-91—close to 400,000 people—created a crisis situation. Israel's population grew by 7.6 percent in this two-year period—the largest influx of immigrants relative to population size of any advanced economy (Alterman 2002, 12).[17] In subsequent years, the rate declined to 50,000 to 80,000 immigrants annually. But even this relatively low rate was still four to seven times higher than the rate of immigration in the 1980s.

As indicated below, the Government became deeply involved in the planning and construction of housing for the immigrants, and in order to finance this expenditure on absorption it raised the value-added tax by three percentage points in a period of less than one year. Not surprisingly, given the history and political culture of the country, the crisis atmosphere of the 1990s was not conducive to strengthening of individual property rights in land. Looking at the history of Basic Law: Human Dignity and Liberty, it is telling in this respect that the first draft of the Basic Law entirely overlooked the right to private property. Property rights were added to the Basic Law at a later stage, creating an awkward structural split between the protection of the rights to life, body and dignity in Section 2 and the protection of property in Section 3. The 1992 constitutional change, to the extent that it elevated the normative status of property rights, was thus in many respects more of a utopian aspiration than the reflection of a dominant national value.

These political, social and cultural dimensions that compromised the discourse of landownership rights in the 1990s must have posed a test for the ability of the Supreme Court to function as an effective source of democratic supervision over land expropriation. True, a major legal move was taken in 1992 with the formal granting of constitutional protection to property rights. But outside the courtroom, the principle of private landownership had to take a back seat to relations between Jews and Palestinians, the social and economic pressures of mass immigration and the history of socialist Zionism.

In the next two sections, I will situate the Supreme Court's post-1992 record land expropriation cases in the context of the conditioned ability of courts to pursue social change. I will argue that the technique of separating rhetoric from substantive decisions reflected the political weakness of the Court, while at the same time elevating and developing a legal culture of the protection of private property. The Court refrained from declaring expropriations to be illegal in order to avoid damaging its own authority. Yet by recognizing (as it regularly did in these years) private property as a valued right deserving of protection, it strengthened the status of private property as one of the symbols of Israeli democracy, and assisted in

---

17 Between 1990 and 1996, Israel's population increased by more than 15 percent. Such an enormous inflow would be equivalent to nearly 40 million immigrants to the United States (as against the five million actually admitted during this same period (Kleiman 1997, 164).

bringing about a gradual change in the hegemonic culture of emphasizing security considerations in the context of Jewish land control.

Nusseibeh I and II

It was perhaps unfortunate for the development of the new land expropriation jurisprudence that the first case to reach the Supreme Court in the post-1992 era involved land in the emotionally and politically charged setting of East Jerusalem. Nusseibeh was the owner of a small parcel of land, 610 square meters, located in the Arab neighborhood of Sheikh Jarrah. In 1968, Nusseibeh's land was expropriated along with other parcels of land situated along the old line of demarcation between East and West Jerusalem. The total area expropriated in 1968 in various parts of Jerusalem amounted to 4,485 dunams. The purpose of this extensive expropriation was to enable the construction and development of several new Jewish neighborhoods, including Ramot Eshkol, Givat Hamivtar, the French Hill and Ma'alot Dafna.

Despite the expropriation, Nusseibeh's land lay undeveloped for 21 years. In 1989, the Jerusalem municipality approved a new plan for a commercial center to be built on the tract originally owned by Nusseibeh and on three other adjoining plots that had been expropriated at the same time as his. This plan was subsequently abandoned, and in 1991, Nusseibeh petitioned the Court to invalidate the 1968 expropriation on the grounds that the authorities had abandoned the purpose for which his land had been taken. Alternatively, he argued, he should be allowed to develop the commercial center himself.

In 1994, the Court accepted the petition by a majority of two to one, and ordered the return of the land to Nusseibeh.[18] It was the first time that the Supreme Court had ever invalidated an expropriation order issued under the AO.[19] This was a dramatic break from the traditional non-interventionist approach of the Court. According to Justice Levin who wrote the majority opinion, the unlawfulness of the expropriation lay in the excessive delay in implementing the public purpose. The long period of time that had passed since the intention to expropriate was first officially announced, and during which no practical steps had been taken either to wrest actual possession of the land from its owner or to put into effect the intended public purpose, tipped the balance of interests against the state and in favor of the private landowner. The circumstances made plain 'that the authorities [had] no urgent need which the land was intended to fill.' Justice Maza concurred, focusing on the public use requirement. A commercial center might be considered a permissible public purpose, Justice Maza explained, as self-sufficient neighborhoods require designated areas for public facilities such as schools, parks and commercial centers. Nevertheless, in the case at hand, the state had failed to show that it planned to use Nusseibeh's land to serve the commercial needs of a specific new Jewish community. According to Justice Maza,

---

18   H.C. 5091/91, *Nusseibeh v. Minister of Finance*, Takdin – Supreme Court Precedents 1994(3) 1765.

19   Prior to *Nusseibeh*, the Court had invalidated an expropriation order only once, in a case that involved the Planning Law. *See* in Chapter 1 above the discussion on H.C. 174/88, *Amitai v. Local Planning and Building Commission, Central Region*, P.D. 42(4) 89.

the Basic Law's requirement that property rights should not be injured beyond what was necessary placed a burden on the state to prove the existence of specific public needs. Furthermore, Justice Maza interpreted the Basic Law to require a reappraisal of the existing doctrine that allowed the authorities to change the intended use of the expropriated land. 'The existing case law cannot be reconciled with the new constitutional status of property rights,' he stated.

Justice Or's minority opinion displayed a position consistent with the traditional deferential approach. 'The political sensitivity of the expropriation policy in Jerusalem,' he wrote, 'inevitably entails a slow process of construction of new Jewish neighborhoods.' In this light, a 20-year delay in taking action to realize the public purpose of creating suitable infrastructure for a major new Jewish residential construction project in the unified city should not be viewed as abandonment of the public purpose, nor as an unjustified infringement of property rights. According to Justice Or, the question of whether the authorities had begun to realize the public purpose ought to be examined in relation to the entire area expropriated, not solely in the narrow context of the specific plot of land at issue. In fact, other plots included in the original act of expropriation were already under development. Addressing Nusseibeh's alternative proposal to undertake the construction of the commercial center himself, Justice Or maintained that the facts of the particular case justified expropriation, and that the project would be better implemented if all four parcels were sold to a single entrepreneur, rather than if Nusseibeh and the three other owners were permitted to undertake the project (*cf.* Haviv-Segal 1998).

Nusseibeh I was groundbreaking. But the decision did not last long as a valid precedent. The state applied for and was granted a rehearing.[20] In 1995, *Nusseibeh II* reversed the holding of *Nusseibeh I*, the Supreme Court now affirming the expropriation of Nusseibeh's land by a vote of four to three.[21] Justice Goldberg, joined by Chief Justice Shamgar and Justices Or and Tal, adopted the reasoning of Justice Or's earlier minority opinion. The new minority opinion by Justices Dorner, Levin and Maza reiterated the majority opinion of *Nusseibeh I*.

Both the majority and the minority acknowledged that the new constitutional status of property rights granted by the Basic Law required a change in the balance of interests between the individual and the public. In the words of Justice Dorner:

> Israeli law inherited the [AO] from the days of the British mandate, and [it] remains, in its character, a product of its time. It is based on principles that characterized a colonial government, such as the interests of the monarchy, and as a consequence bears no relation to the values of democracy or the basic rights of the individual. While prior to 1992 the democratic character of Israel influenced to a degree the interpretation of the [AO] in its provisions, the constitutional revolution demands further improvements.[22]

---

20 Israeli law provides that the Supreme Court may revisit a case previously heard by three Justices. Such a rehearing, conducted before a wider panel, may be justified if the ruling is inconsistent with previous decisions or if the Court deems that the importance, complexity or novelty of its ruling justifies such a rehearing. The decision on whether to rehear a case is the Supreme Court's alone.

21 F.H. 4466/94, *Nusseibeh v. Minister of Finance*, P.D. 49(4) 68.

22 *Id.* at 86.

The minority, and Justice Dorner in particular, went a step further and called for enforcing a new interpretation of the AO. In a lengthy, forceful minority opinion, Justice Dorner identified three bases for concluding that the particular expropriation violated the constitutional requirement of minimal injury to property. First, she proposed an innovative interpretation, according to which a commercial project did not constitute a permissible public purpose for which land could be compulsory taken. 'In my opinion even the construction of a commercial center in a built-up neighborhood does not meet the definition of a "public use" justifying expropriation. The fulfillment of such needs should be left to market forces.' Second, even if the commercial development could be considered a legitimate public purpose, there was no reason why Nusseibeh should not be allowed to reap the financial rewards. The land in question was a small plot, and the petitioner could easily develop it himself. Finally, the long delay in implementing the public purpose was additional ground for nullifying the expropriation order. 'A delay in realizing the purpose for which the expropriation was carried out upsets the requisite balance between the harm caused to the property owner and the benefit to the public. A delay in executing the public purpose casts doubt as to the existence of a definite and specific public purpose.'

It may be that the makeup of the Supreme Court contributed to the outcome in *Nusseibeh II*. All the Justices who reheard the case were Jewish, and all except for Justices Dorner and Tal had been on the Court for many years.[23] The veteran Justices may have been accustomed to applying the broad pre-1992 interpretation of the AO, while Justice Dorner, appointed to the Supreme Court as recently as 1994, brought a fresh perspective to the issue. By contrast, Justice Tal, a religious Jew, was known for his strong identification with the interests of Israel as a Jewish state. That being said, it should be noted that two veteran Justices, Maza and Levin, joined Justice Dorner's dissenting opinion. It should further be noted that some of the longer-serving Justices joined in a groundbreaking decision that same year which interpreted Basic Law: Human Dignity and Liberty as granting the Court the power of judicial review over legislation.[24]

Another factor that may have contributed to *Nusseibeh I* being reversed was the concern of the Justices about potential negative reactions to the original ruling. Given the politically charged issue of Jerusalem and the five-year-long spate of violence in the city (1987-93), it may well be that the Court was concerned that reaffirming *Nusseibeh I* would result in a weakening of its public legitimacy. The decision by the Jerusalem municipality to approve a new plan for a commercial center on Nusseibeh's land was taken in 1989, in the middle of the first intifada. Two years later, the expropriation of 1850 dunams in Har Homa was pursued with the strategic goal of preventing the Jerusalem Arab neighborhoods of Beit Sahur and Sur Bahir from linking up to Bethlehem in the West Bank.

---

23   The first appointment of a non-Jew to the Supreme Court was in 2004 when Salim Joubran, a Christian Arab, was elevated to the Supreme Court.

24   C.A. 6821/93, *Bank Hamizrachi United Ltd. v. Migdal Communal Village*, 49(4) P.D. 221. That case dealt with a law restricting the freedom to own property, but did not deal with property rights in land.

However, it is important to emphasize that the Har Homa expropriation could not have been pursued had the land in question been mainly Arab-owned. The tense political reality in Jerusalem of the early 1990s (before the Oslo Accords were signed) did not permit another large-scale taking of Arab land. In Har Homa, the majority of the land was in fact Jewish-owned. The state could therefore use its expropriation powers to create new facts on the ground in East Jerusalem. By contrast, although the Nusseibeh case involved Arab-owned land, it did not involve a new expropriation. The municipality sought to utilize reserves of land that had been created in 1968. As mentioned in the previous chapter, an integral component of Israel's expropriation strategy in Jerusalem and in the Galilee had historically been to expropriate more land than was needed for immediate purposes, leaving the remainder undeveloped until the need for it arose.

This policy was challenged in *Aton*, which also involved land in Jerusalem and was decided in 1986, almost a decade before *Nusseibeh I*.[25] The land in question, some 500 dunams, was expropriated in 1970 as part of a larger expropriation of 2,240 dunams nearby the Arab village of Sur Bahir. On the majority of this expropriated land the state constructed the Jewish neighborhood of East Talpiyot. A small part, however, was left unused. Then, in the mid-1980s, presumably in response to illegal Arab construction in Sur Bahir which expanded the village in the direction of East Talpiyot, a joint decision was taken by the Jerusalem municipality, the ILA and the JNF to turn the undeveloped area into woodland. This particular use had, from the perspective of the planners, the merit of blocking further illegal Arab construction, thus preserving the original function of the expropriation. In addition, it would allow a swift and politically painless rezoning of the land for urban development purposes to relieve demographic pressure in East Talpiyot in the future. When the original Arab owner petitioned the Supreme Court for the return of his land, claiming that the new land use was incompatible with the original public use designation, and that the expropriation had been carried out in bad faith, the Court dismissed the petition, holding that the original public use definition of 'developing unified Jerusalem' included not only brick and mortar, but also the provision of green spaces for the city (Cohen 1993, 134-48).

Given that both creation of land reserves and delays in implementing designated land use played central roles in Israel's strategy for preserving the Jewishness of Jerusalem, *Nusseibeh I*, which held that the expropriation was illegal, posed a clear challenge to the prevailing consensus. Although judicial intervention along the lines of *Nusseibeh I* was in the spirit of Basic Law: Human Dignity and Liberty, in the political reality of Jewish-Palestinian relations in the early 1990s, this opinion conflicted with the perceived strategic needs of the state, and therefore was bound to be either overridden, ignored or, as ultimately happened, reversed. Furthermore, *Nusseibeh I* was decided in 1994, less than a year after the signing of the Oslo Accords which officially ended the first intifada (1987-93). But by *Nusseibeh II* in 1995, prospects for peace with the Palestinians had dimmed and the focus was once again on the dangers to security posed by Palestinians. The spate of Hamas suicide

25 H.C. 704/85, *Aton v. Ministry of Finance*, Takdin – Supreme Court Precedents 1986(3) 14.

bombing had left the majority of Israelis with the impression that it would be quite some time before the country's borders were safe.[26]

Another factor that may have influenced the reversal of *Nusseibeh I* was the housing shortage created by the wave of immigrants from the former Soviet Union. Between 1990 and 1999, the construction of close to half a million apartments was completed, meeting the demands of newcomers as well as those of long-time residents (Carmon 2002). The perception that it was the duty of the state to ensure adequate housing for its new citizens, rather than to let the market respond to the crisis in its own time and in its own manner, guided the government in its actions. In 1991, the Minister of Interior added 'housing for immigrants' to the list of permissible public purposes for land expropriation identified in Section 188 of the Planning Law. Coincidently, emergency regulations were issued and a special law enacted to speed planning approvals and to provide for shorter bureaucratic time frames for construction projects.[27] About 50 percent of the housing starts in 1990-94, and 30 percent of the housing starts in 1995-99, fell into the category of 'public housing,' which is to say that their construction was executed or at least initiated by the government.[28] The majority of these housing units were in the ex-urban periphery, due to both population dispersal goals and the availability of land for construction on the scale needed for housing the immigrants. However, social and political changes did not allow for the direct transfer of immigrants to development towns as had been done in the 1950s. Instead, attempts were made to lure immigrants to peripheral areas using financial incentives. Buyers of homes in outlying regions of the country or in areas designated by the government as 'national priority zones' were offered mortgages on more advantageous terms than the ones offered to buyers of homes in the center of the country. Jerusalem was defined for such purposes as a 'national priority zone,' although it was lower on the scale of national priorities than the Negev or the Galilee, judging by the benefits offered to home buyers.

About 20,000 immigrants settled in Jerusalem in 1989-91, a number that rose to 53,000 by the end of the decade (*Statistical Yearbook of Jerusalem* 2001). Jerusalem was the fourth city in the country in terms of the number of immigrants that it absorbed. The high cost of housing in the western neighborhoods of the city drove many of the immigrants to look for apartments in the Jewish neighborhoods in East Jerusalem, creating demographic pressure for public facilities in that part of the city and an undercurrent of social and political pressure on the Supreme Court to reverse its *Nusseibeh I*.

---

26   In the five years following Oslo (1993-98), 256 Israelis (civilians and security personnel) were killed, a number that exceeded by more than 50 percent the number of Israeli casualties during the five years of the intifada. During that same period, 400 Palestinians were killed by Israeli soldiers and civilians. See B'Tselem, n.d., *Statistics: Fatalities in the First Intifada.*

27   These regulations, called the Emergency Plans for Construction of Housing Units, 1990, replaced the 1990 Planning and Building Procedures (Interim) Law, which sought to achieve the same objective of shortening procedures by establishing special planning legislation (Alterman 2002).

28   Compared to 28 percent of the housing starts in 1980-89.

Finally, it should be noted that *Nusseibeh II* may also be related to the constitutional status of the Court, which, despite the fundamental changes of the 1990s is still uncertain. While the constitutional change has introduced judicial review of new legislation, the judiciary's ability to hold in check the power of the parliamentary majority is in fact restricted. For example, Basic Law: Freedom of Occupation has been amended three times since it was first enacted in 1992. With few exceptions, under current law, a simple parliamentary majority is all that is required in order to amend a basic law. This is not to say that in practical political terms, amending the Israeli constitution is as easy as the formal requirements for amending it would suggest. Nevertheless, the simplicity of the procedure highlights the precariousness of the constitutional safeguards of civil rights in Israel, as well as the limitations on the powers of the Supreme Court itself. The controversial new standards that were established in *Nusseibeh I* could have led to the introduction of legislation that was hostile to the Court, and to executive sanctions against it. [29]

Facing these considerations, the majority in *Nusseibeh II* deferred to the authorities, noting the Court's limited ability to bring about social change in this highly charged area. Yet the liberal arguments in favor of a change in the existing land expropriation law that were articulated in *Nusseibeh I* remained untouched in *Nusseibeh II*. This liberal rhetoric was a signal of what the Court would have done based on the new Basic Law had the sociopolitical conditions been different. It also was a first step in developing a constitutional discourse of property rights that would allow such a change to take place.

After *Nusseibeh*: The Rulings in *Mehadrin* and *Mahul*

Nusseibeh II was not the only post-1992 expropriation case in which the Supreme Court refrained from intervening. Its decision in the controversial Har Homa case was equally characteristic of its inclination to pursue change only to the extent practical, making up for the rest in its rhetoric. This tendency was by no means limited to cases involving Jerusalem. Another such case was *Mehadrin*.[30]

Mehadrin involved an agricultural company that leased land under a long-term contract from the ILA. The company received a notice of expropriation that designated its land (as well as other adjoining tracts) for the expansion of Israel's international airport. Mehadrin's land was to be used to build a conference center, with offices, banks, shops, restaurants and parking areas. Mehadrin claimed that such uses were not permissible public purposes, or that, in the alternative, it had a right to undertake the commercial development itself. The arguments it presented in

---

29   A 1991 study on the sources of Israel's Supreme Court legitimacy indicates that the spirit of Americanization, that is, respect for a discourse of individual rights, was confined to the Jewish community. The Jewish majority was reluctant to include the Arab-Palestinian minority in its liberal discourse of individual rights. The Court was perceived as a Jewish institution that was supposed to grant rights to Jewish litigants. Negative and mixed relations were traced in relation to specific decisions perceived as granting the Palestinians procedural or substantive rights (Barzilai et al. 1994).

30   H.C. 3028/94, *Mehadrin Ltd. v. Minister of Finance*, 51(3) P.D. 85.

its petition reflected the post-1992 understanding that expropriation should not be exercised unless absolutely necessary.

Writing for the Court, Justice Goldberg quoted approvingly from the opinion of Justice Or in the 1992 Har Homa case:

> The fact that expropriation entails a severe harm to property should be before the court when it comes to interpret the provisions of the [AO]. Thus, if it is possible to reach the same result of fulfilling public needs without expropriation, this route should be chosen. For example, if there is a public need to build a residential housing project and the owner can undertake the project in an appropriate matter and timeframe, expropriation should not be considered necessary.[31]

Rhetoric aside, in practice there was very little change. The Court rejected the lessee's request to develop the project, concluding that it would be more efficient to allow the authorities to expropriate the land and transfer it to private developers.

Justice Goldberg also wrote the majority opinion in *Mahul*, handed down a year later in 1996.[32] *Mahul* involved Arab-owned agricultural land located in the western Galilee near the city of Acre. The land had been designated for expropriation in 1976. At the time, no specific public purpose was identified. In 1987, the landowner petitioned for the revocation of the expropriation order on the grounds that his land had not been put to any use. In the course of the subsequent judicial proceedings, the State revealed that the land was earmarked for Acre's future development needs, and that it could be used for any one of a number of municipal projects, such as providing industrial facilities, expanding the road network or satisfying the housing, hostelry or recreational needs of the city. The landowner agreed to withdraw his petition, reserving his right to petition the Supreme Court at a later date if there was further delay in implementing the public purpose. In 1995, the landowner approached the Supreme Court for the second time, claiming that the authorities had still not taken action to implement the public purposes for which his land had been expropriated, and asked that the expropriation be set aside. In their response, the authorities stated that in light of the recent wave of immigration, there had been a decision taken to change the use of the expropriated land, on which 4900 housing units for immigrants would now be built. But this plan too was left unimplemented because of the objections of the National Planning Council. The Ministry of Construction and Housing then changed the plans yet again, designating part of the land for a hospital and a cemetery. Mahul argued before the Supreme Court that a delay of nearly 20 years in implementing the public purpose indicated that the authorities had abandoned the public use for which the land was taken. He also pointed to the fact that the public use designation had been changed twice, which suggested that the authorities had never had in mind a definite public use for his land.[33]

Writing for the Court, Justice Goldberg opened his opinion with a long exposition of the irreparable harm that expropriation causes to property rights. Nonetheless, he

---

31 H.C. 3956/92, *Makor Issues and Rights Ltd. v. Prime Minister*, Takdin Supreme Court Precedents (1994)(4) 479 (par. 6).

32 H.C. 2739/95, *Mahul v. Minister of Finance*, 50(1) P.D. 309.

33 *Id.* at 314-19.

held, the 20-year delay in implementing the purpose for which Mahul's land was taken was reasonable, given the difficulties the authorities had encountered in getting the necessary approvals for the project. Justice Goldberg also dismissed Mahul's claim regarding the authority's abandonment of the original public use. 'Unless the authority acts in bad faith,' he wrote, 'the Court should not restrict the authority's ability to adapt the use of the expropriated land to changing public needs.'

Justice Maza, while agreeing with Justice Goldberg's legal conclusion that the Court should not intervene on the side of the petitioner, wrote a concurring opinion asserting the need for greater judicial supervision by the Supreme Court over changes in public use designations. Consistent with his opinion in *Nusseibeh I*, Justice Maza stated that when the public purpose for which the land was expropriated ceased to exist, the expropriation should be rescinded, and the land returned to its owners. There was one exception, he believed, namely, when the changes to the original public use were the result of objective difficulties such as land use constraints. In such cases, the authorities' redefinition of the public use should not be regarded a misuse of power, since it had not been their intention to 'bank' the land for future use.[34]

The tensions inherent in *Mehadrin* and *Mahul* reflect, in my opinion, both the impact of *Nusseibeh I* and Har Homa decisions that preceded them, and a concern that a pro-landowner precedent might have serious repercussions for Jewish demography and geographic expansion. Obviously, the Court could not set different precedents for Jerusalem and the densely populated Arab Galilee on the one hand, and for the rest of the country on the other. The Court therefore stepped back in a case like *Mehadrin* to avoid confrontation in future cases.[35] Still, the Court was comfortable leaving untouched the liberal arguments in favor of a change in the existing land expropriation law.

As will be shown in the next chapter, the use of liberal arguments in the Court's rhetoric not only helped it avoid confrontation with the legislature and the executive, but also created a strengthened legal discourse of liberal values that the Court itself, as well as the legislature and the executive, would eventually no longer be able to ignore.

---

34 *Id.* at 327-30.

35 Although not stated explicitly, a perceived demographic threat was presented in *Mahul*, relating to the Arab population of Acre, which was almost entirely Muslim and which constituted roughly 25 percent of the population of the city. The proposed development of 4900 units for immigrants was intended to strengthen the Jewish majority in the city.

Chapter 9

New Millennium, New Directions?

In 2001, nine years after enactment of Basic Law: Human Dignity and Liberty, the Supreme Court delivered two decisions that narrowed the scope of some of the more troubling provisions of Israeli expropriation law. In *Holzman*, the owner's entire parcel of land had been expropriated in order to construct a sports facility.[1] In accordance with the 1965 Planning Law, the local planning authority compensated the landowner to the extent of 60 percent of the value of the land. The owner successfully challenged the limited compensation in the Haifa District Court. The local authority appealed, and an expanded panel of seven Justices unanimously approved the lower court's decision, ruling that the 40 percent reduction in the amount of compensation was unlawful. Writing for the Court, Justice Dorner explained that where the landowner's property was expropriated in its entirety, the reduced level of compensation conflicted with Basic Law: Human Dignity and Liberty, which granted property a superior normative status. In such circumstances, clearly, the landowner did not gain any benefit from the public use to which the expropriation was put, since he was left with no property to which any betterment could attach. The effect was to shift a disproportionate share of the economic burden of local public services to an arbitrarily selected landowner, harming the individual beyond what was strictly necessary, thus failing the Limitation Clause test. *Holzman* thus put an end to a long-standing practice, sanctioned by the Supreme Court in the 1979 *Feitzer* decision.[2]

The second case, *Karsik*,[3] focused on an issue that had previously been raised in *Nusseibeh* and *Mahul*, as well as in pre-1992 cases such as *Spolansky*, *Avivim*, *Ge'ulat Hakrach* and *Banin*. In all these cases, the Court had let stand the authorities' right to leave the expropriated land unused or to pursue a different project from the one originally planned. *Karsik* involved 137 dunams in the vicinity of the town of Hadera, which had been expropriated in the late 1950s for use as an army training ground. The land was used for the designated purpose until 1993 when, as part of its wider response to the wave of immigration from the former Soviet Union, the government decided to relocate the military facility and to construct a housing project on the land.

Basing their arguments on the 1992 legislation, the petitioners, the heirs of the original owners, petitioned the Court to have the property returned to them, on the grounds that the public need for which the land had originally been expropriated had been abandoned, and that the construction of residential housing units should not be

---

1   C.A. 5546/97, *Local Planning and Building Commission Kiryat Ata v. Holzman*, 55(4) P.D. 629. The plaintiff in this case was the author's father.
2   See the discussion in Chapter 3.
3   H.C. 2390/96, *Karsik v. State of Israel*, 55(2) P.D. 625.

considered a public need. In the alternative, the petitioners demanded compensation in an amount reflecting the land's current value. Sitting as the High Court of Justice, an extended panel of nine Justices reviewed the petition and unanimously concluded that an expropriation order could remain in effect only for as long as the land was used for the purpose for which it had originally been expropriated. Once that purpose ceased to exist, the land should be returned to the original owner.[4] The decision fell short of ordering the return of the land to the petitioners. The Court left open the question of whether *Karsik* should take retroactive effect, even with respect to the *Karsik* petitioners themselves, leaving this highly charged question to the Knesset to decide.[5]

These decisions, taken one year apart, overturned long-standing legal doctrines, and hint at the wider rethinking by Israeli Jewish society of the Zionist ideology of public land ownership. Indeed, the late 1990s witnessed a dramatic change in the dominant Zionist narrative of land as a national asset that should not be manipulated for personal profit. The underlying cause of the changes was, once again, the housing shortage created by the influx of immigrants from the former Soviet Union. Their arrival created pressure to rezone agricultural land for residential use. This was particularly the case with respect to the numerous agricultural communities located near the Tel-Aviv metropolitan area, where the majority of the Israeli population (old-timers and newcomers alike) wanted to live. In 1992, the Israel Lands Council (the body in charge of determining policy of the ILA), under instructions from then Minister of Housing and Construction, Ariel Sharon, established a compensation scheme to encourage lessees of state-owned agricultural land to surrender their leases, the incentive being that they would be allowed to participate in the economic windfall that the rezoning of agricultural land represented.[6] Under the new compensation formula, the land newly rezoned for residential purposes was now valued at between

---

4   The original owners in *Karsik* had refused to accept compensation. The Court left open the question of whether payment of compensation to the owner cancelled his right to sue once the original purpose for which the land was expropriated was abandoned.

5   As a result of *Karsik*, a bill for the Amendment of the AO was placed before the Knesset in 2003. The bill would have made the lawfulness of an expropriation conditioned on the ongoing existence of the 'public purpose'. In the event that the public purpose was not realized within ten years of the expropriation, the land would be returned to its original owner. If the original public purpose was implemented but the state subsequently sought to replace it with private development, the original owner should be notified and be accorded the opportunity to reacquire the land at its current value. If the authorities wished to replace the original public purpose with another public purpose, this could be done without granting the owner a right to repurchase the land. These provisions would take retroactive effect, but only with respect to expropriations undertaken within the 25-year period prior to enactment of the law (that is, not earlier than 1980). As of this writing the proposed bill has not been enacted.

6   Out of 20.3 million dunam of state land, some 3.7 million dunam are fit for agricultural use. Kibbutzim and moshavim lease about 2.8 million dunam as agricultural land. Notably, there is disproportion between the amount of land held by kibbutzim and moshavim (some 4.7 million dunam, constituting approximate a fifth of the national territory), and the population of these agricultural settlements, (some 650,000 as of 2000, or roughly one tenth of the total population of Israel).

US$54,000 and US$108,000 per dunam, compared to values of between US$1,000 and US$5,500 per dunam for the same land for agricultural use (Benchetrit and Czamanski 2004, 50-1).

This windfall to the kibbutzim and moshavim that participated in this arrangement was highly controversial, not least because it came at public expense, and two organizations petitioned the High Court of Justice to block it.[7] In August 2002, the High Court ruled that the agricultural compensation scheme was unreasonable, in that it created inequality in the distribution of land between various segments of Israeli society. The Court ordered the Israel Lands Council to establish a more modest compensation formula.[8]

What is interesting here is not so much the outcome of the legal issues involved, as the public discourse that developed in the late 1990s on the economic meaning of rights in the land. The ILA's compensation formula was indeed revolutionary, as the High Court noted. It severed the tenure system of public land from its historic purpose—social equality and the prevention of market manipulation and speculation. The compensation scheme proposed to transfer millions of dollars to kibbutzim and moshavim. Members of agricultural settlements, once the symbols of idealism, modest means and virtuous commitment to agriculture, had become the land speculators of the 1990s. The new compensation formula thus symbolized the weakening of the Zionist rationales for maintaining a tenure system of public landownership.[9] The enrichment of the kibbutzim and moshavim, seen by many as unjust, made it hard for the Court to ignore the claims of the private landowners such as those in *Holzman* and *Karsik*.

Another landmark case was *Ka'adan*, which challenged the link between communal land ownership and control, epitomized since 1901 by the JNF, and the political goals of Zionism itself. The Ka'adans, an Arab couple from the town of Baqa-al-Gharbiyya, wanted to purchase land in the newly established suburban settlement of Katzir, south of Hadera, in order to build a home. Katzir was established in 1992 on state land that was allocated to, and developed by, the Jewish Agency. The Ka'adans were refused permission to acquire land in Katzir because they were Israeli Arabs. The Katzir Cooperative Society, in collaboration with the Jewish Agency, explained

---

7   One was the Society for the Protection of Nature in Israel, which argued that the arrangement ignored the important societal interest in the preservation of open spaces. The second was Hakeshet Hademocratit Hamizrahit (Sephardic Democratic Rainbow), an organization established to promote equality and social justice in Israel. Its claim was that the ILA's decision unjustly discriminated in favor of the agricultural sector and thus against oriental Jews who historically were under-represented in this sector.

8   H.C. 244/00, *Kibbutz Sdeh Nahum v. Israel Lands Administration*, 56(6) P.D. 25. The Court ordered the ILA to formulate new guidelines for compensation that would take into account principles of just distribution. At the same time, the Court acknowledged that the old scheme to compensate for the loss of agricultural leases was not reasonable either. The issue of compensation has not yet been resolved. See, www.hakeshet.org.il/english/land_struggles. htm.

9   A further weakening of the public ownership tenure system occurred in 2005 when the Government of the day approved the Gadish Commission recommendation to privatize urban land. See Chapter 3 above.

that the group's policy was to accept Jewish members only. Until *Ka'adan*, no one had challenged the nationally biased policy by which the ILA, a state organ, leased state-owned land to the Jewish Agency, which would then develop rural settlements that were open only to Jewish applicants. Dozens of new agricultural settlements have been established since the foundation of Israel in this way, but none were open to members of the Arab minority.

The Association for Civil Rights in Israel (ACRI) filed a petition with the High Court on behalf of the couple. The Supreme Court avoided ruling on the case for five years, in the course of which Chief Justice Aharon Barak described the case as one of the most difficult he had ever faced. Finally, in March 2000, the Court accepted the Ka'adans' petition by a four-to-one majority, ruling that that the state could not allocate land to the Jewish Agency on a discriminatory basis.[10] The majority was careful to limit its ruling to the facts of the case, indicating that there were different kinds of settlements whose special requirements might call for particular arrangements. The Justices were clearly aware of the unprecedented nature of their decision.[11] Chief Justice Barak wrote: 'We are today taking the first step on a difficult and delicate path. It is therefore appropriate that we proceed very slowly on this path, from case to case, so that we do not trip and fall.'

It is probably not a coincidence that *Ka'adan* was decided at the culmination of a year and a half of optimism in Israel regarding the chances of resolving the Israeli-Palestinian conflict. The 1999 election of Ehud Barak as Prime Minister, the long-overdue withdrawal from southern Lebanon, and the preparations for what were supposed to be final status negotiations at Camp David—all these helped Israeli Jews countenance the increasing assertiveness of the Israeli Arab community without particular alarm (Reches 2002). In early 2000 (prior, that is, to the outbreak of the second intifada), support among Israeli Jews for the establishment of a Palestinian state in the West Bank and Gaza within the framework of a peace agreement reached 60 percent (Arian 2004, 201). The public mood of toleration in the spring of 2000 was undoubtedly one of the factors that enabled the Court to decide as it did in *Ka'adan* (Saban 2007).

As the first step on the road towards equal treatment of Arabs in the allocation of public land, *Ka'adan* had direct ramifications for the jurisprudence of land expropriation. The Court proposed a less polarized perception of Jewish-Arab relations in Israeli society, and approached the issue of the status of Israeli Arabs by regarding them as citizens of the state rather than as a potential fifth column. It is indicative of the Court's correct reading of public reaction to its decision that its signal for the need for change in the status of Arabs in Israeli society was not overridden by the legislature. *Ka'adan* generated intensive public debate,[12] and gave

---

10   H.C. 6698/95, *Ka'adan v. Israel Lands Administration*, 54(1) P.D. 258, Par. 40.

11   In 1978, the Supreme Court had upheld the exclusion of an Arab from the Jewish Quarter in the Old City of Jerusalem. H.C. 11/78, *Burkan v. Minister of Finance*, 32(2) P.D. 800.

12   On the right, *Ka'adan* was viewed as 'effectively defining Israel as a democratic country only', that is, as obliterating its Jewish identity. Yair Sheleg, 'Katzir and a State of all its Citizens', *Ha'aretz* (Hebrew daily), March 14, 2000. Under the heading 'Zionism on Trial',

rise to a Knesset bill (which did not, however, pass) to overrule the decision. Even so, the ILA dragged its feet and refused to allocate land to the Ka'adans for another four years.[13]

Ka'adan preceded *Karsik* by a year, and it laid the ground for the restrictions that *Karsik* placed on the powers of expropriation. The challenge to the link between the Jewish character of Israel and Jewish control of the land was further manifested in *Karsik*. Although *Karsik* involved Jewish owners, the ruling, which tied the legality of an expropriation to the continued justification for public ownership of the land, clearly affected large-scale Arab land expropriations, as well. If *Karsik*'s restrictions had been given unlimited retroactive effect, many of the historic expropriations of Arab land would have been brought into question, including many of the expropriations undertaken throughout the country in the 1950s, in the Galilee in the early 1970s and in East Jerusalem post-1967. The extended panel of nine Justices who decided *Karsik* was clearly aware of these potentially far-reaching implications and therefore avoided addressing the issue of retroactivity full on, calling instead on the legislature to do so.[14]

The legal developments in *Karsik* and *Holzman* and the proposed bill to amend the AO, in what would have been its first such amendment since 1948, raise the question of whether Israel's Supreme Court will continue to strengthen the protection of landowners. The history of Israel's land expropriation jurisprudence suggests that its future will be closely linked to the wide range of political and social factors that inform this highly public and emotive issue.

The deepening of the domestic Jewish-Arab rift in light of the eruption of the second (El-Aqsa) intifada in September 2000, in which, for the first time, Israeli Arabs played a significant role, strengthened the general perception of Israeli Jews that national security still required demographic superiority and control of the land (Bar-Tal and Teichman 2004; Evans 2006; Reches 2002). In June 2004, the

---

JNF chairman Yehiel Leket wrote that when Chaim Herzog publicly tore to shreds the UN resolution equating Zionism with racism 'he surely never imagined that a generation later, an Israeli court would be called on to debate the question of whether one of Zionism's central organizations [the Jewish Agency] was guilty of racism.' Akiva Eldar, 'Zionism on Trial', *Ha'aretz*, January 31, 2005. Elsewhere it was hailed as 'one of the most powerful and positive decisions in decades.' ACRI executive director Vered Livne, 'The Right of an Israeli Arab Couple to Build their Home in Katzir,' at www.acri.org.il.

13   After the ACRI submitted a second petition asking that the ILA be sanctioned for ignoring the Court's ruling, the Ka'adans were finally granted the right to purchase a plot in Katzir.

14   At the time *Karsik* was being decided, another petition was pending before the Supreme Court, one concerning the former residents of the village of Iqrit who wished to return to their homes from which they had been forcibly evacuated during the War of Independence. One of the arguments that the petitioners ultimately raised as a direct result of the *Karsik* decision was that the new doctrine enunciated in *Karsik* entitled them to return to their land, given that the land was no longer needed for security purposes. Facing this potential precedent for Arab Israelis to return to their land, Justice Dorner, writing for the Court, rejected the claim, pointing to Prime Minster Ariel Sharon's affidavit that a public need for the expropriated land still existed. H.C. 840/97, *Sbeit v. Government of Israel*, 57(4) P.D. 803.

Land Expropriation in Israel

Government of the day decided to apply the Absentees' Property Law of 1950 to East Jerusalem, in order to confiscate thousands of dunams of land from owners who lived in the West Bank.[15] This law, originally enacted after the War of Independence, had been dormant for several decades, and was now reactivated in an attempt to preserve the demographic status quo in Jerusalem. After the daily *Ha'aretz* reported on this decision, which was taken in secret and not published in the *Official Gazette*, the Attorney General ordered the Government to cease applying the Absentees' Property Law to East Jerusalem properties owned by West Bankers.[16] The Attorney General's intervention did not, however, address (let alone influence) the prevailing belief held by many Israelis on both the left and the right that a strong Jewish majority in Jerusalem and the containment of Arab demographic expansion in the city were issues of fundamental national security. Yitzhak Herzog, member of the Labour Party and Minister of Construction and Housing in Ariel Sharon's Government of national unity stated in an interview that 'strengthening Jerusalem in a smart manner, without damaging Israel's political standing,' was one of the issues at the top of his agenda. This interview was conducted following the government decision to expand the Jewish settlement of Ma'ale Adumim in order to create a possible link between this settlement located in the West Bank and East Jerusalem. Herzog opposed the plan, but strongly supported an expansion of Har Homa settlement. By February 2005, the first stage of construction in Har Homa, comprising 2,400 apartments, had been completed. The second stage included a further 2,000 apartments, while the third stage, as yet uncompleted, is to include 3,000 apartments. Herzog, a Zionist leftist, explained that Har Homa 'differs from other, harmful plans.'

Plans for the expansion of the Jewish presence in the Galilee and the Negev are also continuing. In 2003, the government launched a drive to establish 30 new settlements in attempt to increase the Jewish population of both regions by 20 percent within five years. Economic incentives for Jews to move to the Galilee and the Negev center on the offer to lease land from the ILA at only 10 percent of the market value of such leases. This benefit has been offered only to discharge soldiers, meaning that most Arabs are ineligible.

While such policies may hinder the Supreme Court's ability to supervise land expropriation effectively, there are also grounds for cautious optimism. To begin with, the Supreme Court has made a number of controversial decisions that affect the status of the Arab minority in Israel. The Court has ruled, for instance, that principles of equality must be respected in the allocation of resources to Arab communities, and that Arabs are entitled to representation on the Israel Lands Council.[17] The Court also declared, in a 2004 decision which gained international attention, that sections

---

15   One of the results of the intifada was that West Bank residents were barred entry to Jerusalem for security reasons.

16   The government decision was kept secret for almost six months until exposed by *Ha'aretz*. The newspaper ran editorials on the decision with titles such as 'Like Thieves in the Night,' and 'Injustice and Stupidity in Jerusalem,' *Ha'aretz* January 21, 2005; February 2, 2005.

17   H.C. 6924/98, *Association for Civil Rights in Israel v. Government of Israel*, 55(5) P.D. 15.

of the route of the security fence around Jerusalem were illegal because they did not properly balance the security needs of the state and the welfare of the Palestinian population.[18]

There has also been open admission by government authorities of past and present discrimination against Arabs in land allocation, planning and construction, and an acknowledgement that discrimination needs to be abolished. The *Report of the National Commission of Inquiry to Examine the Clashes between the Security Forces and Israeli Citizens* (State of Israel 2003) detailed various oppressive land policies that have been used against the Arab minority over the years, and which remain very much alive in the collective consciousness of Arab-Israelis. The Attorney General recently further weakened the discriminatory legal mechanisms of land allocation by applying the *Ka'adan* ruling to JNF land. This despite the fact that the Court did not comment directly on the legality of the JNF practice of leasing land to Jews only.[19]

Even so, it would naïve to assume that such improvements can go very far, as long as the conflict continues at a high level of intensity. The future of Israel's land expropriation jurisprudence, like the future of human rights in Israel in general, is closely linked to the wider political situation. This is one area that the Supreme Court is powerless to affect.

---

18   H.C. 2056/04, *Beit Sureik Village Council v. Government of Israel*, 58(5) P.D. 807 The security fence, also known as the separation barrier, is part electronic fence with barbed-wire and trenches on both sides, part concrete wall, 6 to 8 meters high. It was introduced to prevent the entry of suicide bombers crossing from the West Bank into Israel unobserved. The extent of Palestinian land expropriated for construction of the fence amounts to about 7,000 acres, 0.5 percent of the territory of the West Bank.

19   Yuval Yoaz and Amiram Bareket, 'AG Mazuz Rules that JNF Land Can be Sold to Arabs', *Ha'aretz*, January 27, 2005.

Bibliography

Ackerman, Bruce (1979), *Private Property and the Constitution*, Yale University Press, New Haven.

Aharoni, Yair (1991), *The Israeli Economy: Dreams and Realities*, Routledge, London.

Al-Haj, Majid (1996), *Arab Education in Israel: Control and Social Change*, Magness Press, Jerusalem (Hebrew).

Al-Haj, Majid (2004), 'The Status of the Palestinians in Israel: A Double Periphery in an Ethno-National State' in Alan Dowty (ed.), *Critical Issues in Israeli Society*, Praeger Publishers, Westport, pp. 109-26.

Al-Haj, Majid (2005), 'Whither the Green Line? Trends in the Orientation of the Palestinians in Israel and the Territories', *Israel Affairs*, vol. 11, pp. 183-206.

Almog, Shmuel (1990), 'Redemption in Zionist Rhetoric', in Ruth Kark (ed.), *Redemption of the Land of Eretz Israel*, Yad Yitzhak Ben-Zvi, Jerusalem, pp. 13-32 (Hebrew).

Almog, Oz (2000), *The Sabra: The Creation of the New Jew*, University of California Press, Berkeley.

Alterman, Rachelle (1985), 'Exactions of Land for Public Services: Toward Revaluation', *Mishpatim*, vol. 15, pp.179–244 (Hebrew).

Alterman, Rachelle and Hill, Morris (1986), 'Land Use Planning in Israel', in Nicholas N. Patricious (ed.), *International Handbook on Land Use Planning*, Greenwood Press, Westport, pp. 119-50.

Alterman, Rachelle and Kayden, Jerold S. (1988), 'Developer Provision of Public Benefits: Toward a Consensus Vocabulary', in Rachelle Alterman (ed.), *Private Supply of Public Services, Evaluation of Real Estate Exactions, Linkage and Alternative Land Policies*, New York University Press, New York, pp. 22-32.

Alterman, Rachelle (1990), 'From Expropriation to Development Agreements: Developer Obligations for Public Services in Israel', *Israel Law Review*, vol. 24, pp. 28-81.

Alterman, Rachelle et al. (1990), *Municipal Land Policy in Israel: Does it Exist?*, Center for Urban and Regional Studies, Haifa (Hebrew).

Alterman, Rachelle (1991), *From Expropriations to Agreements: Methods for Obtaining Land For Public Purposes*, Center for Urban and Regional Studies, Haifa (Hebrew).

Alterman, Rachelle and Churchman, Arza (1991), *Israel's Neighborhood Rehabilitation Program: The Great Experiment and its Lessons*, Samuel Neaman Institute for Advanced Studies in Science and Technology, Haifa (Hebrew).

Alterman, Rachelle and Na'im, Orna (1992), *Compensation for Value Reductions of Land Caused by Changes in Plans*, Center for Urban and Regional Studies, Haifa (Hebrew).

Alterman, Rachelle and Rosenstein, Miriam (1992), *Agricultural Land: Conservation or Waste?*, Center for Urban and Regional Studies, Haifa (Hebrew).

Alterman, Rachelle (1997), 'The Challenge of Farm Land Preservation: Lessons from a Six-Country Comparison', *Journal of the American Planning Association*, vol. 63, pp. 220-43.

Alterman, Rachelle (2001), 'National-Level Planning in Israel: Walking the Tightrope Between Government Control and Privatisation', in Rachelle Alterman (ed.), *National-Level Planning in Democratic Countries*, Liverpool University Press, Liverpool, pp. 257-88.

Alterman, Rachelle (2002), *Planning in the Face of Crisis: Land Use, Housing and Mass Immigration in Israel*, Routledge, London and New York.

Alterman, Rachelle (2003), 'The Land of Leaseholds: Israel's Extensive Public Land Ownership in an Era of Privatization', in Steven C. Bourassa and Yu-Hung Hong (eds.), *Leasing Public Land: Policy Debates and International Experiences*, Lincoln Institute of Land Policy, Cambridge, pp. 115-50.

Altshuler, Alan A., Howitt, Arnold M., Gomez-Ibanez, Jose A. (1993), *Regulations for Revenues: The Political Economy of Land Use Regulations*, Brookings Institution, Washington DC.

Amiran, David (1996), 'Urbanization and the Preservation of Agricultural Land in Israel', *Karka, vol. 41, pp. 6-14 (Hebrew)*.

Amirav, Moshe (1992), *Israel's Policy in Jerusalem since 1967*, Stanford Center on Conflict and Negotiation, Stanford University, Stanford.

Amitai, Yossi (1998), 'The Arab Minority in Israel: The Years of Military Rule, 1948-1966', in Anita Shapira (ed.), *Independence – The First Fifty Years*, Zalman Shazar Center, Jerusalem, pp.129-48 (Hebrew).

Arian Asher (1991), 'Israeli Public Opinion and the Intifada' in Robert Freeman (ed.), *The Intifada*, Florida International University Press, Miami, pp. 269-92.

Arian, Asher (1995), *Security Threatened: Surveying Israeli Opinion on Peace and War*, Cambridge University Press, Cambridge.

Arian Asher (2004), 'Public Opinion and the Peace Process,' in Alan Dowty (ed.), *Critical Issues in Israeli Society*, Praeger Publishers, Westport, pp. 195-220.

Arlosoroff, Chaim (1934), 'The Settlement Funds of the Jewish Agency', in *Ktavim II*, Tel-Aviv, pp. 123-287 (Hebrew).

Arlosoroff, Chaim (1934a), 'Conclusions', in *Ktavim II*, Tel-Aviv, pp. 46-60 (Hebrew).

Avineri, Shlomo (1981), *The Making of Modern Zionism: The Intellectual Origins of the Jewish State*, Basic Books, New York.

Avneri, Aryeh L. (1984), *The Claim of Dispossession: Jewish Land Settlement and the Arabs, 1878-1948*, Transaction Books, New Brunswick.

Bachi, Roberto (1974), *The Population of Israel*, Scientific Translation International, Jerusalem.

Barak, Aharon (1987), *Judicial Discretion*, Yale University Press, New Haven.

Barak, Aharon (1992), 'The Constitutional Revolution: Protected Human Rights', *Mishpat Umimshal*, vol.1, pp. 9-35 (Hebrew).

Barak, Aharon (1997), 'Constitutionalization of the Israeli Legal System as a Result of the Basic Laws and its Effect on Procedural and Substantive Criminal Law', *Israel Law Review*, vol. 31, pp. 3-23.

Barak-Erez, Dafna (1995), 'From an Unwritten to a Written Constitution: The Israeli Challenge in American Perspective', *Columbia Human Rights Law Review*, vol. 26, pp. 309-55.

Barkai, Haim (1990), *The Beginnings of the Israeli Economy*, Bialik Institute, Jerusalem (Hebrew).

Barzel, Yoram (1997), *Economic Analysis of Property Rights*, Cambridge University Press, Cambridge.

Barzilai, Gad, Yuchtman-Yaar, Ephraim, Segal, Zeev (1994), *The Israeli Supreme Court and the Israeli Public*, Papyrus Publishing House, Tel-Aviv (Hebrew).

Barzilai, Gad (1998), 'The Argument of "National Security" in Politics and Jurisprudence', in Daniel Bar-Tal, Dan Jacobson and Aharon Kleiman (eds.), *Security Concerns: Insights from the Israeli Experience*, JAI Press, Stamford, pp. 243-66.

Barzilai, Gad (1999), 'Courts as Hegemonic Institutions: The Israeli Court in a Comparative Perspective', *Israel Affairs,* vol. 5, pp. 15-33.

Barzilai, Gad (2004), 'How Far Do Justices Go: The Limits of Judicial Decisions', in Alan Dowty (ed.), *Critical Issues in Israeli Society*, Praeger Publishers, Westport, pp. 55-68.

Bar-Gil, Yoram (1999), *An Agent of Zionist Propaganda: The Jewish National Fund, 1924-1947*, Haifa University Press, Haifa (Hebrew).

Bar-Joseph, Uri (2000), 'Towards a Paradigm Shift in Israel's National Security Conception' in Efraim Karsh (ed.), *Israel: The First Hundred Years*, vol. II, Frank Cass Publishers, London, pp. 99-114.

Bar-Tal, Daniel and Teichman, Yona (2004), *Stereotypes and Prejudice in Conflict: Representations of Arabs in Israeli Jewish Society*, Cambridge University Press, Cambridge.

Bein, Alex (1945), *The History of Agricultural Settlement in Palestine*, Sifriat Kav-le-Kav, Jerusalem (Hebrew).

Bein, Alex (1971), 'Franz Oppenheimer and Theodore Herzl', *Herzl YearBook*, vol. 7, pp. 71-128.

Benchetrit, Gilat and Czamanski, Daniel (2004), 'The Gradual Abolition of the Public Leasehold System in Israel and Canberra: What Lessons Can be Learned?', *Land Use Policy*, vol. 21, pp. 45-57.

Benchetrit, Gilat and Czamanski, Daniel (2005), 'Homeownership Extension Policy in Israel During the 1990s: Capitalism Sponsored by Government Intervention?', *Israeli Sociology*, vol. 6, pp. 39-67 (Hebrew).

Bentwich, Norman (1932), *England in Palestine*, K. Paul & Co., London.

Benvenisti, Eyal (1989), *Legal Dualism: The Absorption of the Occupied Territories into Israel*, Westview Press, Boulder.

Benvenisti, Meron (1976), *Jerusalem, The Torn City*, University of Minnesota Press, Minneapolis.

Benvenisti, Meron (1984), *The West Bank Data Project: A Survey of Israel's Policies*, American Enterprise Institute for Public Policy Research, Washington and London.

Benvenisti, Meron (1996), *City of Stone: The Hidden History of Jerusalem*, University of California Press, Berkeley.

Benvenisti, Meron (2000), *Sacred Landscape: The Buried History of the Holy Land since 1948*, University of California Press, Berkeley.

Ben-Ami, Shlomo (2005), 'So Close and Yet so Far: Lessons from the Israeli-Palestinian Peace Process', *Israel Studies*, pp. 72-90.

Ben-Elia, Nahum and Cnaani, Shai (1996), *"Costless" Local Autonomy: The Issue of Educational Facilities Funding*, Floersheimer Institute for Policy Studies, Jerusalem (Hebrew).

Ben-Elia, Nahum (1999), *Government Finance and Fiscal Crisis in Israeli Local Authorities*, Floersheimer Institute for Policy Studies, Jerusalem (Hebrew).

Ben-Elia, Nahum (2000), *The Fiscalization of Local Planning and Development*, Floersheimer Institute for Policy Studies, Jerusalem (Hebrew).

Ben-Porat, Amir (1999), *The Bourgeoisie: The History of the Israeli Bourgeoisie*, Magness Press, Jerusalem (Hebrew).

Ben-Porath, Yoram (1986), 'The Entwined Growth of Population and Product 1922-1982', in Y. Ben-Porath (ed.), *The Israeli Economy: Maturing through Crises*, Harvard University Press, Cambridge, pp. 27-41.

Ben-Zadok, Efraim (1993), *Local Communities and the Israeli Polity: Conflict of Values and Interests*, SUNY Press, Albany.

Berlin, Meyer (1932), 'The Significance of the National Fund', in *Eretz Israel: Jubilee Volume of the Jewish National Fund*, Jewish National Fund of America, New York, pp. 7-9.

Bernstein, Deborah (1981), 'Immigrant Transit Camps: The Formation of Dependent Relations in Israeli Society', *Ethnic and Racial Studies*, vol. 4, pp. 26-43.

Bisharat, George H. (1994), 'Land, Law and Legitimacy in Israel and the Occupied Territories', *The American University Law Review*, vol. 43, pp. 467-561.

Blander, Dana (2004), 'Nation-Building from the Perspective of Public Opinion', *Israeli Sociology*, vol. 6, pp. 9-39 (Hebrew).

Blank, Yishai (2002), *Local Frontiers: Local Government Law and Its Impact on Space and Society in Israel*, unpublished S.J.D dissertation, Harvard University Law School (on file with author).

Blank, Yishai (2004), 'Decentralized National Education: Local Government, Segregation and Inequality in the Public Education System', *Tel-Aviv University Law Review*, vol. 28, pp. 347-416 (Hebrew).

Blume, Lawrence and Rubinfeld, Daniel L. (1984), 'Compensation For Takings: An Economic Analysis', *California Law Review*, vol. 72, pp. 569-624.

Bohm, Adolf (1932), *The Jewish National Fund*, Jewish National Fund, The Hague.

Borukhov, Eliyahu, Ginsberg, Yona, Werczberger, Elia (1978), 'Housing Prices and Housing Preferences in Israel', *Urban Studies*, vol. 15, pp. 187-200.

Borukhov, Eliyahu (1980), 'Land Policy in Israel', *Habitat International*, vol. 4, pp. 505-15.

Bracha, Baruch (1991), 'Judicial Review of Security Powers in Israel: A New Policy of the Courts', *Stanford Journal of International Law*, vol. 28, pp. 39-102.

Bracha, Baruch (2003), 'Checks and Balances in a Protracted State of Emergency – The Case of Israel', *Israel Yearbook on Human Rights*, vol. 33, pp. 123-52.

Brecher, Michael (1972), *The Foreign Policy System of Israel*, Yale University Press, New Haven.

Breemer, David J. (2002), 'The Evolution of the "Essential Nexus": How State and Federal Courts Have Applied Nollan and Dolan and Where They Should Go from Here', *Washington & Lee Law Review*, vol. 59, pp. 373-408.

Brutzkus, Eliezer (1964), *Physical Planning in Israel: Problems and Achievements*, Jerusalem.

B'Tselem (n.d.), *Statistics: Fatalities in the First Intifada*, available online at www.btselem.org.il.

B'Tselem (n.d.), *Statistics on Land Expropriation in East Jerusalem*, available online at www.btselem.org.il.

Burt, Robert A. (1989), 'Inventing Judicial Review: Israel and America', *Cardozo Law Review*, vol. 10, pp. 2013-97.

Callies, David L. and Malcolm, Grant (1991), 'Paying for Growth and Planning Gain: An Anglo-American Comparison of Development Conditions, Impact Fees and Development Agreements', *Urban Law*, vol. 23, pp. 221-48.

Carmi, Ram (1977), 'Human Values in Urban Architecture', in *Israel Builds*, Ministry of Housing and Construction, Jerusalem, pp. 31-44 (Hebrew and English).

Carmon, Naomi (1988), *Neighborhood Rehabilitation in Israel: Evaluation of Outcomes*, Nachman Books, Haifa (Hebrew).

Carmon, Naomi and Czamanski, Daniel (1990), *Housing In Israel: From Planned Economy to Semi-Free Market Management, 1948-1988*, University of California Press, Los Angeles.

Carmon, Naomi, Czamanski D., Amir S., Law Yone H., Kipnis B., and Lipshitz G. (1990), *The New Jewish Settlement in the Galilee: An Evaluation*, Center for Urban and Regional Research, Technion, Haifa (Hebrew).

Carmon, Naomi (2002), 'Housing Policy in Israel: Review, Evaluation and Lessons', in David Nachmias and Gila Menachem (eds.), *Public Policy in Israel*, Frank Cass Publishers, London, pp. 181-208.

Cattan, Henry (1969), *Palestine, The Arabs and Israel: The Search for Justice*, Longman, London.

Central Bureau of Statistics (CBS) (1955-57), *Judicial Statistics*, Special Publication Series, State of Israel, Jerusalem (Hebrew).

Central Bureau of Statistics (CBS) (1992), *Statistical Abstract of Israel*, State of Israel, Jerusalem (Hebrew).

Central Bureau of Statistics (CBS) (2003), *Family Expenditure Survey*, Special Publication Series, State of Israel, Jerusalem (Hebrew).

Central Bureau of Statistics (CBS) (1992), *Statistical Abstract of Israel*, State of Israel, Jerusalem (Hebrew).

Cheshin, Amir, Hutman, Bill and Melamed, Avi (1999), *Separate and Unequal: The Inside Story of Israeli Rule in East Jerusalem*, Harvard University Press, Cambridge.

CIA (n.d.) *CIA World Fact Book*, available online at www.cia.gov/library/ publications/the-world-factbook/index.html.

Cohen, Barak (2003), 'Empowering Constitutionalism with Text from an Israeli Perspective', *American University International Law Review*, vol. 18, pp. 585-650.

Cohen, Erik (1970), *The City in the Zionist Ideology*, Institute of Urban and Regional Studies, Jerusalem.

Cohen, Erik (1972), 'The Black Panthers in Israeli Society', *Jewish Journal of Sociology*, vol. 14, pp. 93-110.

Cohen, Hilel (2000), *The Present Absentees: The Palestinian Refugees in Israel since 1948*, Institute for Israeli Arab Studies, Jerusalem (Hebrew).

Cohen, Shaul E. (1993), *The Politics of Planting: Israeli-Palestinian Competition for Control of Land in the Jerusalem Periphery*, University of Chicago Press, Chicago.

Connors, Donald L. and High, Michael E. (1987), 'The Expanding Circle of Exactions: From Dedication to Linkage', *Law & Contemporary Problems*, vol. 50, pp. 69-84.

Dagan, Hanoch (1999), 'Takings and Distributive Justice', *Virginia Law Review*, vol. 85, pp. 741-804.

Dagan, Hanoch (2000), 'Just Compensation, Incentives and Social Meanings', *Michigan Law Review*, vol. 99, pp. 134-56.

Dana, David A. (1997), 'Land Use Regulation in the Age of Heightened Scrutiny', *North Carolina Law Review*, vol. 75, pp. 1243-303.

Dana, David A. and Merrill, Thomas W. (2002), *Property: Takings*, Foundation Press, New York.

Darin-Drabkin, Haim (1957), *Housing in Israel: Economic and Sociological Aspects*, Gadish Books, Tel-Aviv.

Davies, Keith (1994), *Law of Compulsory Purchase and Compensation*, Butterworths, London.

Davies, William D. (1982), *The Territorial Dimension of Judaism*, University of California Press, Berkeley.

Delaney, John J., Gordon, Larry A. and Hess, Kathryn, J. (1987), 'The Needs-Nexus Analysis: A Unified Test for Validating Subdivision Exactions, User Impact Fees and Linkage', *Law & Contemporary Problems*, vol. 50, pp. 139-66.

Doeblele, William A. (ed.) (1982), *Land Readjustment: A Different Approach to Financing Urbanization*, Lexington Books, Lexington.

Doleve-Gandelman, Tsili (1987), 'The Symbolic Inscription of Zionist Ideology in the Space of Eretz Israel: Why the Native Israeli is Called Tsabar', in Harvey E. Goldberg (ed.), *Judaism Viewed From Within and From Without: Anthropological Studies*, SUNY Press, Albany, pp. 257-84.

Dominitz, Yehuda (1997), 'Israel Immigration Policy and the Dropout Phenomenon', in Noah Lewin-Epstein et al. (eds.), *Russian Jews on Three Continents: Migration and Resettlement*, Franc Cass, London, pp. 113-27.

Dorner, Dalia (1999), 'Does Israel Have a Constitution?', *Saint Louis University Law Journal*, vol. 43, pp. 1325-35.

Dotan, Yoav (2002), 'Judicial Accountability in Israel: The High Court of Justice and the Phenomenon of Judicial Hyperactivism', *Israel Studies*, vol. 8 (4), pp. 87-106.

Drori, Moshe (1982), 'The Israeli Settlements in Judea and Samaria: Some Legal Aspects', in D.J. Elazar (ed.), *Judea, Samaria and Gaza: Views on the Present and Future*, American Enterprise Institute for Public Policy Research, Washington, pp. 44-80.

Drori, Ze'ev (2006), 'Society Strength as a Base for Military Power: The State of Israel during the Early 1950s', *Israel Affairs* vol. 12, pp. 412-29.

Duckan-Landau, Leah (1979), *The Zionist Companies for Land Purchase in Palestine*, Yad Yitzhak Ben-Zvi, Jerusalem (Hebrew).

Dumper, Michael (1994), *Islam and Israel: Muslim Religious Endowments and the Jewish State*, Institute for Palestine Studies, New York.

Dumper, Michael (1997), *The Politics of Jerusalem Since 1967*, Columbia University Press, New York.

Edelman, Martin (1994), *Courts, Politics and Culture in Israel*, University Press of Virginia, Charlottesville.

Efrat, Elisha (2000), 'Jerusalem: Partition Plans for a Holy City', in Efraim Karsh (ed.), *Israel: The First Hundred Years*, vol. II, Frank Cass Publishers, London, pp. 238-55.

Eisenman, Robert H. (1979), *Islamic Law in Palestine and Israel*, E.J. Brill, Leiden.

Eisenstadt, Shmuel N. (1954), *The Absorption of Immigrants: A Comparative Study Based Mainly on the Jewish Community in Palestine and in the State of Israel*, Routledge & Paul, London.

Eisenstadt, Shmuel N. (1967), *Israeli Society*, Weidenfeld and Nicolson, London.

Eisenstadt, Shmuel N. (1985), *The Transformation of Israeli Society*, Westview Press, Boulder.

Erasmus, Gavin M. (ed.) (1990), *Compensation for Expropriation: A Comparative Study*, Oxford.

Erzt, Donna E. (1997), *Refugees into Citizens: Palestinians and the End of the Arab-Israeli Conflict*, Council on Foreign Relations Books, New York.

Etzioni-Halevy, Eva (1977), *Political Culture in Israel: Cleavage and Integration Among Israeli Jews*, Praeger Publishers, New York.

Evans, Matt (2006), 'Defending Territorial Sovereignty Through Civilian Settlement: The Case of Israel's Population Dispersal Policy', *Israel Affairs*, vol. 12, pp. 578-96.

Falah, Ghazi (1991), 'Israeli "Judaization" Policy in Galilee', *Journal of Palestine Studies*, vol. 20(4), pp. 69-85.

Falah, Ghazi (1996), 'The 1948 Israeli-Palestinian War and Its Aftermath: The Transformation and De-signification of Palestine's Cultural Landscape', *Annals of the American Association of Geographers*, vol. 86(2), pp. 256-85.

Felner, Eitan (1995), *A Policy of Discrimination: Land Expropriation, Planning and Building in East Jerusalem*, B'Tselem Report, Jerusalem (Hebrew), available in English online at www.btselem.org.il.

Fenster, M. (2004), 'Takings Formalism and Regulatory Formulas: Exactions and the Consequences of Clarity', *California Law Review*, vol. 92, pp. 609-81.

Firer, Ruth (1985), *The Agents of Jewish Education*, Sifriat Poalim, Tel-Aviv (Hebrew).

Fischbach, Michael R. (2002), 'The United Nations and Palestinian Refugee Property Compensation', *Journal of Palestine Studies*, vol. 31(2), pp. 34-50.

Fischbach, Michael R. (2003), *Records of Dispossession: Palestinian Refugee Property and the Arab-Israeli Conflict*, Columbia University Press, New York.

Flapan, Simha (1987), *The Birth of Israel: Myth and Realities*, Pantheon, New York.

Forman, Geremy (2002), 'Settlement of Title in the Galilee: Dowson's Colonial Guiding Principles', *Israel Studies*, vol. 7(3), pp. 61-83.

Forman, Geremy and Kedar, Alexandre (2004), 'From Arab Lands to "Israel Lands" The Legal Dispossession of the Palestinians Displaced by Israel in the Wake of 1948', *Environment and Planning D: Society and Space*, vol. 22, pp. 809-30.

Forman, Geremy (2006), 'Military Rule, Political Manipulation, and Jewish Settlement: Israeli Mechanisms for Controlling Nazareth in the 1950s', vol. 25(2), *Journal of Israeli History* 335-59.

Frankel, Jonathan (1981), *Prophecy and Politics*, Cambridge University Press, Cambridge.

Friedlander, Dov and Goldscheider, Calvin (1979), *The Population of Israel*, Columbia University Press, New York.

Friedman, Daniel (1975), 'The Effect of Foreign Law on the Law of Israel: Remnants of the Ottoman Period', *Israel Law Review*, vol. 10, pp. 192-206.

Gabriel, Stuart A. (1986), 'Housing Policy', in Ya'akov Kop (ed.), *Changing Social Policy, Israel 1985-1986*, Center for Social Policy Studies in Israel, Jerusalem, pp. 227-59.

Gavison, Ruth (1985), 'The Controversy over Israel's Bill of Rights', *Israel Yearbook on Human Rights*, vol. 15, pp. 113-54.

Gavison, Ruth (1990), 'Forty Years of Constitutional Law', *Israel Law Rev.*, vol. 24, pp. 431-50.

Gavison, Ruth (1997), 'The Constitutional Revolution-Description of Reality or Self-fulfilling Prophecy?', *Mishpatim*, vol. 28, pp. 21-147 (Hebrew).

Gavison, Ruth (2005), *The Israeli Constitutional Process: Legislative Ambivalence and Judicial Resolute Drive*, Center for the Study of Rationality, The Hebrew University of Jerusalem.

Gazit, Shlomo (1999), *Trapped*, Zmora-Bitan, Tel-Aviv (Hebrew).

Gelber, Yoav (1998), 'Difficulties and Changes in the Zionist Attitude to Aliya', in Dvora Hacohen (ed.), *Ingathering of Exiles: Aliyah to the Land of Israel: Myth and Reality*, Zalman Shazar Center for Jewish History, Jerusalem, pp. 249-85 (Hebrew).

George, Henry (1879), *Progress and Poverty*, Robert Schalkenbach Foundation, San Francisco.

Gerner, Deborah J. (1991), *One Land, Two Peoples: The Conflict over Palestine*, Westview Press, Boulder.

Giladi, Dan (1966), 'Private Enterprise, National Wealth and the Political Consolidation of the Right', in S.N. Eisenstadt et al. (eds.), *The Social Structure of Israel: A Collection of Readings and Research*, Jerusalem, pp. 85-97 (Hebrew).

Giladi, Dan (1973), *Jewish Palestine During the Fourth Aliya Period*, Am-Oved, Tel-Aviv (Hebrew).

Giladi, Dan and Naor, Mordechai (1982), *Rothschild: 'Founder of the Yishuv': His Activities in Eretz Israel*, Keter Publishing House, Jerusalem (Hebrew).

Goadby, Frederic M. and Doukhan, Moses J. (1935), *The Land Law of Palestine*, Shoshany's Print, Tel-Aviv.

Golan, Arnon (1995), 'The Transfer to Jewish Control of Abandoned Arab Lands during the War of Independence', in S. Ilan Troen and Noah Lucas (eds.), *Israel, The First Decade of Independence*, SUNY Press, Albany, pp. 403-40.

Golan, Arnon (2001), *Wartime Spatial Changes: Former Arab Territories within the State of Israel 1948-1950*, Ben-Gurion University Press, Be'er Sheva (Hebrew).

Goldstein, Stephen (1994), 'Protection of Human Rights by Judges: The Israeli Experience', *St Louis University Law Journal*, vol. 38, pp. 605-18.

Gonen, Amiram (1985), 'The Changing Ethnic Geography of Israeli Cities', in Alex Weingrod (ed.), *Studies in Israeli Ethnicity: After the Ingathering*, Gordon and Breach Science Publishers, New York, pp. 25-38.

Gonen, Amiram (1995), *Between City and Suburb: Urban Residential Patterns and Processes in Israel*, Avebury, Aldershot.

Gracier, Iris (1983), 'The JNF's Urban Land Policy and its Influence on the Development of Planning During the Mandate', 1983 *Karka*, pp. 70-86 (Hebrew).

Gracier, Iris (1989), 'Social Architecture in Palestine: Conceptions in Working-Class Housing 1920-38', in Ruth Kark (ed.), *The Land that became Israel: Studies in Historical Geography*, Magnes Press, Hebrew University, Jerusalem, pp. 287-307.

Granott (Granovsky), Avraham (1936), *The Land Issue in Palestine*, Goldberg Press, Palestine.

Granott (Granovsky), Avraham (1940), *Land Policy in Palestine 1890-1962,* Bloch Publishing, New York.

Granott (Granovsky), Avraham (1952), *The Land System in Palestine: History and Structure*, Eyre & Spottiswoode, London.

Granott (Granovsky), Avraham (1956), *Agrarian Reform and the Record of Israel*, Eyre & Spottiswoode, London.

Gross, Nahum (1997), 'Israel's Economy', in Zvi Zamereth and Chana Yablonka (eds.), *The First Decade*, Yad Izhak Ben-Zvi, Jerusalem, pp. 137-50 (Hebrew).

Gvati, Haim (1985), *A Hundred Years of Settlement: The Story of Jewish Settlement in the Land of Israel*, Keter Publishing House, Jerusalem.

Haber, Aliza (1975), *Population and Building in Israel, 1948-1973*, Ministry of Housing, Jerusalem.

Hacohen, Dvorah (1994), *Immigrants in Turmoil: The Great Wave of Immigration to Israel and its Absorption 1948-1953*, Yad Izhak Ben-Zvi, Jerusalem (Hebrew).

Hacohen, Dvorah. (1998), 'Immigration Policy in the First Decade of Statehood: The Attempts to Restrict Immigration to Israel and their Outcome', in Dvorah Hacohen (ed.), *The Ingathering of Exiles: Aliyah to the Land of Israel: Myth and Reality*, Zalman Shazar Center for Jewish History, Jerusalem, pp. 285-316 (Hebrew).

Hadawi, Sami (1963), *Palestine: Loss of a Heritage*, The Naylor Co., San Antonio.

Halevi, Nadav and Klinov-Malul, Ruth (1968), *The Economic Development of Israel*, Praeger, New York.

Halperen, Ben (1969), *The Idea of the Jewish State*, Harvard University Press, Cambridge.

Harris, Ron (1997), 'Israeli Law', in Zvi Zameret and Hana Yablonka (eds.), *The First Decade 1948-1953*, Yad Izhak Ben-Zvi, Jerusalem, pp. 243-62 (Hebrew).

Harris, Ron (2002), 'Arab Politics in a Jewish Democracy: El-Ard Movement and the Israeli Supreme Court', *Plilim*, vol. 10, pp. 107-55 (Hebrew).

Haviv-Segal, Irit (1998), 'Coordination Problems and the Question of Public Goal in Real Estate Expropriation', *Tel-Aviv University Law Review*, vol. 21, pp. 449-89 (Hebrew).

Heap, Desmond (1996), *An Outline of Planning Law*, Sweet and Maxwell, London.

Heller, Michael A. and Krier, James E. (1999), 'Deterrence and Distribution in the Law of Takings', *Harard Law Review*, vol. 112, pp. 997-1025.

Herzel, Theodor (1902), *Altneuland*, Seemann Nachf, Austria (German).

Hofnung, Menachem (1996), *Democracy, Law and National Security in Israel*, Dartmouth, Aldershot.

Hofnung, Menachem (1996a), 'The Unintended Consequences of Unplanned Constitutional Reform: Constitutional Politics in Israel', *The American Journal of Comparative Law*, vol. 44, pp. 585-604.

Holzman-Gazit, Yifat (2002), 'Law as a Symbol of Status: The Jewish National Fund Law of 1953 and the Struggle of the Fund to Maintain its Status after Independence', *Tel-Aviv University Law Review*, vol. 26, pp. 601-44 (Hebrew).

Holzman-Gazit, Yifat (2002a), 'Mass Immigration, Housing Supply and Supreme Court Jurisprudence of Land Expropriation in Early Statehood', in Ron Harris et al. (eds.), *The History of Law in a Multi-Cultural Society: Israel 1917-1967*, Ashgate, Aldershot, pp. 273-305.

Horowitz, Dan and Lissak, Moshe (1978), *Origins of the Israeli Polity: Palestine Under the Mandate*, University of Chicago Press, Chicago.

Horowitz, Dan and Lissak Moshe (1989), *Trouble in Utopia: The Overburdened Polity of Israel*, SUNY Press, Albany.

Horowitz, David (1972), *The Enigma of Economic Growth: A Case Study of Israel*, Praeger, New York.

Hunt, Alan (1985), 'The Ideology of Law: Advances and Problems in Recent Application of the Concept of Ideology to the Analysis of Law', *Law & Society Review*, vol. 19, pp. 11-37.

Hurwitz, Maximilian (1932), 'The Father of the National Fund', in *Eretz Israel: Jubilee Volume of the Jewish National Fund*, Jewish National Fund for America, New York, pp. 9-24.

Israel Lands Administration (1995), *Report by the Committee for Determining the Reorganization of Urban Land* (Tsaban Commission), ILA, Tel-Aviv (Hebrew).

Israel Lands Administration (2003), *Annual Report*. available online at www.mmi.gov.il

Israel Year Book and Almanac (1998), IBRT Tranlsation/Documentation, Jerusalem.

Israel Year Book and Almanac (1999), IBRT Tranlsation/Documentation, Jerusalem.

Jacobsohn, Gary J. (1993), *Apple of Gold: Constitutionalism in Israel and the United States*, Princeton University Press, Princeton.

Jiryis, Sabri (1972), 'The Legal Structure for the Expropriation and Absorption of Arab Lands in Israel', *Journal of Palestine Studies*, vol. 2, pp. 82-103.

Jiryis, Sabri (1976), The Arabs in Israel, Monthly Review Press, New York.

Jones, Clive (1996), *Soviet Jewish Aliya 1989-1992: Impact and Implications for Israel and the Middle East*, Frank Cass, London.

Kalchheim, Chaim (1988), 'The Division of Functions and Interrelationship Between Local and State Authorities', in Daniel Elazar and Chaim Kalchheim (eds.), *Local Government in Israel*, University Press of America, Lanham, pp. 41-82.

Kallus, Rachel and Law Yone, Hubert (2002), 'National Home/Personal Home: Public Housing and the Shaping of National Space in Israel', *European Planning Studies*, vol. 10, pp. 765-77.

Kallus, Rachel (2004), 'The Political Construct of the "Everyday": The Role of Housing in Making Place and Identity', in Haim Yacobi (ed.), *Constructing a Sense of Place: Architecture and the Zionist Discourse*, Ashgate, Aldershot, pp. 136-61.

Kam, Ephraim (2003), 'Conceptualising Security in Israel', in H. Brauch et al. (eds.), *Security and Environment in the Mediterranean: Conceptualising Security and Environmental Conflicts*, Springer Books, Germany, pp. 357-66.

Kamar, Arieh (2001), *The Law of Land Expropriation*, Merav Publishing, Tel-Aviv (Hebrew).

Kaplow, Louis (1985), 'An Economic Analysis of Legal Transitions', *Harvard Law Review*, vol. 99, pp. 509-617.

Kark, Ruth (1992), 'Land-God-Man: Concepts of Land Ownership in Traditional Cultures in Eretz-Israel', in Alan Baker and Gideon Biger (eds.), *Ideology and Landscape in Historical Perspective*, Cambridge University Press, Cambridge, pp. 63-82.

Kark, Ruth (1995), 'Planning, Housing and Land Policy 1948-1952: The Formation of Concepts and Governmental Frameworks', in S. Ilan Troen and Noah Lucas (eds.), *Israel, The First Decade of Independence*, SUNY Press, Albany, pp. 461-94.

Karp, Judith (1992), 'Basic Law: Human Dignity and Freedom – A Biography of Power Struggles', *Mishpat Umimshal*, vol. 1, pp. 323- 84 (Hebrew).

Katz, Yossi (1994), *The 'Business' of Settlement: Private Entrepreneurship in the Jewish Settlement of Palestine, 1900-1914*, Bar-Ilan University Press, Ramat-Gan and Magness Press, Jerusalem.

Katz, Yossi (2001), *The Battle for the Land: The Jewish National Fund before the Establishment of the State of Israel*, Bar-Ilan University Press, Ramat-Gan and Magness Press, Jerusalem (Hebrew).

Katz, Yossi (2002), *'The Land Shall Not be Sold in Perpetuity' : The Legacy and Principles of the JNF in Israeli Legislation*, Magness Press, Jerusalem (Hebrew).

Kedar, Alexandre (2001), 'The Legal Transformation of Ethnic Geography: Israeli Law and the Palestinian Landholder 1948-1967', *New York University Journal of International Law & Politics*, vol. 33, pp. 923-1000.

Kedar, Alexandre (2002), 'On the Legal Geography of Ethnocratic Settler States: Notes Towards a Research Agenda', *Law and Geography: Current Legal Issues*, vol. 5, pp. 402-41.

Kimmerling, Baruch (1977), 'Sovereignty, Ownership and Presence in the Jewish-Arab Territorial Conflict: The Case of Bir'im and Ikrit', *Comparative Political Studies*, vol. 10, pp. 155-76.

Kimmerling, Baruch (1983), *Zionism and Territory: The Socio-Territorial Dimensions of Zionist Politics*, Institute of International Studies, University of California Press, Berkeley.

Kimmerling, Baruch (1983a), *Zionism and Economy*, Schenkman Publishing Company, Cambridge.

Kimmerling, Baruch (2001), *The Invention and Decline of Israeliness: State, Society and the Military*, University of California Press, Berekley.

Kimmerling, Baruch (2002), 'Jurisdiction in an Immigrant-Settler Society: The "Jewish and Democratic State"', *Comparative Political Studies*, vol. 35, pp. 1119-44.

Kislev, Ran (1976), 'Land Expropriations: History of Oppression', *New Outlook*, vol. 19, pp. 23- 32.

Klausner, Israel (1966), *Land and Soul: The Life and Actions of Professor Zvi Herman Schapira*, Jewish National Fund, Jerusalem (Hebrew).

Kleiman, Ephraim (1997), 'The Waning of Israeli Etatisme', *Israel Studies*, vol. 2, pp. 146-71.

Klinghoffer, Itzhak (1972), 'The Linkage of Expropriated Land to its Declared Object', *Tel-Aviv University Law Review*, vol. 2, pp. 872-7 (Hebrew).

Koren, David (1988), *The Western Galilee in the War of Independence*, The Ministry of Defense, Tel-Aviv (Hebrew).

Kretzmer, David (1984), 'Demonstrations and the Law', *Israel Law Review*, vol.19, pp. 47-153.

Kretzmer, David (1990), *The Legal Status of the Arabs in Israel*, Westview Press, Boulder.

Kretzmer, David (1990a), 'Forty Years of Public Law', *Israel Law Review*, vol. 24, pp. 341-55.

Kretzmer, David (2002), *The Occupation of Justice: The Supreme Court of Israel and the Occupied Territories*, SUNY Press, Albany.

Kretzmer, David (2005), 'Human Rights', *Israel Affairs*, vol. 11, pp. 39-64.

Kroyanker, David (1988), 'The Face of the City', in Yehoshua Prawer and Ora Ahimeir (eds.), *Twenty Years in Jerusalem 1967-1987*, Ministry of Defense and Jerusalem Institute for Israel Studies, Jerusalem, pp. 11-67 (Hebrew).

Lahav, Pnina (1981), 'American Influence on Israel's Jurisprudence of Free Speech', *Hastings Constitutional Law Quarterly*, vol. 9, pp. 21-107.

Lahav, Pnina (1990), 'Foundations of Rights Jurisprudence in Israel: Chief Justice Agranat's Legacy', *Israel Law Review*, vol. 24, pp. 211-69.

Lahav, Pnina (1990a), 'The Supreme Court of Israel: Formative Years, 1948-1955', *Studies in Zionism*, vol. 11, pp. 45-66.

Lahav, Pnina (1993), 'Rights and Democracy: The Court's Performance', in Ehud Sprinzak and Larry Diamond (eds.), *Israeli Democracy Under Stress*, Lynne Rienner Publishers, Boulder & London, pp. 125-51.

Lahav, Pnina (1997), *Judgment in Jerusalem: Chief Justice Simon Agrant and the Zionist Century*, University of California Press, Berkeley.

Landau, Moshe (1996), 'Providing Israel with a Constitution through Court Decisions', *Mishpat Umimshal*, vol. 3, pp. 697-712 (Hebrew).

Laqueur, Walter (1972), *A History of Zionism*, Holt, Rienehart & Winston, New York.

Lehn, Walter (1988), *The Jewish National Fund*, Kegan Paul International, London.

Lein, Yehezkel (2002), *Land Grab: Israel's Settlement Policy in the West Bank*, B'Tselem, Jerusalem.

Lerman, Robert (1976), *A Critical Review of Israeli Housing Policy*, Brookdale Institute, Jerusalem.

Lewinsohn-Zamir, Daphna (1994), 'Development Agreements and Conditions in Building Permits – A Substitute for Formal Planning Processes?', *Israel Law Review*, vol. 28, pp. 57-135.

Lewinsohn-Zamir, Daphna (1996), 'Compensation for Injuries to Land Caused by Planning Authorities: Towards a Comprehensive Theory', *University of Toronto Law Journal*, vol. 46, pp. 47-127.

Lewin-Epstein, Noah, Ro'I, Yaacov and Ritterband, Paul (2004), 'Home Ownership and Social Inequality in Israel', in Karin Kurz and Hans-Peter Blossfeld (eds.), *Home Ownership and Social Inequality in Comparative Perspective*, Stanford University Press, Stanford, pp. 338-64.

Likhovski, Assaf (1998), 'Between "Mandate" and "State": Rethinking the Periodization of Israeli Legal History', *Journal of Israeli History*, vol. 19, pp. 39-68.

Lipow, Jonathan (1996), *Israel's Housing Subsidy Programs* (Research Paper in Land Economics No. 4.), Institute for Advanced Strategy and Political Studies, Jerusalem.

Lipshitz, Gabriel (1998), *Country on the Move: Migration to and Within Israel: 1948-1995*, Kluwer Academic Press, Dordrecht.

Lissak, Moshe (1995), 'The Civilian Components of Israel's Security Doctrine: The Evolution of Civil-Military Relations in the First Decade', in S. Ilan Troen and Noah Lucas (eds.), *Israel: The First Decade of Independence*, SUNY Press, Albany, pp. 575-92.

Lissak, Moshe (2003), 'The Demographic-Social Revolution in Israel in the 1950s: The Absorption of the Great *Aliyah*', *Journal of Israeli History*, vol. 22, pp. 1-31.

Lithwick, Irwin (1980), *Macro and Micro Housing Programs in Israel*, JDC-Brookdale Institute of Gerontology and Human Development, Jerusalem.

Llewellyn, Karl N. (1960), *The Common Law Tradition: Deciding Appeals*, Little Brown, Boston.

Lucas, Noah (1975), *The Modern History of Israel*, Praeger, New York.

Lustick, Ian S. (1980), *Arabs in the Jewish State: Israel's Control of a National Minority*, University of Texas Press, Austin.

Lustick, Ian S.1999), 'Israel as a Non-Arab State: The Political Implications of Mass Immigration of Non-Jews', *Middle East Journal*, vol. 53(3), pp. 417–33.

Maoz, Asher (1988), 'The System of Government in Israel', *Tel-Aviv University Studies in Law*, vol. 8, pp. 9-57.

Maoz, Asher (1988a), 'Defending Civil Liberties Without a Constitution – The Israeli Experience', *Melbourne University Law Review*, vol. 16, pp. 815-36.

Markoe, Zaharah R. (2000), 'Note: Expressing Oneself Without a Constitution: The Israeli Story', *Cardozo Journal of International and Comparative Law*, vol. 8, pp. 319-46.

Mautner, Menachem (1993), *The Decline of Formalism and the Rise of Values in Israeli Law*, Ma'agalay Da'at Publishing House, Tel-Aviv (Hebrew).

McCarthy, Justin (1990), *The Population of Palestine*, Columbia University Press, New York.

Medding, Peter Y. (1972), *Mapai in Israel: Political Organization and Government in a New Society*, Cambridge University Press, Cambridge.

Metzer, Jacob (1978), 'Economic Structure and National Goals – The Jewish National Home in Interwar Palestine', *Journal of Economic History*, vol. 38, pp.101-19.

Metzer, Jacob (1979), *National Capital for a National Home 1911-1921*, Yad Yitzhak Ben-Zvi, Jerusalem (Hebrew).

Michelman, Frank I. (1967), 'Property, Utility and Fairness: Comments on the Ethical Foundations of "Just Compensation" Law', *Harvard Law Review*, vol. 80, pp.1165-258.

Ministry of Construction and Housing (2000), *Planning Guidelines for Land Dedication for Public Services*, Tel-Aviv (Hebrew).

Ministry of Housing (1974), *Housing Subsidy Program for Young Couples*, Jerusalem (Hebrew).

Morris, Benny (1987), *The Birth of the Palestinian Refugee Problem, 1947-1949*, Cambridge University Press, Cambridge.

Morris, Benny (1993), *Israel's Border Wars, 1949-1956: Arab Infiltration, Israel Retaliation and the Countdown to Suez War*, Oxford University Press, Oxford.

Morris, Benny (2004), *The Birth of the Palestinian Refugee Problem Revisited*, Cambridge University Press, Cambridge.

Nakkara, Hanna D. (1985), 'Israeli Land Seizure under Various Defence and Emergency Regulations', *Journal of Palestine Studies*, vol. 14, pp. 13-34.

Naor, Arye (1999), 'The Security Argument in the Territorial Debate in Israel: Rhetoric and Policy', *Israel Studies*, vol. 4, pp.150-77.

Naor, Mordechai (1987), 'The Tsena', in Mordechai Naor (ed.), *Immigrant and Transit Camps*, Yad Itzhak Ben-Zvi, Jerusalem , pp. 97-110 (Hebrew).

National Agency for Enterprise and Housing, (2003), *Housing Statistics in the European Union*, available online at www.ebst.dk/file/2256/housing_statistics_2003.pdf.

Near, Henry (1990), 'Redemption of the Soil and of the Man: Pioneering in Labor Zionist Ideology, 1904-1935', in Ruth Kark (ed.), *Redemption of the Land of Eretz Israel*, Yad Izhak Ben-Zvi, Jerusalem, pp. 33-47 (Hebrew).

Newman, David (1989), 'The Role of Civilian and Military Presence as Strategies of Territorial Control: The Arab-Israel Conflict', *Political Geography Quarterly*, vol. 8, pp. 215-27.

Newman, David (2002), 'The Geopolitics of Peacemaking in Israel-Palestine', *Political Geography*, vol. 21, pp. 629-46.

Nichols, Philip (1997), *The Law of Eminent Domain*, Bender, New York.

Oded, Yitzhak (1964), 'Land Losses Among Israel's Arab Villagers', *New Outlook*, vol. 7, pp. 10-25.

Olshan, Isaac (1978), *Din Udvarim: Memories of the Second Chief Justice of Israel*, Shoken Press, Tel-Aviv (Hebrew).

Oren-Nordheim, Michal (2002), 'And the Land Shall Never be Sold in Perpetuity', *Studies in the Geography of Israel*, vol. 16, pp. 146-81 (Hebrew).

Parker, R.B. (ed.) (1996), *The Six Day War: A Retrospective*, University Press of Florida, Gainesville.

Peleg, Ilan (1995), *Human Rights in the West Bank and Gaza: Legacy and Politics*, Syracuse University Press, Syracuse.

Penslar, Derek J. (1991), *Zionism and Technocracy: The Engineering of Jewish Settlement in Palestine, 1870-1918*, Indiana University Press, Bloomington.

Penslar, Derek J. (2001), *Shylock's Children: Economics and Jewish Identity in Modern Europe*, University of Calirfornia Press, Berkeley.

Peretz, Don (1958), *Israel and the Palestine Arabs*, Middle East Institute, Washington, DC.

Peretz, Don (1986), *The West Bank: History, Politics, Society, and Economy*, Westview Press, Boulder.

Perry, Elizabeth (2003), 'Blueprint for Peace: Planning Law in Israel as a Precursor to the Peace Process', *Transnational Law and Contemporary Problems*, vol. 13, pp. 397-427.

Plessner, Yakir (1994), *The Political Economy of Israel: From Ideology to Stagnation*, SUNY Press, Albany.

Rabinowitz, Dan (1997), *Overlooking Nazareth: The Ethnography of Exclusion in Galilee*, Cambridge University Press, Cambridge.

Rabinowitz, Dan (2000), 'The Abandoned Option: Collective Urban Housing', *Theory and Criticism*, vol. 16, pp. 101-28 (Hebrew).

Razin, Assaf and Sadka, Efraim (1993), *The Economy of Modern Israel: Malaise and Promise*, University of Chicago Press, Chicago.

Reches, Eli (1977), *Israeli Arabs and the Land Expropriation in the Galilee: Background, Events and Implications 1975-1977*, Tel Aviv University Press, Tel-Aviv (Hebrew).

Reches, Eli (2002), 'The Arabs After Oslo: Localization of the National Struggle', *Israel Studies*, vol. 7(3), pp. 1-44.

Reeve, Andrew (1986), *Property*, Macmillan, London.

Regev, Motti and Seroussi, Edwin (2004), *Popular Music and National Culture in Israel*, University of California Press, Berkeley.

Reichman, Shalom (1979), *From Foothold to Settled Territory: The Jewish Settlement, 1918-1948,* Yad Yitzhak Ben-Zvi, Jerusalem (Hebrew).

Roter Rephael and Shamai Nira (1990), 'Housing Policy' in N. Sanbar (ed.), *Economic and Social Policy in Israel – The First Generation*, pp.171-84

Rouhana, Nadim and Ghanem, As'ad (1998), 'The Crisis of Minorities in Ethnic States: The Case of Palestinian Citizens in Israel', *International Journal of Middle East Studies*, vol. 30, pp. 321-46.

Rubinstein, Amnon and Medina, Barak (2005), *The Constitutional Law of the State of Israel*, vol. 1, Shoken Publishing, Jerusalem (Hebrew).

Rudensky, M. (1932), 'Social Justice and the National Fund', in *Eretz Israel: Jubilee Volume of the Jewish National Fund*, Jewish National Fund for America, New York, pp. 71-6.

Ruppin, Arthur (1926), *The Agricultural Colonisation of the Zionist Organisation in Palestine*, Martin Hopkinson and Company, London.

Russell, Peter H. (1998), 'High Courts and the Rights of Aboriginal People: The Limits of Judicial Independence', *Saskatchewan Law Review*, vol. 61, pp. 247-76.

Rynhold, Jonathan and Steinberg, Gerald (2004), 'The Peace Process and the Israeli Elections', *Israel Affairs*, vol. 10, pp. 181-204.

Saban, Ilan (2002), 'The Minority Rights of the Palestinian-Arabs in Israel: What Is, What Isn't and What Is Taboo', *Tel-Aviv University Law Review*, vol. *26*, pp. *241-319* (Hebrew).

Saban, Ilan (2004), 'Minority Rights in Deeply Divided Societies: A Framework for Analysis and the Case of Arab Palestinian Minority in Israel', *New York University Journal of International Law & Politics*, vol. 36, pp. 885-1003.

Saban, Ilan (2007), 'After the Storm? Aftermath of October 2000- The Israeli Supreme Court and the Arab-Palestinian Minority', *Israel Affairs* (forthcoming).

Salzberger, Eli and Oz-Salzberger, Fania (2000), 'The Hidden German Sources of the Israeli Supreme Court', *Tel-Aviv University Studies in Law,* vol. 15, pp. 79-122.

Sandberg, Haim (2000), *Land Title Settlement in the Land of Israel and in the State of Israel*, Hebrew University Faculty of Law, Jerusalem (Hebrew).

Sandberg, Haim (2004), 'Jerusalem: Land Title Settlement and Expropriation', *Journal of Israeli History*, vol. 23, pp. 216-31.

Sandler, Shmuel (1993), *The State of Israel, the Land of Israel: The Statist and Ethnonational Dimensions of Foreign Policy*, Greenwood Press, Westport.

Saskin, A. and Gilai, M. (eds.) (1986), *Report of the Public Committee for the Examination of the Aims of the Land Policy* (Hebrew).

Schiff, Ze'ev and Ya'ari, Ehud (1990), *Intifada*, Simon and Schuster, New York.

Schmelz, Uziel O. (1987), *Modern Jerusalem's Demographic Evolution*, Jerusalem Institute for Israel Studies, Jerusalem.

Schnidman, Frank (1988), 'Land Readjustment: An Alternative to Development Exactions', in Rachelle Alterman (ed.), *Private Supply of Public Services, Evaluation of Real Estate Exactions, Linkage and Alternative Land Policies*, New York University Press, New York, pp. 250-63.

Segev, Tom (1986), *1949: The First Israelis*, The Free Press, New York.

Segev, Tom (2005), *Israel – 1967*, Keter Publishing House, Tel-Aviv (Hebrew).

Shachar, Yoram, Harris, Ron and Gross, Meron (1996), 'Citation Practices of the Supreme Court: Quantitative Analyses', *Mishpatim*, vol. 27, pp. 119-217 (Hebrew).

Shachar, Yoram, Gross, Meron and Goldshmidt, Chanan (2004), '100 Leading Precedents of the Supreme Court - Qualitative Analysis', *Mishpat Umimshal*, vol. 7, pp. 243-303 (Hebrew).

Shafir, Gershon (1989), *Land, Labor and the Origins of the Israel-Palestinian Conflict, 1882-1914*, Cambridge University Press, Cambridge.

Shafir, Gershon (1993), 'Land, Labor, and Population in Zionist Colonization: General and Unique Aspects', in Uri Ram (ed.), *Israeli Society: Critical Approaches*, Breirot, Tel-Aviv, pp.104-19 (Hebrew).

Shafir, Gershon and Peled, Yoav (2002), *Being Israeli: The Dynamics of Multiple Citizenship*, Cambridge University Press, Cambridge.

Shahar, Nathan (1993), 'The Eretz-Israeli Song and the Jewish National Fund', in Ezra Mendelsohn (ed.), *Studies in Contemporary Jewry: Modern Jews and Their Musical Agendas*, pp. 78-91.

Shamgar, Meir (1971), 'The Observance of International Law in the Administrated Territories', *Israel Yearbook on Human Rights*, vol. 1, pp. 262-77.

Shamgar, Meir (1982), 'Legal Concepts and Problems of the Israeli Military Government – The Initial Stage', in M. Shamgar (ed.), *Military Government in the Territories Administered by Israel, 1967-1980: The Legal Aspects*, Harry Sacher Institute for Legislature Research and Comparative Law, Jerusalem, pp. 13-61.

Shamir, Ronen (1991), 'Legal Discourse, Media Discourse and Speech Rights: The Shift from Content to Identity – The Case of Israel', *International Journal of Sociology of Law*, vol. 19, pp. 45-65.

Shamir, Ronen (1996), 'Suspended in Space: Bedouins under the Law of Israel', *Law & Society Review*, vol. 30, pp. 231-57.

Shapira, Amos (1983), 'Judicial Review without a Constitution: The Israeli Paradox', *Temple Law Quarterly*, vol. 56, pp. 405-58.

Shapira, Amos (1993), 'Why Israel Has No Constitution', *Saint Louis University Law Journal*, vol. 37, pp. 283-90.

Shapiro, Yonathan (1976), *The Formative Years of the Israeli Labour Party: The Organization of Power, 1919-1930*, Sage Publications, London.

Shapiro, Yonathan (1977), *Israel's Democracy*, Masada Press, Ramat-Gan (Hebrew).

Sharef, Zeev (1962), *Three Days*, W.H. Allen, London.

Sharkansky, Ira (1987), *The Political Economy of Israel*, Transaction Books, New Brunswick.

Shavit, Yaacov and Biger, Gideon (2000), *History of Tel-Aviv*, vol. 1, Tel-Aviv (Hebrew).

Shavit, Yaacov and Siton, Shoshana (2004), *Staging and Stagers in Modern Jewish Palestine: The Creation of Festive Lore in a New Culture 1882-1948*, Wayne State University Press, Detroit.

Shehadeh, Raja (1988), *Occupier's Law: Israel and the West Bank*, Institute for Palestine Studies, Washington, DC (revised ed.).

Shehadeh, Raja (1993), *The Law of the Land: Settlement and Land Issues under Israeli Military Occupation*, Palestinian Academic Society for the Study of International Affairs, Jerusalem.

Sheleff, Leon (1996), *The Rule of Law and the Nature of Politics*, Papirus, Tel-Aviv (Hebrew).

Shelach, Chaman (1980), 'Judicial Review of Land Expropriations', *Tel-Aviv University Law Review*, vol. 7, pp. 618-52 (Hebrew).

Shetreet, Shimon (1988), 'The Scope of Judicial Review of National Security Considerations in Free Speech and Other Areas: The Israeli Perspective', *Israel Yearbook on Human Rights*, vol. 18, pp. 35-47.

Shetreet, Shimon (1994), *Justice in Israel: A Study of the Israeli Judiciary*, Nijhoff Publishers, Dordrecht.

Shetreet, Shimon (1996), 'Standing and Justiciability', in Itzhak Zamir and Allen Zysblat (eds.), *Public Law in Israel*, Oxford University Press, Oxford, pp. 265-75.

Shilony, Zvi (1990), *Jewish National Fund and Settlement in Eretz Israel 1903-1914*, Yad Yitzhak Ben-Zvi, Jerusalem (Hebrew).

Shlaim, Avi (1999), 'The Debate about 1948' in Ilan Pappe (ed.), *The Israel/Palestine Question* , Routledge, London, pp. 211-20.

Sicron, Moshe (1957), *Immigration to Israel, 1948-1953*, Central Bureau of Statistics, Jerusalem.

Singer, Joseph W. (1991), 'Sovereignty and Property', *Northwestern University Law Review*, vol. 86, pp. 1-56.

Siton, Shoshana (1998), '"Education in the Spirit of the Homeland": The Curriculum of the Teachers' Council for the JNF (1925-1953)', *Dor Ledor*, vol. 14 (Hebrew).

Smith, Marlin R. (1987), 'From Subdivision Improvement Requirements to Community Benefits Assessments and Linkage Payments: A Brief History of Land Development Exactions', *Law & Contemporary Problems*, vol. 50, pp. 5-30.

Smooha, Sammy (1997), 'Ethnic Democracy: Israel as an Archetype', *Israel Studies*, vol. 2, pp. 198-241.

Sprinzak, Ehud (1986), *Every Man Whatsoever is Right in His Own Eyes: Illegalism in Israeli Society*, Poalim Press, Tel-Aviv (Hebrew).

Sprinzak, Ehud (1993), 'Elite Illegalism in Israel and the Question of Democracy', in Ehud Sprinzak and Larry Diamond (eds.), *Israeli Democracy Under Stress*, Lynne Rienner Publishers, Boulder & London, pp. 173-98.

State of Israel, (1951), *Israel Government Yearbook*, State of Israel.

State of Israel, (1998), *Report of the Committee for the Investigation of Israel's Land Policy chaired by Prof. Boaz Ronen* (Hebrew), State of Israel.

State of Israel (2003), *Report of the National Commission of Inquiry to Examine the Clashes between the Security Forces and Israeli Citizens*, State of Israel Publications, Jerusalem (Hebrew).

State of Israel, (2005), *Report of the Public Committee for Reform in Israel Lands Administration, chaired by Ya'acov Gadish* (Hebrew), State of Israel.

Statistical Yearbook of Jerusalem (2001), Jerusalem Institute for Israel Studies, Jerusalem.

Stein, W. Kenneth (1984), *The Land Question in Palestine, 1917-1939*, University of North Carolina Press, Chapel Hill.

Sternhell, Zeev (1998), *The Founding Myths of Israel: Nationalism, Socialism, and the Making of the Jewish State*, Princeton University Press, Princeton.

Stock, Ernest (1988), *Chosen Instrument: The Jewish Agency in the First Decade of the State of Israel*, Herzl Press, New York.

Stone, Alan (1985), 'The Place of Law in the Marxian Structure-Superstructure Archetype', *Law & Society Review*, vol. 19, pp. 39-67.

Tal, Israel (1977), 'Israel's Doctrine of National Security: Background and Dynamics', *Jerusalem Quarterly*, vol. 4, pp. 44-57.

Todd, Erik C.E. (1992), *The Law of Expropriation and Compensation in Canada*, Carswell, Ontario.

Torgovnick, Efraim (1990), *The Politics of Urban Planning Policy*, University Press of America, Lanham.

Treanor, William M. (1995), 'The Original Understanding of the Takings Clause and the Political Process', *Columbia Law Review*, vol. 95 pp. 782-887.

Treanor, William M. (1997), 'The *Armstrong* Principle, the Narrative of Takings and Compensation Statutes', *William & Mary Law Review*, vol. 38, pp. 1151-76.

Tsur, Zeev (1983), 'The Jewish National Fund's Heritage and the Formation of the Public Land in Israel', 1983 *Karka*, pp. 59-69 (Hebrew).

Tushnet, Mark (2000), 'The Universal and the Particular in Constitutional Law: An Israeli Case Study', *Columbia Law Review*, vol. 100, pp. 1327-46.

Tute, Richard C. (1927), *The Ottoman Land Law*, Greek Conv. Press, Jerusalem.

Tuten, Eric E. (2002), 'Courting Private Capital: The Jewish National Fund's Joint Land Purchase Scheme in Mandatory Palestine, 1938-47', *Middle Eastern Studies*, vol. 38, pp. 123-44.

Ulitzur, A. (1939), *The National Capital and the Building of Palestine*, The Foundation Fund, Jerusalem (Hebrew).

Ussishkin, Menahem (1905), *Our Program : An Essay*, Federation of American Zionists, New York (Hebrew).

Ussishkin, Menahem (1929), *The Voice of the Land*, Jewish National Fund, Jerusalem (Hebrew).

Van der Walt, Andre J. (1997), *The Constitutional Property Clause: A Comparative Analysis of Section 25 of the South African Constitution of 1996*, Juta, Cape Town.

Wallfson, Max (1976), *Planning Residential Environment and Providing for Human Needs: Examples from the New Neighborhoods in Jerusalem*, Ministry of Housing and Construction, Jerusalem (Hebrew).

Weeramantry, C.G. (1988), *Islamic Jurisprudence: An International Perspective*, St. Martin's Press, New York.

Weisman, Joshua (1972), *Principal Features of Israel Land Law, 1969*, The Harry and Michael Sacher Institute for Legislative Research and Comparative Law, The Hebrew University of Jerusalem, Jerusalem.

Weisman, Joshua (1980), 'Legal Aspects of Alien Acquisition of Real Property in Israel' in Dennis Campbell (ed.), *Legal Aspects of Alien Acquisition of Real Property*, Kluwer, Deventer, pp. 97-101.

Weisman, Joshua (1995), *Property Law*, The Harry and Michael Sacher Institute for Legislative Research and Comparative Law, The Hebrew University of Jerusalem, Jerusalem (Hebrew).

Weiss, Yfaat (2001), '"The Monster and its Creator" – Or How the Law of Return Made Israel a Multi-Ethnic State', *Theory and Criticism*, vol. 19, pp. 45-69 (Hebrew).

Weitz, Joseph (1950), *The Struggle for the Land*, Twersky, Tel-Aviv (Hebrew).

Weitz, Joseph (1965), *My Diary and Letters to the Children*, Massada Press, Tel-Aviv (Hebrew).

Werczberger, Elia and Borukhov, Eliyahu (1999), 'The Israel Land Authority: Relic or Necessity', *Land Use Policy*, vol. 16, pp. 129-38.

Witkon, Alfred (1962), 'Law in a Developing Country', in Haim Cohen (ed.), *Jubilee Book for Pinhas Rosen*, Jerusalem, pp. 65-88 (Hebrew).

Witkon, Gideon (1998), 'Reform in Land Policy:The Ronen Commission', 44 *Karka*, vol. 14, pp. 15-40 (Hebrew).

Witkon, Gideon (2004), *The Law of Israel Lands*, Hoshen Mishpat, Tel-Aviv (Hebrew).

Yaffe, Nurit and Tal, Dorith (2001), *Immigration to Israel from the Former Soviet Union*, Central Bureau of Statistics, Jerusalem.

Yanai, Nathan (1990), 'Politics and Constitution-Making in Israel: Ben-Gurion's Position in the Constitutional Debate Following the Foundation of the State', in Daniel Elazar (ed.), *Constitutionalism: The Israeli and American Experiences*, University Press of America, Lanham, pp.101-14.

Yaniv, Avner (1993), 'A Question of Survival: The Military and Politics Under Siege', in A. Yaniv (ed.), *National Security and Democracy in Israel*, Lynne Rienner Publishers, Boulder, pp. 81-103.

Yiftachel, Oren (1992), *Planning a Mixed Region in Israel: The Political Geography of Arab-Jewish Relations in the Galilee*, Avebury, Aldershot.

Yiftachel, Oren (1997), 'Israeli Society and Jewish-Palestinian Reconciliation: "Ethnocracy" and Its Territorial Contradictions', *Middle East Journal*, vol. 51(4), pp. 505-19.

Yiftachel, Oren (1997a), 'Nation-building or Ethnic Fragmentation? Frontier Settlement and Collective Identities in Israel', *Space and Polity*, vol. 1(2), pp. 149-70.

Yiftachel, Oren (1998), 'The Internal Frontier: Territorial Control and Ethnic Relations in Israel', in Oren Yiftachel and Avinoam Meir (eds.), *Ethnic Frontiers and Peripheries: Landscapes of Development and Inequality in Israel*, Westview Press, Boulder, pp. 39-68.

Yiftachel, Oren (1998a), 'Nation-Building and the Division of Space: Ashkenazi Domination in the Israeli Ethnocracy', *Nationalism and Ethnic Politics*, vol. 4(3), pp. 33-58.

Yifatchel Oren and Kedar, Alexandre (2000), 'Landed Power: The Making of the Israeli Legal Regime', *Theory and Criticism,* vol. 16, pp. 67-100 (Hebrew).

Zamir, Eyal (1985), *State Lands in Judea and Samaria – The Legal Status*, Jerusalem Institute for Israel Studies, Jerusalem (Hebrew).

Zamir, Itzhak (1996), 'Unreasonableness, Balance of Interests and Proportionality', in I. Zamir and A. Zysblat (eds.), *Public Law in Israel*, Clarendon Press, Oxford, pp. 327-33.

Zerubavel, Yael (1996), 'The Forest as a National Icon: Literature, Politics, and the Archeology of Memory', *Israel Studies*, vol. 1(1), pp. 60-99.

Zinger Zvi [Yaron] (1973), 'State of Israel (1948-1972)', in *Immigration and Settlement*, Keter Publishing House, Jerusalem, pp. 50-74.

Zureik, Elia (1996), *Palestinian Refugees and the Peace Process*, Institute for Palestine Studies, Washington DC.

Zysblat, Allen (1996), 'Protecting Fundamental Rights in Israel without a Written Constitution', in I. Zamir and A. Zysblat (eds.), *Public Law in Israel*, Oxford University Press, Oxford, pp. 1-17.

Index

Galilee 4, 6, 46, 64, 72, 83, 87, 93, 96, 106,
    116, 123, 129, 133-4, 138-41, 147-9,
    154, 162-3, 165-6, 171-2
Ganimat v. State of Israel 153
Gaza Strip 24, 103, 130-1, 139, 154-5, 170
General Zionists 65, 74, 111
George, Henry 59
Ge'ulat Hakrach Ltd. v. Minister of Finance
    16, 46, 167
Gilo 137-8
Givat Hamivtar 137, 159
Golan Heights 24, 130
Goldberg, Eliezer 160, 165-6
*Goldenberg v. Planning and Building
    Commission Tel Aviv District* 52
Granott, Avraham 69
Green Line 155-6
Gush Emunim 132

Ha'aretz 68, 133, 172
Hadera 167, 169
Hagana 106
Haifa 16, 20, 28, 44, 64, 83, 87, 90, 93, 95-
    6, 105, 155
Har Homa 137-8, 145-8, 155, 157, 161-2,
    164-6, 172
Harari Resolution 39, 152
Harzfeld, Avraham 69
Hawaii Housing Authority v. Midkiff (U.S.
    Supreme Court) 13-4
hearing, right to 1, 9, 13-5, 46, 115-6, 120-3,
    127, 140-1, 143
Hebron 137, 156
Heirs of Edith Feitzer v. Minister of Interior
    53; *see also Feitzer v. Ramat Gan
    Local Planning and Building
    Commission*
Herzl, Theodore 59, 62
Herzliya 28, 149
Herzog, Yitzhak 172
High Commissioner for Palestine 11, 13, 19
High Court of Justice, *see* Supreme Court
Histadrut 72, 76, 98
Housing 11, 27, 68-9, 85, 96, 123, 128, 165,
    167
    apartment confiscations 85, 88-92
    in East Jerusalem 137-8, 142-6, 148,
        155, 163
    policies 25, 40, 51, 79, 82, 84-5, 94-5,
        97-8, 158

and population distribution plans 82,
    84, 93
shortages 6, 87, 91, 95, 138, 146, 158,
    163, 168
state-driven housing market 83-4, 95,
    163
subsidies 96, 98-9
transit camps 87, 92
see also immigration

immigration 2, 4-5, 40, 51, 58, 60-1, 67-8,
    79, 81-3, 85-92, 94-9, 101, 105, 123,
    128, 142, 166
and Declaration of Independence 79-80
and geographic dispersal of population
    75, 82, 93, 96, 163
and Holocaust 80
and Law of Citizenship 80
and Law of Return 80
from the Soviet Union 30, 32, 77, 82-4,
    99, 157-8, 163
waves of 57, 64, 69, 71, 80-2, 92, 94-5,
    167-8
intifada 154-7, 161-3, 170-2
Iqrit and Bir'im 116-7, 127, 171
Islamic law 24; *see also* waqf
Israel, State of 3-5, 12, 24-5, 37, 62, 64, 69,
    81, 126
as democratic and Jewish state 33, 36,
    43-5, 51, 79-80, 102, 151-2, 154,
    170-1
demographic policy 30, 75, 82-4, 87, 93,
    98, 101-2, 124, 136, 139-40, 142,
    145, 147, 155, 157, 163, 166, 171-2
and discrimination 4, 71, 80, 103, 113,
    115, 119, 124-5, 139, 144-5, 170,
    172-3
and the Holocaust 80
and the Jewish National Fund 55, 65,
    71-4, 78
and quasi-governmental entities 4, 55,
    65, 68, 73, 98, 169-71
security policy 6, 38, 79-82, 85-8,
    102-3, 109, 112, 124, 129-30, 134,
    137-9, 142, 154-7, 162-3, 171-2
state-owned land 26, 40, 55-6, 70-1, 73,
    76-7, 103-4, 106, 116
sovereignty 70, 101, 103, 105, 109, 136,
    138, 156
and Zionism 69-70, 72, 79

For Product Safety Concerns and Information please contact our EU
representative GPSR@taylorandfrancis.com
Taylor & Francis Verlag GmbH, Kaufingerstraße 24, 80331 München, Germany